Cases in Finance

Third Edition

David F. Scott, Jr.
Phillips-Schenck Chair in American Private Enterprise;
Executive Director of the Dr. Phillips Institute
for the Study of American Business Activity;
and Professor of Finance,
University of Central Florida

John D. Martin
Margaret and Eugene McDermott Professor
of Banking and Finance,
University of Texas at Austin

J. William Petty
W.W. Caruth Endowed Chair
of Entrepreneurship,
Professor of Finance,
Baylor University

Arthur J. Keown
R.B. Pamplin Professor of Finance,
Virginia Polytechnic Institute and
State University

John G. Thatcher
Associate Professor of Finance,
University of Wisconsin–Whitewater

Sharon S. Graham
Associate Professor of Finance,
University of Central Florida

Prentice Hall, Englewood Cliffs, New Jersey 07632

To our wives, Peggy, Sally, Donna, Barbara, and Janet, and our families

Library of Congress Cataloging-in-Publication Data
Cases in finance / David F. Scott, Jr. . . . [et al.].—3rd ed.
   ISBN 0-13-117995-0
    1. Corporations—Finance—Case studies. 2. Business enterprises–
–Finance—Case studies. I. Scott, David F.
HG4015.5.C36 1992
  658.15—dc20
                                                      92-1342
                                                       CIP

Editorial/production supervision and
  interior design: Keith Faivre
Acquisitions editor: Leah Jewell
Cover design: Karen Salzbach
Pre-press buyer: Trudy Pisciotti
Manufacturing buyer: Bob Anderson

 © 1993 by Prentice-Hall, Inc.
A Simon & Schuster Company
Englewood Cliffs, New Jersey 07632

Printed in the United States of America

10 9 8 7 6 5 4 3 2

ISBN 0-13-117995-0

Prentice-Hall International (UK) Limited, *London*
Prentice-Hall of Australia Pty. Limited, *Sydney*
Prentice-Hall Canada Inc., *Toronto*
Prentice-Hall Hispanoamericana, S.A., *Mexico*
Prentice-Hall of India Private Limited, *New Delhi*
Prentice-Hall of Japan, Inc., *Tokyo*
Simon & Schuster Asia Pte. Ltd., *Singapore*
Editora Prentice-Hall do Brasil, Ltda., *Rio de Janeiro*

Contents

iii

✍ SECTION II ॐ
―――――――――― *Working Capital Management* ―――――――――

✍ SECTION III ॐ
―――――――――― *Capital Investment Decisions* ―――――――――

❧ SECTION IV ❧
————————Valuation and the Cost of Capital————————

❧ SECTION V ❧
————————Long-Term Financing Decisions————————

❧ *SECTION VI* ☙
————————*Noteworthy Financial Management Problems*————

Preface

THE CASE METHOD OF INSTRUCTION

In order to truly understand problems of the financial manager and the role of financial theory in the real world, it is necessary for you as the student to actually experience real world problems. It is the purpose of the case method of study to expose you to actual decision making situations in the hope that this will provide you with greater insight into the problems of the financial manager in addition to improving your decision making ability. Since it is impossible for you to gain actual business experience in the classroom, the case method of instruction becomes a valuable tool in simulating the functioning of the financial manager.

In the past, you probably have been exposed to problems rather than cases. The difference between problems and cases is more than merely length. In cases, the business situation is described, giving you a feel for the conditions, attitudes and practices of a particular company. Moreover, the financial situation being examined will be of a more complex nature than those you might have experienced in previous problem exercises. Additionally, cases differ from problems in three major respects. First, there is usually room for more than one correct answer. The correct answer depends upon the assumptions being made and in many cases there is room for varying assumptions. Secondly, whereas problems traditionally deal with only one aspect of a financial problem, cases recognize the complexity of the various financial problems and portray them in this state. It is for this reason that cases in finance generally require you to answer multiple and interacting questions in attempting to solve a problem. Finally, in many cases you will find irrelevant information, just as in the real world, which requires you to differentiate between relevant and irrelevant facts in solving the problem.

With this in mind, the case method approach should provide you with a broad learning experience as decision-making experience is gained through the simulation of the financial business environment. Additionally, it should enable you to focus on the role of financial theory in actual business situations. In the end, it must be added that learning by the case method is an individual proposition, requiring a maximum effort, and so the value of the educational experience depends upon the effort put into it.

THE THIRD EDITION

This third edition of *Cases in Finance* contains 56 cases compared to 44 different case settings in the second edition. Eighteen new cases are in the volume and six others have undergone revision. Six cases from the second edition have been dropped.

Both complex and shorter situations have been added. Many have been added to the high use subject categories of ratio analysis, cash budgeting, capital budgeting, valuation, financial leverage analysis, bond refunding, and agency theory.

Risk-adjusted discount rates, the use of simulation in a capital budgeting setting, the capital asset pricing model, and small business valuation are all addressed by means of new cases. Many of the cases are particularly suited for spreadsheet analysis.

Once more, we offer our sincere gratitude to the many people who have discussed their ideas with us for improving the text. Please continue to let us know what can be done to make this volume more useful.

CASE 1

Abington-Hill Toys, Inc.

Part I: Financial Ratio Analysis

On December 2, 1991, Vernon Albright assumed the position of president of the Abington-Hill Toy Company (A-H), following the death of Lewis Hill, the last of the original founders of the firm. Neither Abington nor Hill had a son or daughter who was interested in taking over the firm's management. The financial condition of the firm had deteriorated during the final years of Hill's control; however, the firm's owners[1] felt that the company's prospects were good if a capable manager could be found to take over the leadership. A key concern of the owners was the lack of financial planning and general crisis-to-crisis pattern that had characterized the firm's operation in recent years.

It was decided to seek a manager from outside the firm who, in the owners' opinion, could reshape the company into the prosperous concern it once had been. Advertisements placed in a number of trade journals provided the owners with a list of six individuals who were willing and apparently capable of rebuilding A-H. After extensive correspondence and several personal interviews with each of the applicants, Vernon Albright was chosen to head the firm.

---

[1]The firm is closely held, with 85 percent of the stock held by the combined Abington and Hill families. The remaining minority interest is primarily held by company employees who acquired it through the company stock option plan.

One of the first actions of the new president was to hire a company comptroller.[2] David Hartly, an assistant comptroller of a major electric appliance manufacturing firm, was hired and took over his duties on December 28, 1991. Hartly had been with the appliance company since receiving his MBA in 1977 and had moved up in the comptroller's office to the position of assistant to the comptroller in charge of general accounts and budgeting. His experience in budgetary procedures was viewed with particular favor by Albright in light of A-H's recent financial problems.

Hartly's first task was to undertake a complete analysis of the firm's financial condition. Specifically, Albright had requested a statement of the firm's condition, including an enumeration of specific strengths and weaknesses. He also requested a brief statement of a feasible solution to the firm's most pressing problems.

QUESTIONS

1. Using ratio analysis and a statement of sources and uses of funds, prepare Hartly's statement of the firm's financial condition. (Financial statements are found in Exhibit 1 and industry standard ratios in Exhibit 2.)

2. Based on your analysis, what areas of the firm's operations are in greatest need of immediate attention? Prepare a planned course of action for the solution of the firm's most pressing problems.

---

[2] In the past, Hill had handled most of the comptroller functions with the assistance of the firm's chief accountant, Jerald Cohen, who had been with the firm for the 28 years of its existence and planned to retire within the year. He agreed to remain with the firm, at the request of the owners, until the new president could be selected and the company was on its feet. However, Cohen was in poor health and would probably be forced to retire within the year.

———————— **EXHIBIT 1** ————————

Abington-Hill Toys, Inc.

Comparative Balance Sheets
December 31, 1990–1991

	December 31, 1990	December 31, 1991
Assets		
Cash	$ 50,000	$ 10,000
Accounts receivable	100,000	120,000
Inventory	150,000	150,000
Total current assets	$ 300,000	$ 280,000
Plant and equipment	1,200,000	1,480,000
Less: Allowance for depreciation	(500,000)	(560,000)
Total fixed assets	$ 700,000	$ 920,000
Total assets	$ 1,000,000	$ 1,200,000
Liabilities and Net Worth		
Accounts payable	$ 40,000	$ 42,000
Short-term notes	50,000	224,000
Accrued expenses	20,000	24,000
Total current liabilities	$ 110,000	$ 290,000
Long-term debt	200,000	200,000
Common stock, $10 par	200,000	200,000
Capital surplus	490,000	510,000
Total liabilities and net worth	$ 1,000,000	$ 1,200,000

Income Statement
for Year Ended December 31, 1991

	Actual 1991
Sales	$ 1,200,000*
Cost of goods sold	900,000
Gross profit	$ 300,000
Operating expenses	
Variable cash operating expense	84,000
Fixed cash operating expense	30,000
Depreciation	60,000
Total operating expenses	$ 174,000
Net income before interest and taxes	126,000
Interest	39,600
Net income before taxes	$ 86,400
Taxes @ 30%	25,920
Net income	$ 60,480

*Includes 60 percent credit sales.

3

———————————— **EXHIBIT 2** ————————————

Abington-Hill Toys, Inc.

Standard Industry Ratios

Ratio	Industry*
Current ratio	3.50X
Acid-test ratio	1.50X
Average collection period	60.0 days
Inventory turnover (COGS to ending inventory)	5.00X
Fixed asset turnover	1.43X
Total asset turnover	1.00X
Debt ratio (total debt to total assets)	45.0%
Times interest earned (overall interest coverage)	4.10X
Gross profit margin	25.0%
Net profit margin	8.0%
Return on total assets	8.0%
Return on net worth	14.55%

*All ratios based on year-end (rather than average) figures and on 360 (rather than 365) days in a year.

CASE 2

Abington-Hill Toys, Inc.

Part II: Financial Planning

David Hartly, comptroller of A-H, completed the financial analysis of the firm and, based upon his findings, suggested the following course of action:[1]

1. Seek a long-term loan to raise the firm's long-term debt to a level of $386,000.
2. Take steps to make the following ratios conform to industry averages:
    a. Average collection period
    b. Inventory turnover
3. Reduce short-term notes payable to $30,000.
4. Sell plant and equipment with an original cost of $140,000 and accumulated depreciation of $65,000 for its book value of $75,000.

In his final report to the president, Hartly wanted to show the effect of the successful implementation of his plan on the financial condition of the firm. The plan could conceivably be fully implemented by the end of January if approved by the president.

---

[1]See Abington-Hill Toys, Inc., Part I.

QUESTIONS

1. Prepare a set of pro forma financial statements for the end of January reflecting Hartly's proposed plan. In preparing these statements, you may assume the following:
   a. Sales for 1992 are estimated to be $1,200,000 and January sales are equal to one-twelfth of that amount.
   b. Variable expenses including cost of goods sold remain at a constant proportion of sales.
   c. Fixed operating expenses and depreciation for January are equal to one-twelfth of the 1991 totals.
   d. Interest expense of $2,500 is incurred and is paid in January.
   e. Accounts payable increase to $46,000 and accrued expenses remain constant at $24,000.
   f. The January tax liability is paid during that month and the tax rate is 30%.

2. Using the pro forma balance sheet and income statement developed, prepare a cash budget for the month of January.

3. Evaluate the financial condition of the firm after the successful implementation of Hartly's proposal. (A ratio analysis of the firm's pro forma statements for January 31, 1992 would be one way in which to assess the financial condition of the firm after implementing the plan.)

CASE 3

Abington-Hill Toys, Inc.

Part III: Financial Planning

Upon completion of his financial analysis of A-H (see Abington-Hill Toys, Inc., Part I), the company comptroller, David Hartly, concluded that the principal action to be taken immediately was to seek out a term loan whose proceeds could be used to repay $194,000 of the firm's short-term notes. The particular note in question was due in March of the coming year. Part of the needed funds was expected to come from operations and another portion from the sale of fixed assets during January for $75,000 (accumulated depreciation on the assets is $65,000, while the original purchase price was $140,000).

In addition to paying off the short-term note in March, Hartly felt that the firm should increase its cash balance to a minimum level of $40,000. Although he believed that the firm should attempt to reach this cash balance goal as soon as possible, Hartly recognized the fact that additional short-term loans would be prohibitively expensive (factoring of accounts receivable or an inventory loan is possible but would cost an estimated 20 percent per annum). Thus, Hartly hoped to be able to hold out with the firm's existing cash balance ($10,000), plus cash flow from operations, until March, when he intended to seek the long-term loan. The proceeds from the loan in conjunction with funds from operations would be used to clear up $194,000 in notes payable and reach the desired cash balance of $40,000.

EXHIBIT 1

Abington-Hill Toys, Inc.

Sales Data, 1991–1992

1991		1992	
October	$100,000	January	$90,000
November	$100,000	February	$90,000
December	$150,000	March	$90,000
		April	$100,000
		May	$110,000
		June	$100,000
		July	$90,000

Sales estimates for the next seven months, as well as past monthly sales for the previous three months, are presented in Exhibit 1.

Traditionally, A-H's sales have been 60 percent credit and 40 percent cash. Of the credit sales, roughly half are collected one month after the sale and the remainder collected two months after the sale, with negligible bad-debt losses. Purchases are approximately 75 percent of sales and are made one month in advance, with payment following in 60 days. Variable cash operating expenses (including selling costs, wages, advertising, and miscellaneous cash expenses) are 7 percent of sales and are paid in the month in which they are incurred. Fixed cash operating expenses are roughly $2,500 a month, with payment made in the same month. Taxes are paid quarterly (April for the quarter ended in March, and so on) based on estimated earnings for the quarter. Annual depreciation expense is $60,000 on the net assets remaining after the January 1, 1992 sale of fixed assets. Interest expense for the notes payable is 12 percent and is payable quarterly in March and June. Interest on the outstanding long-term debt is at a rate of 6.06 percent and is paid semiannually in June and December. The term loan is expected to carry a 9.5 percent rate of interest, with interest payable semiannually beginning in September and the entire principal amount due in five years.

QUESTIONS

1. Based on the information provided, prepare a cash budget for A-H covering the first quarter of 1992.
2. Based on your answer to question 1, how much should A-H seek in additional long-term debt to pay off the $194,000 note and increase cash to a level of $40,000?
3. Prepare a cash budget for the second quarter of 1992. You may assume that A-H was successful in renegotiating its line of credit with its bank

carrying a $100,000 line and an 8.5 percent rate of interest with interest paid monthly.

4. Based on your answers to the preceding questions, prepare a pro forma income statement and balance sheet as of the end of the six-month budget period.

CASE 4

Sundown Ski Wear

Financial Ratio Analysis

In August 1991, Rebecca Swank, a recent M.B.A. graduate, was hired as a loan-lending officer for Massachusetts State American Bank. Swank graduated with honors and had previous experience working at the bank during the past three summers. One of her first assignments in her new position was to review the account of Sundown Ski Wear (SSW), a long-standing client of the bank. SSW had recently applied for an increase in its line of credit from $3 million to $4 million, and it also requested a 10-year extension on a $2 million bank loan issued 10 years ago and due in October 1992.

Swank's initial approach to the problem was to do some research into the background of the company. She found that SSW had been formed in 1947 by Andrew Todd, a man then in his mid-40s who was making his first attempt at owning and operating his own business. SSW specialized in the manufacture and sale of a line of sophisticated, high-quality ski sweaters. The company had remained very small until the ski industry boom in the 1970s. Then, along with an increased interest in skiing, SSW's sales grew steadily, going from $4.3 million in 1976, to $9.2 million in 1981, to $20.1 million in 1986, and to $25.7 million in 1991. Of these, approximately 70 percent were credit sales.

Until 1986, SSW had been owned and operated by the Todd family, with James Todd taking over from his father in 1965. James Todd was very proud of the fact that under his management, although he kept within the guidelines originally set by his father, SSW had realized tremendous growth in sales and profits. Upon Todd's retirement in 1986, SSW was sold twice within the next year—first to a group of Chicago businessmen and then to a syndicate of Boston businessmen headed by Ben Pinkerton; thus ended the 36-year Todd control of the firm.

The Todd family had been very conservative in its management of SSW, limiting the product line to high-quality ski sweaters sold only in ski shops and in specially approved menswear stores, but the Pinkerton syndicate took a more aggressive approach. It expanded the product line to include ski pants, ski jackets, shirts, and high-fashion sweaters and drastically expanded the types of sales outlets to include department stores and some chain discount stores. This expansion in product line was financed in large part through the issuance of $7.5 million of 10 percent long-term debt on September 1, 1990. This debt was due in 15 years (2005), and it carried an annual sinking fund provision of $500,000, with the first sinking fund payment due one year after the bonds were issued. Aside from the $2 million bank loan due in October 1992, this was the first long-term debt that SSW had employed; it had previously limited the capital structure to common and preferred stocks. The Pinkerton syndicate, relying heavily on the good name of SSW, was hoping that this aggressive expansion would help to recapture the company's growth recorded in the 1970s and 1980s.

Swank further found that the preferred stock outstanding is nonparticipating and has a cumulative feature. This means that while the preferred stockholders cannot participate in the residual earnings of the firm, any unpaid dividends to preferred stockholders are carried forward and must be fully paid off before any dividends to common stockholders can be paid. In addition, preferred stockholders are allowed to elect one-half of the board of directors in the case of a dividend default (arrearages on two quarterly dividend payments constitute a default). Thus, the management of SSW has no intention of ever passing up a preferred dividend. The common stock is currently selling at around $40 per share and is paying $1.50 in annual dividends, with the dividends growing at about 10 percent per year, except between 1990 and 1991, when they remained constant. SSW had not missed or lowered its annual dividend payment in over 10 years, and because of this had become a favorite of pension and trust funds, which has resulted in a relatively stable stock price.

For the past four years, Massachusetts State American Bank has granted SSW a line of credit of $3 million. The need for seasonal borrowing for SSW is a result of its highly seasonal sales pattern and limited production facilities. Throughout the year SSW is forced to keep production at nearly full capacity, building large inventories that will be reduced from mid-July through December, when 90 percent of the sales take place. Thus, for SSW, short-term borrowing generally reaches a peak in August and is

———————————————— **EXHIBIT 1** ————————————————

Sundown Ski Wear

Balance Sheet
As of August 31, 1989–1991
(thousands)

		1989		1990		1991
Assets						
Cash		$ 2,100		$ 1,800		$ 1,600
Accounts receivable		1,400		1,800		1,500
Raw materials and						
supplies	$ 800		$ 1,000		$ 1,200	
Work in process	2,600		3,500		4,600	
Finished goods	200		300		500	
Inventory		$ 3,600		$ 4,400		$ 6,300
Total current assets		7,100		8,000		9,400
Fixed assets at cost	$22,900		$27,000		$34,000	
Less: accumulated						
depreciation	6,300		6,200		6,400	
Net fixed assets		$16,600		$20,800		$27,600
Goodwill		12,000		12,000		12,000
Total assets		$35,700		$40,800		$49,000
Liabilities and Stockholders' Equity						
Line of credit		$ 2,400		$ 2,600		$ 2,400
Accounts payable		700		1,000		1,600
Accruals		300		500		800
Total current liabilities		$ 3,400		$ 4,100		$ 4,800
Bank loan (due October 1992)		2,000		2,000		2,000
Long-term debt		0		0		7,500
Preferred stock*		12,000		12,000		12,000
Common stock†		4,000		5,000		5,000
Paid-in surplus		10,000		13,000		13,000
Retained earnings		4,300		4,700		4,700
Total stockholders' equity		$30,300		$34,700		$34,700
Total liabilities and equity		$35,700		$40,800		$49,000

*On August 31, 1991 there were 120,000 shares of preferred stock outstanding with a par value of $100 each and yielding 7.5 percent.

†On August 31, 1991 there were 625,000 shares of common stock outstanding.

completely repaid by the end of November. Although SSW has had a line of credit of $3 million for the past four years, the company's high credit was only for $2.6 million in August 1990.

In preparing her report for Massachusetts State American Bank, Swank will be required to prepare sources and uses of funds statements for the past two years to provide some insight into how SSW has used its funds

---
EXHIBIT 2

Sundown Ski Wear

Income Statements for Years Ending
August 31, 1989–1991
(thousands)

	1989	1990	1991
Net sales	$20,600	$24,400	$25,980
Cost of goods sold	14,700	17,300	18,400
Gross profit	$ 5,900	$ 7,100	$ 7,580
Selling, general and administrative expenses	993	1,968	2,233
Depreciation	650	710	930
Earnings before interest and taxes	$ 4,257	$ 4,422	$ 4,417
Interest expense	310	340	974
Earnings before taxes	$ 3,947	$ 4,082	$ 3,443
Taxes	1,797	1,844	1,605
Net income	$ 2,150	$ 2,238	$ 1,838
Dividends paid			
Common	$ 750	$ 938	$ 938
Preferred	$ 900	$ 900	$ 900

EXHIBIT 3

Sundown Ski Wear

Industry Averages for
Selected Ratios, 1989–1991

Ratio	Average
Current ratio	1.943
Acid-test ratio	.969
Average collection period ratio	40.3 days
Inventory turnover ratio	3.877 X
Total debt to total tangible stockholder's equity	.636
Long-term debt to total capitalization	.487
Gross profit margin	23.4%
Net profit margin	9.64%
Total tangible asset turnover ratio	.826 X
Return on assets (earning power)	7.96%
Interest coverage ratio	4.133 X

in the past. A complete ratio analysis of the firm that focuses on liquidity, debt, coverage, and profitability ratios will also be necessary. In addition to doing the calculations of these ratios and an analysis of them, Swank must make a tentative recommendation on both the line of credit and the loan extension. This analysis is based upon the financial data given in Exhibits 1, 2, and 3.

QUESTIONS

1. Calculate the following financial ratios for Sundown Ski Wear for 1989, 1990, and 1991.
    a. Current ratio
    b. Acid-test ratio
    c. Average collection period ratio[1]
    d. Inventory turnover ratio[2]
    e. Total debt to total tangible stockholders' equity
    f. Long-term debt to total capitalization
    g. Gross profit margin
    h. Net profit margin
    i. Total tangible asset turnover ratio
    j. Return on tangible assets ratio (earning power ratio)
    k. Interest coverage ratio (times interest earned ratio)

2. Comment on the strengths and weaknesses uncovered by this analysis.

3. If a value for annual cash flow before interest and taxes were available, what other coverage ratio might be useful? Why is this ratio somewhat more meaningful than the simple interest coverage ratio?

4. Assuming that a value for annual cash flow before interest and taxes is not available, how might the simple interest coverage ratio be modified to examine coverage of other fixed charges for SSW? What does this analysis indicate? (Use 50 percent as the federal tax rate.)

5. Explain why depreciation charged on the income statement is not the same as the increase in accumulated depreciation on the balance sheet.

6. Prepare a sources and uses of funds statement for SSW for 1990 and 1991. What is the purpose of this analysis?

7. Prepare a percentage income statement for SSW for 1990 and 1991. What is the purpose of this analysis?

8. If you were Rebecca Swank, what would be your recommendation as to Sundown's request for an extension and increase in its line of credit and refinancing of its $2 million of long-term debt? Why?

[1]Use year-end receivables as average receivables.
[2]Use the value for ending inventory as given on the balance sheet as a surrogate for average inventory.

CASE 5

Bradford Drug, Inc.

Financial Ratio Analysis

In recent years, the ethical drug industry has prospered. While numerous other industries faced financial difficulties in the early 1990s recessionary period, most ethical drug firms did well. The sales of most drug firms continued to grow steadily. However, despite such overall favorable results within the industry, Donald Bradford, president of Bradford Drug, Inc., has been anything but pleased with the financial picture of his organization. Although Bradford was relieved to see a recovery from the downturn in sales encountered by his firm in 1990, he remains very concerned about the profitability being generated from these sales. The firm has maintained a profitable status, but one of Bradford's primary questions relates to the adequacy of the profits. On several occasions he has confronted his vice president, Mike Todd, with such concerns. However, to date, Bradford does not consider his questions to have been satisfactorily resolved. In response to his inquiries, Todd notes that the firm's operating profits have increased by a "staggering 141 percent" within the last four years. Thus, Todd is convinced that the company's financial condition has improved in an impressive fashion. As additional supporting data for his conviction of the corporation's overall prosperity, Todd cites the fact that Bradford's cost of production has consistently been less than half the dollar sales for its products.

--- EXHIBIT 1 ---

Bradford Drug, Inc.

Income Statements for 1988–1992
(thousands)

	1988	1989	1990	1991	1992
Sales*	$ 7,053	$ 8,301	$ 7,694	$ 8,806	$10,046
Cost of goods sold	3,455	3,968	3,526	4,115	4,823
Gross profit	$ 3,598	$ 4,333	$ 4,168	$ 4,691	$ 5,223
Operating expenses†					
General and administrative	2,380	2,499	2,221	2,471	3,033
Selling and advertising	274	307	371	460	353
Depreciation	156	183	174	195	205
Research and development	298	330	354	397	449
Total operating expenses	$ 3,108	$ 3,319	$ 3,120	$ 3,523	$ 4,040
Operating income	490	1,014	1,048	1,168	1,183
Other income‡	154	158	172	173	216
Earnings before interest and taxes	644	1,172	1,220	1,341	1,399
Interest expense	122	140	161	186	253
Earnings before taxes	522	1,032	1,059	1,155	1,146
Income taxes @ 40%	209	413	424	462	458
Earnings after taxes	313	619	635	693	688
Preferred dividends	31	0	0	0	0
Earnings available for common	282	619	635	693	688
Common dividends	258	320	334	350	370
Increase in retained earnings	$ 24	$ 299	$ 301	$ 343	$ 318
Earnings per share	$ 0.82	$ 1.40	$ 1.41	$ 1.52	$ 1.45
Number of common shares	344,803	440,625	451,430	455,250	474,485

*Credit sales normally represent 80 percent of total sales.

†Lease payments included in the operational expenses are $100,000 in 1988 and 1989, $200,000 in 1990 and 1991, and $400,000 in 1992.

‡Other income is made up of profits from Young Industries, a Bradford subsidiary in the cosmetics industry, and long-term security investments.

In spite of Todd's conclusion that the firm is doing well, Bradford continues to desire more specific financial information relating to the strengths and weaknesses of Bradford Drug, Inc. In this regard, he has acquired the financial data of Bradford's principal competitor, M. J. Ellis, Inc. Bradford has for some time felt competitive pressure from this orga-

—————————————— EXHIBIT 2 ——————————————

Bradford Drug, Inc.

Balance Sheets for December 31, 1988–1992
(thousands)

	1988	1989	1990	1991	1992
		Assets			
Current assets					
Cash and equivalent	$ 449	$ 484	$ 559	$ 1,223	$ 1,373
Accounts receivable*	1,206	1,519	1,840	2,017	2,239
Inventories*	1,253	1,570	1,419	1,670	2,218
Other current assets	123	133	478	252	325
Total current assets	$ 3,031	$ 3,706	$ 4,296	$ 5,162	$ 6,155
Fixed assets					
Gross plant	3,811	4,536	4,465	4,790	5,206
Reserve for depreciation	1,522	1,675	1,576	1,694	1,778
Net plant and equipment	$ 2,289	$ 2,861	$ 2,889	$ 3,096	$ 3,428
Other assets					
Investment in subsidiaries	45	50	42	45	40
Investments, other	445	565	856	719	510
Miscellaneous assets	18	28	41	43	48
Total other assets	$ 508	$ 643	$ 939	$ 807	$ 598
Total assets	$ 5,828	$ 7,210	$ 8,124	$ 9,065	$10,181
		Liabilities and Net Worth			
Liabilities					
Current liabilities	$ 1,450	$ 1,687	$ 1,942	$ 1,987	$ 2,326
Long-term debt†	1,196	1,543	1,623	1,992	2,251
Deferred taxes	123	141	243	242	240
Other liabilities	100	122	141	166	189
Total liabilities	$ 2,869	$ 3,493	$ 3,949	$ 4,387	$ 5,006
Net worth					
Preferred stock	1,028	0	0	0	0
Common equity	1,931	3,717	4,175	4,678	5,175
Total net worth	$ 2,959	$ 3,717	$ 4,175	$ 4,678	$ 5,175
Total liabilities and net worth	$ 5,828	$ 7,210	$ 8,124	$ 9,065	$10,181

*Beginning accounts receivable and inventory balances for 1988 were $1,000,000 and $11,000,000, respectively. Also, with respect to the receivables, the policy of the firm is to extend credit for 60 days on credit sales.

†The indenture of the long-term debt places a 10 percent sinking fund requirement upon the firm.

--- EXHIBIT 3 ---

M. J. Ellis, Inc.

Income Statements for 1988–1992
(thousands)

	1988	1989	1990	1991	1992
Sales*	$3,912	$4,368	$5,042	$6,116	$7,038
Cost of goods sold	1,093	1,199	1,168	1,447	1,726
Gross profit	$2,819	$3,169	$3,874	$4,669	$5,312
Operating expenses†					
General and administrative	1,184	1,346	1,574	1,885	2,222
Selling and advertising	380	400	519	606	651
Depreciation	83	80	116	132	147
Research and development	214	252	286	300	371
Total operating expenses	$1,861	$2,078	$2,495	$2,923	$3,391
Operating income	958	1,091	1,379	1,746	1,921
Other income‡	0	11	27	35	64
Earnings before interest and taxes	958	1,102	1,406	1,781	1,985
Interest expense	10	12	15	20	33
Earnings before taxes	948	1,090	1,391	1,761	1,952
Income taxes @ 40%	379	436	556	704	781
Earnings after taxes	569	654	835	1,057	1,171
Preferred dividends	12	11	6	3	2
Earnings available for common	557	643	829	1,054	1,169
Common dividends	176	222	243	291	407
Increase in retained earnings	$ 381	$ 421	$ 586	$ 763	$ 762
Earnings per share	$ 0.72	$ 1.11	$ 1.05	$ 1.33	$ 1.97
Number of common shares	775,000	580,250	788,500	790,500	593,240

*Credit sales normally represent 90 percent of total sales.

†No lease payments are incurred.

‡Other income is provided from a relatively small investment in short-term securities and a 1992 investment in long-term securities.

nization. He believes that an in-depth comparison of the two businesses would specifically demonstrate whether his dissatisfaction is justified. Although Bradford has not had an opportunity to do a complete investigation, he has computed the return on assets (on a before-tax basis) for Ellis, Inc., and found it to be significantly higher than the equivalent figure for Bradford. Furthermore, he has noticed that his institution's earnings per

-------------------------------- EXHIBIT 4 --------------------------------

M. J. Ellis, Inc.

Balance Sheets for December 31, 1988–1992
(thousands)

	1988	1989	1990	1991	1992
			Assets		
Current assets					
Cash and equivalent	$ 627	$ 960	$1,453	$1,800	$1,171
Accounts receivable*	714	745	807	988	1,229
Inventories*	656	633	735	867	1,515
Other current assets	225	280	317	382	444
Total current assets	$2,222	$2,618	$3,312	$4,037	$4,359
Fixed assets					
Gross plant	1,352	1,608	1,822	2,183	2,780
Less: Depreciation	502	566	640	733	846
Net plant and equipment	850	1,042	1,182	1,450	1,934
Other assets					
Investments	0	0	0	74	174
Total assets	$3,072	$3,660	$4,494	$5,561	$6,467
			Liabilities and Net Worth		
Liabilities					
Current liabilities	$ 700	$ 795	$1,010	$1,290	$1,493
Long-term debt	38	131	128	83	7
Deferred taxes	12	11	12	16	53
Other liabilities	56	74	92	110	—
Total liabilities	$ 806	$1,011	$1,242	$1,499	$1,553
Subordinated preferred stock	17	18	22	26	35
Net worth					
Preferred stock	241	206	90	21	0
Common equity	2,008	2,425	3,140	4,015	4,879
Total net worth	$2,249	$2,631	$3,230	$4,036	$4,879
Total liabilities and net worth	$3,072	$3,660	$4,494	$5,561	$6,467

*Beginning accounts receivable and inventory balances for 1988 were $700,000 and $600,000, respectively.

share are less than those for Ellis, Inc., in 1992. On the other hand, he has taken some comfort in discovering that Bradford's return on common is close to that of Ellis, Inc. Also, Bradford has made it a point to compute his competitor's growth in operating income during the most recent four-year period, and found it to be less than the comparable growth rate for

Bradford. Since he has not performed a thorough examination, he cannot definitely explain the reasons for the more narrow margin between the two firms' return on common and Bradford's larger growth rate in operating income; however, he thinks it is the result of recent investment decisions and Bradford's dividend policy.

In a recent meeting with the company's financial officer, Bradford enumerated his concerns

1. Is the business maintaining an adequate liquidity position?
2. Is the management of Bradford Drug, Inc., generating a sufficient return on the firm's operating assets on a before-tax basis?
3. Does the financial mix appear to be appropriate?
4. Is an ample return on common being provided to attract future common stockholders? Bradford is particularly interested in knowing the key variables that have an impact upon the return on common.

QUESTIONS

1. Perform a financial ratio analysis using Exhibits 1–4 that gives detailed attention to Bradford's four questions. Conduct your investigation in terms of both time (the five years given) and relative to M. J. Ellis, Inc. Where relevant, use a 360-day year in your computations.
2. Make recommendations to Bradford with respect to any financial matters needing attention.
3. Evaluate both Bradford's and Todd's beliefs about the financial position of the company.

CASE 6

American Department Stores, Inc.

Financial Ratio Analysis

This August, the Board of Directors of American Department Stores, Inc. (ADS), will meet to discuss the effectiveness of the company's strategies. Five years ago, management recommended implementing certain innovative plans to enhance the corporation's rate of growth. The Board of Directors feels that the time has come to evaluate the success of those plans in maintaining the company's industry leadership position.

American Department Stores is one of the largest retail chains in the United States. Unlike many of its competitors, ADS has been able to expand during the economic recession of the past few years. Currently, the company owns 2,300 discount department stores in 48 states, Puerto Rico, and Canada.

For the past five years, competition within the retail industry has intensified. The U.S. economy experienced eight years of unusually high rates of inflation, peaking in double digits. The economy also had unusually high rates of unemployment and displayed tendencies toward recession. The severe recession actually began three years ago and lasted for two years. Monetary tactics, dubbed "Reaganomics," were employed to combat inflation.

With the relatively high rates of inflation, many consumers turned toward the discount stores. Factory outlet mall, discount chain drugstores, and discount retail department stores expanded dramatically. Price competition forced retailers to take lower markups on their products in order to attract customers by offering better prices. Net income fell, so retailers had to turn to other strategies to maintain their return on equity.

Over the past five years, ADS has restructured their stores in order to improve sales, control costs, and maintain return on equity. The marketing department decided to target a different customer base. Historically, ADS had offered "cheap" products with a low markup. To compensate, all sales had been "cash only." Five years ago, when management sought to raise the gross profit margin, it improved the merchandise mix by adding higher-quality/higher-priced discount merchandise. While ADS still maintained its discount store image, the new products were intended to attract the "upscale" customer to the discount chain.

The strategy was entirely consistent with the company's decision to locate its stores in suburban shopping centers. Customers, who continued to move to the suburbs, were attracted by the convenient shopping locations. New stores were built in company-owned and -developed shopping centers close to suburban housing. Old stores were modernized in an effort to attract the "upscale" discount shopper. While this modernization required a substantial investment of capital, the improvements were designed to lead to a higher turnover of merchandise and a higher return on equity.

Management sought to control costs through several strategies. First, a computerized inventory system was installed and connected to the checkout registers. This system helped to improve inventory turnover by showing the exact count of inventory available for sale. As a result, slow-moving inventory was easily eliminated and purchasing agents were encouraged to maintain better control of inventory that sold quickly. Improved ordering techniques meant that fewer units of quick-selling inventory had to be kept on hand, which decreased the amount of inventory required per dollar of revenue. Thus, management was able to lower the amount of funds required for investment in inventory.

Costs associated with bad check charges were also attacked. Historically, ADS had accepted only cash or checks from its customers. Company credit cards, similar to those issued by Sears and J. C. Penney, were not a feasible alternative because ADS's low markup and gross profit margin would not cover the costs associated with store-owned credit cards. One solution was to accept third-party credit cards, such as VISA and Master Charge. This strategy was implemented four years ago and seemed successful.

All of these strategies had been in place for the past three years. The "upscale" discount department store approach to the retail industry clearly contrasted with the strategies of other large department stores such as Sears. Other retailers frequently issued their own credit cards, maintained high levels of inventory, and located their stores in rented or leased space in shopping malls. Thus, ADS faced retail competition from mall-based department stores as well as factory outlet malls, discount chain drugstores, and other discount department stores.

In preparation for the August meeting, Julie Adamson, the vice president of finance, has requested that you submit a complete financial analysis of ADS relative to the retail industry. To perform this task, you have been provided with ADS financial statements for the past five years (Exhibits 1 and 2). Exhibit 3 summarizes comparable retail industry averages provided by Robert Morris Associates.

EXHIBIT 1

American Department Stores, Inc.

Income Statements
(thousands)

	Current−4	Current−3	Year Current−2	Current−1	Current
Revenue	$12,731,852	$14,208,747	$16,538,981	$16,787,066	$18,616,856
Cost of goods sold	9,284,066	10,420,695	12,369,504	12,309,956	13,655,464
Gross profit	3,447,786	3,788,052	4,169,477	4,477,111	4,961,392
Operating expenses					
General & administrative	1,234,990	1,392,457	1,587,742	1,527,623	1,731,368
Advertising	1,387,772	1,591,380	1,819,288	1,829,790	2,010,620
Research & development	127,319	142,087	165,390	167,871	186,169
Depreciation	140,050	156,296	181,929	201,445	223,402
Other operating expenses	38,196	42,626	49,617	67,148	74,467
Total operating expenses	2,928,326	3,324,847	3,803,966	3,793,877	4,226,026
Operating profit	519,460	463,205	365,511	683,234	735,366
Other income	165,000	175,000	196,000	214,000	235,000
EBIT	684,460	638,205	561,511	897,234	970,366
Interest Expense	103,658	132,125	212,633	259,191	285,519
EBT	580,802	506,081	348,878	638,043	684,847
Taxes	249,745	207,493	114,432	243,732	292,429
Profit after taxes	331,057	298,588	234,446	394,310	392,417
Preferred dividends	79	79	79	79	79
Earnings available for common	330,979	298,509	234,368	394,232	392,339
Common dividends	30,710	34,395	39,309	51,593	56,506
Retained earnings	$ 300,269	$ 264,114	$ 195,059	$ 342,639	$ 335,832
Number shares outstanding	122,840	122,840	122,840	122,840	120,313
Earnings per share	$ 2.69	$ 2.43	$ 1.91	$ 3.21	$ 3.26
Average price per share	$ 23.98	$ 24.54	$ 20.61	$ 29.20	$ 29.67

EXHIBIT 2

American Department Stores, Inc.

Balance Sheets
(thousands)

	Current-4	Current-3	Year Current-2	Current-1	Current
Assets					
Cash	$ 416,884	$ 414,676	$ 493,502	$ 330,118	$ 552,195
Accounts receivable	811,233	890,333	980,335	1,052,873	1,120,167
Inventory	2,743,545	2,847,848	3,134,404	3,298,511	3,581,378
Other current assets	180,274	201,240	206,737	220,882	260,320
Total current assets	4,151,936	4,354,097	4,814,978	5,102,385	5,511,060
Gross fixed assets	6,276,984	6,663,496	7,093,890	7,619,497	8,023,216
Less: Accumulated depreciation	3,781,316	3,937,612	4,119,541	4,320,985	4,511,388
Net property, plant, & equipment	2,495,668	2,725,884	2,974,349	3,298,511	3,178,828
Other fixed assets	315,480	341,498	440,150	655,285	616,857
Total fixed assets	2,811,148	3,067,382	3,414,499	3,953,796	1,125,685
Total assets	$6,963,084	$7,421,478	$8,229,477	$9,056,180	$9,639,715

Liabilities & Net Worth

	Current-4	Current-3	Year Current-2	Current-1	Current
Current liabilities					
Accounts payable	$ 821,644	$ 942,528	$1,103,573	$1,177,303	$1,221,218
Accrued expenses	327,265	326,545	395,015	452,809	191,627
Short-term debt	364,010	593,718	641,899	642,989	597,661
Other current liabilities	410,822	467,553	534,916	470,921	616,911
Total current liabilities	2,123,741	2,330,344	2,675,403	2,744,023	2,930,482
Long-term liabilities					
Long-term debt	2,033,761	1,954,274	2,136,119	2,479,002	2,515,973
Other	118,372	185,537	271,573	314,135	113,128
Total long-term liabilities	2,152,134	2,139,811	2,407,692	2,823,136	2,959,102
Net worth					
Preferred stock	7,852	7,852	7,852	7,852	7,852
Common stock	2,557,607	2,557,607	2,557,607	2,557,607	2,182,615
Retained earnings	121,750	385,864	580,923	923,562	1,259,391
Total net worth	2,687,209	2,951,323	3,146,382	3,489,021	3,719,861
Total liabilities & net worth	$6,963,084	$7,421,478	$8,229,477	$9,056,180	$9,639,715

EXHIBIT 3

American Department Stores, Inc.

Industry Averages—Robert Morris Associates, Annual Statement Studies

				Year		
	Current–4	Current–3	Current–2	Current–1		Current
Percentage Income Statements						
Revenues	100.0	100.0	100.0	100.0		100.0
Gross profit	37.2	34.1	34.6	35.8		35.6
Operating expenses	33.9	31.1	31.6	32.4		32.3
Operating profit	3.3	2.9	3.1	3.4		3.4
All other expenses	0.4	0.4	0.8	0.3		0.7
Profit before taxes	2.9	2.6	2.2	3.1		2.7
Percentage Balance Sheets						
Assets						
Cash	7.4	6.8	7.4	7.2		7.0
Accounts receivable	20.0	18.9	19.2	18.8		19.9
Inventory	45.9	47.2	43.7	43.2		42.4
Other current assets	1.5	1.5	1.8	1.6		1.2
Total current assets	74.7	74.4	72.1	70.8		70.4
Net property, plant, and equipment	19.3	20.0	21.3	20.3		21.4
Other fixed assets	6.0	5.6	6.6	8.9		8.2
Total assets	100.0	100.0	100.0	100.0		100.0

Liabilities & Net Worth

Notes payable	8.9	8.9	7.8	7.5	6.5
Current maturity of long-term debt	2.3	2.2	1.9	1.9	2.1
Accounts payable	12.8	13.8	14.4	14.0	13.9
Accrued expenses	5.0	5.2	5.3	5.6	5.5
Other current liabilities	3.9	5.5	4.0	3.5	4.8
Total current liabilities	33.0	35.6	33.5	32.5	32.8
Long-term debt	17.0	16.5	17.7	14.6	16.2
Other long-term debt	1.7	2.5	3.3	3.8	4.6
Net worth	48.3	45.4	45.4	49.1	46.3
Total liabilities & net worth	100.0	100.0	100.0	100.0	100.0

Ratios

Current	2.3	2.3	2.2	2.3	2.3
Quick	0.9	0.8	0.9	0.8	1.0
Sales/receivable	11.4	12.4	12.2	9.5	8.7
Cost of sales/inventory	3.3	3.3	3.6	3.6	3.5
Sales/working capital	5.5	5.6	5.9	5.4	5.6
EBIT/interest	2.8	2.6	2.3	2.0	2.0
Cash flow coverage	2.6	2.4	3.1	2.5	2.5
Fixed assets/net worth	0.4	0.4	0.4	0.4	0.5
Total debt/net worth	1.1	1.2	1.2	1.2	1.3
% EBT/total net worth	13.4%	12.9%	10.9%	12.7%	11.9%
% EBT/total assets	5.8%	5.1%	4.3%	5.2%	5.0%
Sales/net fixed assets	14.0	14.1	11.9	13.5	11.7
Sales/total assets	2.2	2.2	2.1	2.1	2.1

QUESTIONS*

1. Prepare a percentage income statement and percentage balance sheet for ADS for each of the five years of financial statements.

2. Calculate five years of relevant financial ratios for ADS (including rates of return, profitability ratios, efficiency ratios, leverage ratios, liquidity ratios, measures of valuation, and sustainable growth rates), as well as annual and compound rates of growth in sales and total assets.

3. Calculate four years of statements of cash flow for ADS.

4. Analyze the book value return on equity relative to the company's risk. Comment on the company's strengths and weaknesses uncovered by this analysis.

*The computer spreadsheet model is named "ADS.wk1."

CASE 7

Hasbro, Inc.

Financial Ratio Analysis

In mid-1988, Charles Stevens, vice president for investment analysis at First National Bank of Florida, was looking for a company to recommend to the bank's portfolio committee for inclusion on its "buy list." Portfolio managers selected stocks from this "buy list" for the various trust funds managed by First National's trust department. Stevens's criteria for recommending a company were that it be a "good, fundamentally sound, long-term prospect, not a hot stock." Since the stock market crash in October 1987, portfolio returns had been rather weak. Stevens hoped to convince the portfolio committee to take a long-term view of the market rather than focus on short-term price changes.

Stevens had recently read an article in *The Wall Street Journal* concerning Hasbro, Inc. (HI), a toy manufacturer. HI had posted a six-month pre-tax profit margin of 10 percent. While this was below the 15 percent margins enjoyed during the 1984–1986 period, it was far ahead of the margins for other companies in the industry. Perhaps HI was a good long-term investment.

The toy industry depended on three main factors for growth: the economy, demographics, and product innovations on a regular basis. During most of the 1980s, toy manufacturers had benefited from favorable conditions on all of these factors. The U.S. economy was in its sixth year of expansion, even though the stock market had suffered a sharp decline in October 1987. Unemployment and interest rates were at their lowest in 10 years. Demographics also favored toy manufacturers—birth rates were increasing, the grandparent population was growing, and two-income families were on the rise.

The average life for new products in the toy industry was only one or two Christmas seasons. Companies had two choices to maintain their sales strength. Either they came up with regular product innovations or they relied on strong standby toys.

Hasbro had changed its marketing strategy during the past two years. Management was concentrating on its solid-performing toys and moving away from the highly risky (yet potentially very profitable) promotional, faddish toys that had dominated the toy market in the early 1980s. Since 1986, shipments of these "blockbuster" toys had steadily declined, leaving the manufacturers with obsolete inventory and machinery. Examples of such "hot" toys were Tonka's Pound Puppies and Coleco's Cabbage Patch Kids. Coleco and Tonka had both tried to expand during the uncertain 1987 Christmas market. These attempts had left Coleco filing for Chapter 11 bankruptcy in July of 1988 and Tonka with an excessively leveraged balance sheet (88 percent to total capital).

In contrast, both Hasbro and Mattel had bitten the bullet in 1987. They had trimmed overhead, written down inventories, and closed plants with excess capacity. Hasbro was concentrating on its traditional toy line, including G.I. Joe, board games acquired through the 1984 purchase of Milton Bradley (e.g., Monopoly), and preschool games acquired through the 1985 purchase of Child Guidance.

In 1988, Hasbro had three potential major strengths for the next several years. First, the company had recently announced the purchase from Coleco of two operations that produced ride-on toys and outdoor furniture for children. These were expected to complement Hasbro's solid array of preschool items. Second, Hasbro received the toy license from the hit movie *Who Framed Roger Rabbit?*, which appealed to both adults and children. Third, Hasbro was rumored to be planning a 1989 entry into the high-tech market with a toy its developers called "NEMO" (Never Ever Mentioned Outside). NEMO was rumored to be a computer video game that would compete with Nintendo in the pricey and highly profitable end of the toy market.

In preparation for the necessary analysis, Stevens had collected Hasbro's financial statements and industry data for the past five years. Exhibit 1 contains company income statements for the years 1983 to 1987. Exhibit 2 provides comparable balance sheets. Exhibit 3 contains industry average percentage income statements, balance sheets, and ratios as reported by Robert Morris and Associates.

——————————— **EXHIBIT 1** ———————————

Hasbro, Inc.

Income Statements
(thousands)

	1983	1984	1985	1986	1987
Revenues	$221,522	$714,392	$1,220,352	$1,329,631	$1,345,089
Cost of goods sold	107,136	340,007	556,192	605,071	647,342
Gross profit	114,386	374,385	664,160	724,560	697,747
Operating expenses					
General & admin- istrative	71,871	206,652	382,271	437,221	443,713
Selling expenses	0	0	0	0	0
Research & development	8,794	21,924	40,345	57,701	69,472
Depreciation	5,100	14,100	19,467	34,009	52,077
Other	0	0	0	0	0
Total operating expenses	85,765	242,676	442,083	528,931	565,262
Operating profit	28,621	131,709	222,077	195,629	132,485
Other income	3,343	6,048	10,499	25,828	171
EBIT	31,964	137,757	232,576	221,457	132,656
Interest expense	2,400	27,546	37,661	29,619	33,021
EBT	29,564	110,211	194,915	191,838	99,635
Taxes	14,334	57,823	95,946	92,679	51,412
Profit after taxes	15,230	52,388	98,969	99,159	48,223
Preferred dividend	0	0	2,769	2,559	2,817
Earnings available to equity	15,230	52,388	96,200	96,600	45,406
Common dividend	1,628	2,774	3,858	4,740	4,757
Retained earnings	$ 13,602	$ 49,614	$ 92,342	$ 91,860	$ 40,649
Number of shares outstanding	32,550	46,230	48,220	52,663	52,850
Earnings per share	$0.47	$1.13	$2.00	$1.83	$0.86
Average price per share	$3.85	$8.55	$15.55	$23.75	$18.25

EXHIBIT 2

Hasbro, Inc.

Balance Sheets
(thousands)

	1983	1984	1985	1986	1987
			Assets		
Current assets					
Cash	$ 40,972	$ 62,786	$182,385	$116,061	$ 161,770
Accounts receivable	48,726	200,797	241,786	305,489	339,556
Inventory	9,797	76,753	67,856	122,902	133,585
Other current assets	7,906	23,757	38,407	57,010	57,721
Total current assets	107,401	364,093	530,434	601,462	692,632
Gross fixed assets	28,240	107,755	146,553	231,508	297,900
Less: Accumulated depreciation	13,850	18,136	37,233	70,038	121,647
Net property, plant, and equipment	14,390	89,619	109,320	161,470	176,253
Other fixed assets	9,468	211,810	205,879	218,928	207,107
Total fixed assets	23,858	301,429	315,199	380,398	383,360
Total assets	$131,259	$665,522	$845,633	$981,860	$1,075,992
		Liabilities and Net Worth			
Current liabilities					
Accounts payable	$ 20,122	$ 30,349	$ 45,856	$ 91,142	$ 88,239
Accrued expenses	18,995	105,742	142,685	107,950	115,089
Accrued taxes	10,956	23,991	24,486	30,853	26,183
Short-term debt	1,303	83,404	26,687	42,475	74,397
Total current liabilities	51,376	243,486	239,714	272,420	303,908
Long-term liabilities					
Long-term debt	3,063	127,537	185,746	124,977	127,127
Other	1,035	1,524	2,240	4,191	3,414
Total long-term liabilities	4,098	129,061	187,986	129,168	130,541
Net worth					
Preferred stock	2,051	35,728	3,517	3,517	3,517
Common stock	36,443	170,342	235,169	305,648	326,269
Retained earnings	37,291	86,905	179,247	271,107	311,757
Total net worth	75,785	292,975	417,933	580,272	641,543
Total liabilities and net worth	$131,259	$665,522	$845,633	$981,860	$1,075,992

EXHIBIT 3
Hasbro, Inc.

Industry Averages—Robert Morris Associates, Annual Statement Studies

	1983	1984	1985	1986	1987
Percentage Income Statements					
Revenues	100.0%	100.0%	100.0%	100.0%	100.0%
Gross profit	34.7%	35.0%	34.6%	35.1%	35.0%
Operating expenses	29.8%	28.2%	29.9%	28.3%	29.6%
Operating profit	4.8%	6.8%	4.7%	6.8%	5.4%
All other expenses	3.0%	2.7%	2.1%	3.1%	2.0%
Profit before taxes	1.8%	4.1%	2.7%	3.7%	3.4%
Percentage Balance Sheets					
Assets					
Cash	9.5%	8.3%	7.4%	8.9%	8.5%
Accounts receivable	29.0%	30.4%	28.7%	31.0%	28.0%
Inventory	34.1%	31.2%	33.7%	29.7%	33.1%
Other current assets	2.3%	3.2%	1.9%	3.4%	2.6%
Total current assets	74.9%	73.1%	71.7%	73.0%	72.2%
Net property, plant, & equipment	19.0%	19.7%	20.5%	19.1%	18.4%
Other fixed assets	6.1%	7.4%	7.7%	7.8%	9.3%
Total assets	100.0%	100.2%	99.9%	99.9%	99.9%
Liabilities & Net Worth					
Notes payable	14.3%	12.2%	18.6%	14.5%	15.1%
Current maturity of long-term debt	2.8%	2.8%	2.8%	4.6%	4.0%
Accounts payable	13.0%	13.5%	14.6%	13.0%	13.3%
Accrued taxes	0.0%	0.0%	0.7%	1.6%	1.7%
Other current liabilities	10.2%	11.6%	11.2%	8.7%	8.2%
Total current liabilities	40.3%	40.1%	47.9%	42.4%	42.3%
Long-term debt	14.7%	16.2%	13.9%	13.5%	13.4%
Other long-term debt	4.7%	3.5%	3.4%	2.8%	3.1%
Net worth	40.5%	40.4%	34.0%	41.3%	41.0%
Total liabilities & net worth	100.2%	100.2%	99.2%	100.0%	99.8%
Ratios					
Current	1.9	1.9	1.6	1.8	1.8
Quick	0.9	1.0	0.8	1.0	1.0
Sales/receivable	6.9	6.1	6.5	5.7	5.9
Cost of sales/inventory	3.7	3.4	3.8	4.5	4.1
Cost of sales/payables	10.8	9.5	9.5	11.1	10.2
Sales/working capital	6.0	5.1	6.7	5.3	5.5
EBIT/interest	1.8	2.2	2.0	1.9	3.6
Cash flow coverage	1.9	2.3	3.3	1.4	3.8
Fixed assets/net worth	40.0%	50.0%	60.0%	50.0%	40.0%
Total debt/net worth	160.0%	150.0%	190.0%	150.0%	170.0%
% EBT/total net worth	14.8%	20.2%	18.5%	17.1%	28.9%
% EBT/total assets	6.5%	5.9%	4.9%	6.7%	7.8%
Sales/net fixed assets	11.3	10.3	11.2	10.2	11.6
Sales/total assets	1.9	1.6	1.7	1.7	1.6

QUESTIONS*

1. Prepare a percentage income statement and percentage balance sheet for Hasbro for each of the years 1983 to 1987.

2. Calculate five years of relevant financial ratios for Hasbro (including rates of return, profitability ratios, efficiency ratios, leverage ratios, liquidity ratios, measures of valuation, and sustainable growth rates), as well as annual and compound rates of growth in sales and total assets.

3. Calculate four years of cash flow statements.

4. Analyze the book value return on equity relative to the company's risk. Comment on the company's strengths and weaknesses uncovered by this analysis.

*The spreadsheet model is named "HASBRO.wk1."

CASE 8

Hokie Pool Sales

Cash Budgeting

In mid-March, Eric Swank, president of Hokie Pool Sales (HPS), contacted Financial Advisors, Inc., to arrange for a professional consultant to come into his company. In the past year, it had become increasingly evident that HPS was having definite problems in formulating its cash flows. On March 31, Financial Advisors sent over Julie Lynn. It was planned that she would work with HPS for a one-month period to help HPS analyze its cash inflows and outflows and thereby manage its cash budget more efficiently. Lynn spent her first week working closely with Swank, learning company background and basic operational strategies. She set for her first goal the formulation of a cash budget covering the next six months.

During her first week with the company, Lynn learned that HPS was founded in 1968 by Swank as a pool construction firm based in Crown Point, Indiana. It was a small business that grew very rapidly, surrounded as it was by some of the wealthier counties in northern Indiana.

Although HPS had shown good growth and profit-making ability in the past, it always had considerable cash flow problems resulting from its highly seasonal sales pattern. Therefore, in 1990, in an attempt to smooth out this seasonal fluctuation, HPS set up winter operations in Merritt Island, Florida. Although this effort did have a stabilizing effect on the monthly sales pattern, it did not eliminate the problem, since, as of 1992, Indiana sales remained three times greater than Florida sales.

In July 1991, cash flow problems caused by this seasonal pattern of sales forced the postponement of the purchase of some badly needed construction equipment, which resulted in long construction delays. Consequently, HPS was forced to take a three-year loan of $120,000 at 10 percent per annum at the First American Bank of Crown Point.

In September 1991, in an attempt to speed up HPS's cash flows, Jenny Bellich, bookkeeper for HPS, contacted Mainline Billing, Inc., to handle billing and to aid in the collection of delinquent accounts. This resulted in a significant improvement in average collection time, primarily in those accounts over one month past due. Bellich reported to Swank that currently 10 percent of the sales were for cash and the remainder of the sales were on credit. Twenty percent of the credit sales were paid 30 days after the sale, 70 percent of the credit sales were paid 60 days after the sale, 7 percent of the credit sales were paid 90 days after the sale, and the remaining 3 percent of credit sales resulted in bad debts. Although instituting the new billing system for customers and developing tighter credit checks and collection procedures did not totally solve HPS's cash flow problem, it did bring about significant improvement in its average collection period and in its bad debts to total sales ratios. Bellich has also approached Swank about the possibility of offering trade discounts to customers as a method of speeding up collection of accounts receivable. Swank has seriously considered this alternative, but has not adopted it because, he says, "Why should we bribe customers to pay their bills on time when that is what they are legally obligated to do anyway? The whole idea sounds shady, costs money, and doesn't make much sense." Actual sales through March 1992 and forecasted sales for the following seven months are given in Exhibit 1.

In looking at HPS's cash flow patterns, Lynn found that the cash outflows are largely tied to expected future sales, with expenditures on cost of goods sold amounting to 60 percent of the following month's sales. In addition, HPS pays sales and administrative expenses, and wages and salaries amounting to $5,000 per month plus variable wages resulting from unskilled labor hired to help in peak seasons. Expected variable wages are given in Exhibit 2. HPS's rent expenditures are constant over the year, running approximately $2,000 per month. Moreover, a semiannual interest payment on the $120,000, 10 percent loan from the First American Bank is due in July, along with the first sinking fund payment on that loan of $40,000. Besides these cash outflows, a dividend payment of $10,000 is expected to be declared in May and made during the coming June, and tax payments of $5,000 are due on the calendar quarters. In addition, the capital expenditure associated with the construction equipment, originally planned for purchase in 1991, is to be made in May of 1992 and will involve $30,000. One-third of this expenditure will be paid immediately in cash, with the second third being paid in June and the remaining third in Sep-

—————— EXHIBIT 1 ——————

Hokie Pool Sales

Actual and Expected Sales,
First 10 Months of 1992

	Sales
January	$ 15,000
February	10,000
March	25,000
April	30,000
May	60,000
June	100,000
July	100,000
August	60,000
September	25,000
October	20,000

—————— EXHIBIT 2 ——————

Hokie Pool Sales

Expected Variable Wages

	Wages
April	$1,000
May	3,000
June	6,000
July	6,000
August	3,000
September	1,000

tember. The final expense incurred by HPS during this planning period is monthly depreciation of $3,000.

Through discussions with Swank, Lynn learned that HPS always has a minimum cash balance of $25,000 on hand. Swank feels that any less would interfere with HPS's ability to conduct its ordinary business—that is, making purchases and sales—given the unpredictability of cash inflows and outflows. On March 31, 1992, this cash balance was $80,000—$55,000 over the minimum. On April 30, 1992, Lynn's cash budget was due.

QUESTIONS

1. If Hokie Pool Sales can estimate its profit in the upcoming months, is it necessary for the firm also to estimate its cash budget? Why or why not?

2. What time period (monthly, daily, hourly) should you attempt to analyze in preparing a cash budget?

3. Prepare a monthly cash budget for April through September.

4. If inflows and outflows are not constant during each month, might the analysis be affected?

5. What was the most important estimate required in making this analysis? Why?

6. Comment on Swank's opinion of trade credit discounts.

7. What cash strategy should Julie Lynn recommend to Swank?

CASE 9

Harlington Manufacturing Company

Cash Budgeting

In July 1991, Jim Hunter purchased the Harlington Manufacturing Company for $200,000. Hunter is 48 years old and was vice president of a large manufacturing firm prior to his acquisition of Harlington. Although he had been very successful, he had long dreamed of having his own business and settling down to a less hectic life-style. The opportunity to purchase Harlington came suddenly, and Hunter was quick to recognize the opportunity as a sound one.

Hunter's industrial experience was primarily in marketing and sales; however, he had some limited contact with the financial aspects of a firm's management. Harlington's primary problem at the time of acquisition related to the rather loose control exercised by its former owner, who had been trying to sell the firm and retire for the past four years. During the first five months of his management, Hunter was able to reduce operating costs substantially and in general "tighten up" the firm's operations. This reorganization resulted in some minor personnel changes, but primarily it took the form of better control over production scheduling, materials management, and direct labor cost.

Although significant improvements had been made in the firm's overall operations, Hunter felt that his decisions could best be characterized as "seat of the pants," and he wanted to implement a better system for planning future expenditures. In the past, the firm had utilized a very loosely constructed cash flow statement and depended on its line of credit with the Mercantile National Bank for any cash deficiencies from operations.[1] Hunter believed that this system was simply inadequate in light of his plans for expansion of the firm's operations over the next two years.

Just before closing down the plant for a one-week period at Christmas, Hunter asked his production and sales supervisors to provide him with a complete set of monthly sales and expense estimates covering the first half of 1992. This information, along with the company's past operating history, was used to compile the predicted revenue and expense data found in Exhibit 1.

In addition to those items included in Exhibit 1, Hunter was told that purchases were 75 percent of sales and were made one month in advance on credit terms of 1/15, net 60.[2] Also, direct labor cost (wages) was estimated at 10 percent of cost of sales, with wages paid weekly. Finally, sales commissions amounted to 2 percent of sales and were paid one month following the month in which the sales occurred.

Beyond these operating revenue and expense items, the firm incurs a number of expenses related to overhead, loan repayments, interest, insurance, and dividends. The predicted amounts of these expenses for the next six months are shown in Exhibit 2.

After inquiring about the firm's collections, Hunter learned that approximately 60 percent of the firm's customers take advantage of the cash discount terms (1/15, net 60) offered by the firm, with another 10 percent paying within 30 days after the sale and 29 percent making payment during the second month after the sale. Bad debts are estimated at 1 percent of sales.

EXHIBIT 1

Harlington Manufacturing Company

Predicted Revenue and Expense Data

	Jan.	Feb.	Mar.	Apr.	May	June	July
Sales	$250,000	$260,000	$270,000	$260,000	$250,000	$250,000	$260,000
Salaries	5,800	5,800	5,800	5,800	5,800	5,800	5,800
Utilities	1,250	1,250	1,250	1,250	1,250	1,250	1,250
Rent	1,200	1,200	1,200	1,200	1,200	1,200	1,200
Advertising	500	500	500	500	500	500	500
Depreciation	200	200	200	200	200	200	200
Office supplies*	450	450	450	450	450	450	450

*Postage, stationery, coffee room supplies, and so on.

[1] Hunter had continued the good working relationship with the Mercantile National Bank and had arranged for a $50,000 line of credit at 1 percent over prime.

[2] The firm follows the practice of taking all cash discounts.

--- EXHIBIT 2 ---

Harlington Manufacturing Company

Projected Expenses

Amount	Date Due	Explanation
$1,000	February	Last installment on two delivery vans purchased in 1991
2,000	March	Semiannual interest on long-term debt
400	March and June	Common stock dividends*
1,000	March	Payroll taxes
20,000	January	Quarterly income tax payment
20,000	April	Quarterly income tax payment
52,000	April	Bank note due
650	June	Semiannual insurance premium

*$0.40 per share on 1,000 outstanding shares, all of which are held by Hunter.

Hunter plans to embark on a major expansion as soon as the firm has generated sufficient funds internally. The expansion will require approximately $50,000 as an initial expenditure, followed by a total outlay of $200,000 over the next two years. In light of the firm's past use of debt funds (primarily a $50,000 five-year note with an insurance company), Hunter feels that the initial outlay must come from internally generated funds.

QUESTIONS

1. Based on the information provided, prepare a monthly cash budget for Harlington covering the next six months. Sales for November and December of 1991 were $250,000 and $270,000, respectively.

2. If Hunter believes that the firm should maintain a minimum cash balance of $5,000 and if the beginning balance for January is $6,000, identify the months and the amounts of funds that Harlington will have to borrow in the budget period. You may assume borrowing in minimum increments of $1,000 with interest payable at 12 percent per annum in the month for which the loan is outstanding. Repayments should be made as soon as sufficient funds are available. Also, excess cash can be invested for minimum periods of 90 days and in units of $10,000 to earn a net return of 8 percent (before taxes but after brokerage fees).

3. When approximately will the firm have sufficient funds available to make the down payment on the planned expansion?

CASE 10

The Jackson Farm

Part I: Cash Budgeting

It is the day after the Thanksgiving holiday, and Howard Jackson is a contented man. He has just finished an early, country-style breakfast with his wife and two sons. Both boys, only a year apart in age, are home from college until Monday; during this period they enjoy taking over the operation of the farm. This gives Jackson some "time away from the fields." He is using the pause to attend to bookkeeping matters, and he does so with great attention to detail. This business attribute is unlike that possessed by many of his neighbors, who own and make a living running similar farms.

Jackson settles into the comfortable den of his large farmhouse and lights the logs that rest in the stone-faced fireplace. The den directly faces the sharp winds that blow east over the foothills of the Allegheny Mountains, and he wants to remove the chill that pervades the den during the morning hours.

Running this farm is a pleasure for Jackson. Three years ago, he effected a major career change, which appeared drastic to many, but to him was the fulfillment of a dream. He is now 45 years old. Prior to the purchase of his 540-acre farm near Monterey, Virginia, Jackson had put in exactly 20 years with Bethard-Wheeling Iron and Steel. Those years saw him rise from the position of cost clerk to that of director of cost accounting systems for the entire firm. While with Bethard-Wheeling, Jackson occupied positions in the four-state region of Pennsylvania, West Virginia, Virginia, and Maryland.

Three events that occurred almost simultaneously resulted in his leaving the post with the steel manufacturer and entering the agribusiness industry. First, Jackson suffered a slight coronary warning, as it was described by his physician. Although no actual damage affected the heart muscle, Sally Jackson (his wife) strongly suggested that the sometimes heavy demands of his executive position (which regularly translated into 16-to-18-hour workdays) had taken an unreasonable toll on his physical condition. Second, the fact that Jackson had served Bethard-Wheeling for 20 years meant that he could retire and draw immediate pension benefits. The vesting provisions of the pension plan, run privately by this manufacturer, were among the more liberal in the steel industry. The requirement for a fully vested right in the pension plan was that the worker's age plus years of work service total 62. Howard had reached that milestone at such a relatively young age (then 42) because he had not switched employers during his career within the Financial Controls Department of Bethard-Wheeling. Upon retirement, he began drawing (on a monthly basis) annual benefits totaling exactly 55 percent of the average of his last five years' annual salary. That turned out to be 55 percent of $38,000. The third situation that prompted Jackson's leaving the world of manufacturing was the opportunity to purchase, through an estate auction, the farmland and operation he now managed.

Located in east-central Virginia, The Jackson Farm (TJF) consists primarily of 540 acres of open, fertile, limestone-based land, a few wooded acres, and several buildings. Jackson is especially concerned on this day after Thanksgiving with the preparation of an estimate of cash receipts and disbursements covering the upcoming year for TJF. A 150-acre parcel of land that he especially prizes is to be put on the market in January. The land lies adjacent to his present operation and will be easy to meld into the overall activities of the farm. Jackson knows that he cannot pay cash for the 150-acre parcel, but he has discussed a real estate loan with the credit analyst at the Farmers' Loan Association. As one piece of information to evaluate, the credit analyst requested that Jackson prepare a formal cash budget to cover the next January-December period of operations. Jackson has turned to this task, which he does regularly each year at this time, though not in quite the detail that will characterize the present budget.

The heart of TJF is its herd of Hereford cattle. One hundred brooder cows are owned. These cows (recognizable by their white faces, reddish coats, and white markings) have produced, on the average, one calf each per year. Last week Jackson purchased 50 feeder calves. These calves individually weighed about 380 to 420 pounds and cost an average of $140 each. Payment for the calves will occur at the rate of one-third of the total price during each of the first three months of next year. Also, at this time next year, another 40 feeder calves will be acquired, but the first payment will occur during December, with the remaining two of the three equal payments taking place in January and February of the budget period subsequent to this one. The price of the calves to be acquired next year is estimated at the lower level of $132 per animal.

All the feeders acquired last week, combined with 88 of the calves reared from the brooder herd, will be sold within the cash planning period. These 138 yearlings will weigh in the neighborhood of 750 to 900 pounds each. The projected selling price is an average of $290 per head. The timing of the sales is noted in Exhibit 1.

The terms of sale for the yearlings is 10 percent cash down and 90 percent to be received in the month following sale. At present, none of the brooder herd is unproductive, so no older cows will be marketed. Jackson realizes, however, that in future years some feeder calves might have to be retained and a few older cows sold to maintain an acceptable rate of production.

Another central facet of TJF is its sheep flock, which consists of 90 ewes. These livestock produce offspring at a normal annual rate of 130 percent per sheep. Jackson believes that the market will bring $52 for each lamb. The number of lambs TJF sells during specific months has varied quite a bit in the past three years. Jackson reviews his ledgers and settles upon the data displayed in Exhibit 2 as a reasonable estimate of the market liquidation pace for next year's lamb flock. Full payment for the lambs is received in the month immediately following the sale.

A by-product of raising sheep is the sheared wool available from the flock. Jackson is forecasting that 650 pounds of wool will be sheared next spring. Although he is rather certain of the amount of wool that can be sold, the price at which it can be marketed is subject to more variability. Recalling (1) what he has received per pound in the past, (2) what neighboring farm owners have received, and (3) his recent discussion with an agricultural extension agent from a major state university, he puts together some price estimates and their related chances of occurring (Exhibit 3). Half the wool will be sold for cash in May and the other half in June. After some deliberation, Jackson decides to weigh all possible sales prices for the wool by their respective chances of occurring and use the resultant expected value as the price per pound in his final budget presentation. Further, as the price of wool this year was depressed below a subsidy level computed by the Agricultural Conservation Service, TJF will receive a cash payment amounting to $170 in April.

Jackson now reflects on deriving useful projections for payments arising from the purchase of feed, seed, and fertilizer. The timing of these sources of farm operating expense is highly certain, but rising prices in recent years make estimation of their cost levels somewhat hazy. Continued

─────── EXHIBIT 1 ───────

The Jackson Farm

Sale of Yearlings

Month	Number to Be Sold
April	28
July	41
September	41
October	28

─────── EXHIBIT 2 ───────

The Jackson Farm

Sale of Lambs

Month	Percentage to Be Sold
May	26%
June	40
July	17
August	17

─────── EXHIBIT 3 ───────

The Jackson Farm

Estimated Wool Prices

Possible Price per Pound	Probability of Occurrence
$0.33	.05
0.34	.10
0.35	.15
0.36	.20
0.38	.20
0.39	.15
0.40	.10
0.41	.05

prospects of this inflationary spiral cloud the pleasant feeling that engulfed Howard Jackson earlier in his preparation of the budget. During the current year, $1,800 will be spent on the acquisition of feed for the livestock possessed by TJF. Jackson feels that this will rise to $2,000 over the next planning period. The feed purchases will be of equal amounts concentrated in two periods of each year: (1) January through May and (2) October through December. Cash outflows for these eight payments will be made in the same month the feed is acquired.

Besides selling cattle, sheep, and wool, TJF also benefits from the sale of grain. The grain is raised mainly to feed the livestock, but because of the size of the farm and its fertile land, some excess is always available for market. Oats and corn are regularly planted. The seeds for these crops will cost $720 in total and will be purchased in the middle of March. Payment will occur 30 days later. When the grain is harvested, another expense results. Both because of the high cost of harvesting equipment and the fact that he only uses such machinery twice a year, Jackson rents the equipment when it is needed. The oats are combined during July, the corn is harvested in October. The equipment is hired on a cash basis and will cost $220 for each rental. Based upon recent experience, Jackson believes that he will get $1,500 for the excess oats. This surplus will be sold in July, with payment being received in August. From the current season, some $4,000 worth of "extra" corn is available. Half will be sold within two weeks (during December) and the other half during January. Cash receipts from the corn sale will occur in the month immediately following the sale. Next year, Jackson plans to accelerate the pace of liquidation of his surplus corn crop. Three years of operating TJF have provided him with enough confidence to estimate accurately the feed requirements of his cattle and sheep herds. Thus, the corn above his own forecasted needs will be sold in equal amounts upon harvest in October and during the month of November, about a year from now. Jackson estimates that the value of the subsequent corn crop will be the same as this year's, and payment will follow the existing pattern.

Jackson recognizes well the benefits of effective fertilization of the corn crop. He anticipates spending $1,300 for such purposes during the one-year planning horizon. Plow-down fertilizer amounting to $540 will be purchased in May. In July, he will buy $760 worth of liquid nitrate and some herbicide. The terms of sale for these materials are 30 days net. On such terms, it is Jackson's policy to delay payment until the very last day; therefore, the actual cash drain occurs in the month after receipt of the goods.

TJF employs part-time laborers on a continual basis to operate effectively. The average monthly labor expense has been in the area of $1,000 to $1,100. Jackson decides to play it safe on this input to the budget and uses the upper limit of this historical range as the projected monthly labor expense. In addition to this figure, seasonal variation affects the labor cost estimates. Extra help has to be taken on during hay season to speed up the harvest and mitigate risk caused by the natural elements. TJF makes two-thirds of its hay in June, one-sixth in May, and one-sixth in July. The total added labor cost during hay season is projected to be $600. All labor is paid on a weekly basis.

Because of the rather random nature of their occurrence, Jackson decides to allocate evenly to each month of the year one-twelfth of the

---
EXHIBIT 4

The Jackson Farm

Randomly Occurring Cash Expenditures

Source	Annual Outflow
Gas and oil	$1,400
Veterinary services and medicine	800
Miscellaneous supplies	500
Repairs	1,800

annual expected total of four categories of cash expenses. These items are (1) gas and oil, (2) veterinary services and medicine, (3) miscellaneous supplies, and (4) building and machinery repairs. The totals forecast for these expenditure sources are tabulated in Exhibit 4.

Other areas of expenditure that regularly draw upon the cash resources of TJF and have to be considered are (1) its monthly interest and principal payment of $600, (2) a $2,000 county real estate tax paid every November, and (3) insurance payments of $300 each March and November. While pondering these noncontrollable outflows, Howard Jackson also notes that he will incur depreciation expense of $375 every month of the coming year.

Adding some stability to the revenue picture of TJF are the four small wood-frame houses located on each of the extreme corners of the farmland. Howard Jackson rents these houses, and because of his extraordinary attention to basic maintenance, he has no trouble in finding local families willing to sign one-year leases. As each of the houses is of about the same size, they rent for identical annual amounts of $1,560 each. Rental payments are received monthly.

A final source of income to TJF is the sale of firewood. Jackson has been clearing a few wooded acres on the farm and selling the preponderance of the wood at $25 per pickup truckload, payable on delivery. During the next calendar year, he estimates that 40 loads will be sold. The sales are forecasted to occur in equal amounts in January, February, November, and December.

The current year has not been a good one for most cattle raisers. As a result, TJF will have no taxable income this year; thus, no tax payment will be built into the cash budget. Moreover, as the loss will be quite small for the current year, no tax refund resulting from the carryback procedure of net operating losses will be incorporated into the construction of the budget.

When the planning year begins, Howard Jackson will have a cash balance of $7,000 in his farm-related demand deposit account at a local bank.

He uses a completely separate account for the personal needs of his family. For the most part, he is unconcerned with strict adherence to the maintenance of a minimum cash balance. This is because the local bank appreciates the demand deposit of TJF and has informally (orally) agreed to a line of credit, not to exceed $5,000, which may be drawn down as needed. Because of a personal preference, however, Jackson dislikes the demand deposit balance of TJF to slip below $1,000. This $1,000 minimum cash level, then, will be a part of his formal budget.

QUESTIONS

1. Using all available information, construct a cash budget for The Jackson Farm covering the upcoming January-December period.

2. In your final budget package, include a schedule or financial worksheet that details by month the timing and amount of any necessary borrowing. Assume repayments on any needed borrowings are made as soon as cash is available for that purpose. Surplus funds will be accumulated as cash and not invested in any short-term financial assets. Further, the analyst from the Farmers' Loan Association has instructed Jackson not to include in the final budget schedules interest payments that may arise from any short-term borrowing.

3. As a secondary consideration, review your budget schedules and comment upon whether you think Jackson's commercial bank will be wary of, or highly concerned with, the financial position of the farm after the 12-month planning period has ended.

CASE 11

The Jackson Farm

Part II: Financial Ratio Analysis

On this ninth day of January, Eliot Dudley finishes his morning coffee at the small diner in the center of the business district of Verona, Virginia. He then begins to walk briskly the four blocks to his office. He is anticipating receiving some documents in today's mail that will permit him to take action on a real estate loan request made by Howard Jackson.

Dudley is the manager of the regional Farmers' Loan Association located in Verona. As manager, he serves as executive officer of this local association, a post he has occupied for the past 12 years. The Verona Farmers' Loan Association is regulated by the Federal Land Bank of Hagerstown, Maryland. The Maryland District consists of the five-state region encompassing Delaware, Maryland, Pennsylvania, Virginia, and West Virginia. Each regional association is actually a corporation, is organized by borrowers from its district, and is operated in a specifically defined geographic area under a federal charter. The local associations perform the critical function of originating business for the national Farm Credit System. By being close to the public, the local association is best able to determine the borrowing needs and capabilities of the farm businesses in its area. From a national perspective, the Federal Land Banks are a major supplier of real estate credit to agriculture. Dudley often speaks to local service clubs and groups as a means of subtly advertising the financing services available through his association. Recently, he has drawn upon the

information shown in Exhibit 1 to point out that in terms of outstanding
real estate debt, the Federal Land Banks are the largest institutional lender.

The increasing role played by the Federal Land Banks and their local
associations in financing farm real estate needs has been accompanied by
tighter reporting requirements initiated by the Federal Land Banks. The
local associations have had to pay more attention in recent years to making
accurate assessments of the financial condition of their loan applicants. Accuracy is satisfied in part by a financial analysis (ratio analysis) of the farm
business that is seeking the credit.

Dudley's office is involved in making three major types of loans. First,
loans are made to farmers, both incorporated and unincorporated, who
are mainly involved in a farming-type operation. Second, loans are extended to individual economic units and business economic units that perform farm-related services. These loans involve the extension of credit to
applicants who provide a custom-type service to the farmer. Third, loans
are available to the owners of rural residences. Usually, the loans are limited to 85 percent of the value of the property offered as security for the
credit. In almost every case, the current market value of the property is
used as the appraised value in setting the upper limit on the amount of the
loan. The maturity period of the loans granted by the Farmers' Loan Associations ranges from 5 to 40 years.

Last month Eliot Dudley received from Howard Jackson a 12-month
cash budget covering the current year for The Jackson Farm (TJF). Dudley
had requested the budget as part of the information needed to evaluate
Jackson's request for a loan to purchase 150 acres of prime farming land
near Monterey (see The Jackson Farm, Part I). Dudley was impressed by
the budget's detail and Jackson's overall understanding of the assumptions

--- **EXHIBIT 1** ---

Farm Real Estate Debt Outstanding

Year-End Totals, 1964 versus 1974

	1964		1974	
Lender	Dollar Volume (in millions)	As a % of Total	Dollar Volume (in millions)	As a % of Total
Commercial banks	$ 2,417	12.8%	$ 5,966	12.9%
Farmers Home Administration	1,285	6.8	3,212	6.9
Federal Land Bank	3,687	19.5	13,402	28.9
Life insurance companies	4,288	22.7	6,317	13.6
Individuals and others	7,218	38.2	17,408	37.6
Total	$18,895	100.0%	$46,305	100.0%

Source: Monthly Review, Federal Reserve Bank of Kansas City (November 1975), p. 13.

built into it. He visited with Howard Jackson on two separate occasions at his farm to inspect the assets and get a feel for Jackson's grasp of the farming business. Dudley was well satisfied that even though Howard Jackson had spent most of his working life in the steel manufacturing world, he was an energetic farmer with a thorough knowledge of his business. The land that Jackson desired to acquire would be utilized fully as part of the regular agribusiness operation that he owned and managed. The parcel had recently been appraised at $400 per acre for purposes of this loan request. Jackson also had assurances from the present owner that if he would pay the appraised price of the land, it would be sold to him. Dudley needed information from Jackson concerning the amount he actually wanted to borrow from the local association, as Jackson had indicated that a substantial amount of the purchase price would be met out of his own personal financial resources.

As usual, Dudley's secretary had arrived at the office before him and placed the morning mail along with another cup of coffee on his desk. On top of the stack is the hoped-for letter and set of documents from Howard Jackson.

Dudley quickly reads the memorandum from Jackson (Exhibit 2). He then takes the financial statements (Exhibits 3 and 4) and performs a preliminary analysis of the cash flow–generating ability of the firm (Exhibit 6). He observes that during the past three years the cash flow return on total assets has ranged from 5.53 percent to 10.01 percent. The past year has been a bad one for most farms in the district served by the Verona Farmers' Loan Association. Dudley estimates that 80 percent of all farm businesses in the region will report a negative net farm income before taxes. Dudley feels highly confident that TJF will continue to earn at least a cash flow return on total assets of 8.0 percent. This compares favorably with a norm for farms in the Verona district of 6.9 percent.

At this time, Robert Walker, a credit officer who works for Dudley, returns with the loan amortization schedule that he had been directed to draw up a few minutes earlier. Jackson's loan request of $25,500 will carry an annual interest rate of 9 percent and be paid off in equal annual installments over a 10-year period, as indicated in Exhibit 7.

Dudley now pulls three tabulations from his file cabinet (Exhibits 8, 9, and 10). With reference to Exhibit 8, Dudley notes that farms with outstanding debt in the Fifth District (which includes Verona) are probably paying at least 7 percent on their loans. Exhibit 9 contains a common-size balance sheet for the entire U.S. farming sector. Exhibit 10 contains a summary of data compiled over the years by Dudley. Recognizing many years earlier the value of standards of comparison in the analysis of financial statements, Dudley had taken it upon himself to review every year the financial characteristics of the farms that had been successful in obtaining credit at his office. With this information, Dudley continues with his evaluation of Howard Jackson's loan request.

─────────────── **EXHIBIT 2** ───────────────

The Jackson Farm, II

January 8

Mr. Eliot Dudley, Manager
Farmers' Loan Association
Verona, VA 24482

Dear Mr. Dudley:

I enjoyed talking with you last week and appreciate the opportunity I had to show you around The Jackson Farm. I hope I was able to give you a clear picture of our operation.

Enclosed you will find the three documents that you requested at our last meeting. The balance sheets (Exhibit 3), income statements (Exhibit 4), and loan amortization schedule (Exhibit 5) are attached. The last schedule was prepared by my commercial bank. At my preference I pay the bank one-twelfth of the annual payment each month, even though the interest expense is computed on an annual basis.

Apart from my incorporated business, you also inquired as to the percentage of my adjusted gross (personal) income that income tax payments absorbed during the past three years. The average has been 25 percent. As most of my outside income from personal sources is from my pension and a securities portfolio designed for safety of income, I do not believe this 25 percent figure will change much over the next few years.

Finally, I plan to use $34,500 of savings to help purchase the subject 150-acre parcel. Thus, I am asking for a mortgage loan of $25,500, which I would like to pay off over a 10-year period.

If you need any further information related to this matter, please phone or write and I will attend to the request immediately.

Sincerely,

Howard Jackson
The Jackson Farm

EXHIBIT 3

The Jackson Farm, II

Balance Sheets
December 31

	Most Recent Year	One Year Ago	Two Years Ago
Assets			
Cash	$ 6,800	$ 6,150	$ 4,969
Accounts receivable	2,000	1,600	1,293
Feed and seed	5,000	4,000	3,232
Livestock held for sale	9,340	8,000	6,464
Total current assets	$ 23,140	$ 19,750	$ 15,958
Hereford cattle (held for breeding)	11,000	10,800	8,725
Ewes (held for breeding)	3,150	3,100	2,428
Machinery and equipment	9,200	7,900	6,364
Autos and trucks	6,100	5,174	4,189
Total intermediate assets	$ 29,450	$ 26,974	$ 21,706
Real estate	121,500	121,500	121,500
Homes and buildings	90,000	90,000	90,000
Total fixed assets	211,500	211,500	211,500
Total assets	$264,090	$258,224	$249,164
Liabilities and Equity			
Accounts payable	$ 7,000	$ 3,000	$ 5,000
Current portion of long-term debt	1,946	1,802	1,668
Total current liabilities	$ 8,946	$ 4,802	$ 6,668
Mortgage (held by local commercial bank)	63,729	65,675	67,477
Common stock (family owned)	166,326	166,326	166,326
Retained earnings	25,089	21,421	8,693
Total liabilities and equity	$264,090	$258,224	$249,164

──────────── EXHIBIT 4 ────────────

The Jackson Farm, II

Income Statements
December 31

	Most Recent Year	One Year Ago	Two Years Ago
Net sales	$55,000	$57,000	$54,000
Cost of goods sold	24,750	21,860	24,900
Gross profit	$30,250	$35,140	$29,100
Operating expenses	13,350*	7,190	6,800
Depreciation	4,500	4,000	3,700
Administrative expenses	2,300	2,100	1,800
Interest expense	5,398	5,532	5,655
Farm income before tax	$ 4,702	$16,318	$11,145
Tax @ 22%	1,034	3,590	2,452
Net farm income	$ 3,668	$12,728	$ 8,693
Dividends paid	0	0	0
Total retained earnings	$ 3,668	$12,728	$ 8,693

*Includes a $5,000 expenditure to replace roof and make structural improvements to the main barn.

──────────── EXHIBIT 5 ────────────

The Jackson Farm, II

Repayment Schedule of Outstanding
8% Real Estate Loan

End of Year	Total Payment	Principal	Interest	Balance
0				$70,690
1	$7,200	$1,545	$5,655	69,145
2	7,200	1,668	5,532	67,477
3	7,200	1,802	5,398	65,675
4	7,200	1,946	5,254	63,729
5	7,200	2,102	5,098	61,627
6	7,200	2,270	4,930	59,357
7	7,200	2,451	4,749	56,906
8	7,200	2,648	4,552	54,258
9	7,200	2,859	4,341	51,399
10	7,200	3,088	4,112	48,311
11	7,200	3,335	3,865	44,976
12	7,200	3,602	3,598	41,374
13	7,200	3,890	3,310	37,484
14	7,200	4,201	2,999	33,283
15	7,200	4,537	2,663	28,746
16	7,200	4,900	2,300	23,846
17	7,200	5,292	1,908	18,554
18	7,200	5,716	1,484	12,838
19	7,200	6,173	1,027	6,665
20	7,200	6,665	535	0

EXHIBIT 6

The Jackson Farm, II

Preliminary Analysis of Cash Flow Return

	Most Recent Year	One Year Ago	Two Years Ago
Farm income before tax	$ 4,702	$ 16,318	$ 11,145
Depreciation expense	4,500	4,000	3,700
Interest expense	5,398	5,532	5,655
Before-tax cash flow available to service financing costs	$ 14,600	$ 25,850	$ 20,500
Total investment in assets	$264,090	$258,224	$249,164
Before-tax cash flow return on total assets	5.53%	10.01%	8.23%

EXHIBIT 7

The Jackson Farm, II

Repayment Schedule for Requested 9% Real Estate Loan with Farmers' Loan Association

End of Year	Total Payment	Principal	Interest	Balance
0				$25,500
1	$3,973	$1,678	$2,295	23,822
2	3,973	1,829	2,144	21,993
3	3,973	1,994	1,979	19,999
4	3,973	2,173	1,800	17,826
5	3,973	2,369	1,604	15,457
6	3,973	2,582	1,391	12,875
7	3,973	2,814	1,159	10,061
8	3,973	3,068	905	6,993
9	3,973	3,344	629	3,649
10	3,973	3,649	324	0

─────────────────────── **EXHIBIT 8** ───────────────────────

The Jackson Farm, II

Measures of Farm Operator's Financial Position
Fifth Federal Reserve District, 1970

Item	Unit	Average per Farm Reporting
Average size of farm	acres	172
Value of land and buildings per farm	dollars	58,761
Net cash farm income per farm	dollars	3,523
Off-farm income per farm	dollars	6,755
Total net cash income per farm	dollars	10,278
Total debt per farm	dollars	15,717

Source: *Economic Review*, Federal Reserve Bank of Richmond (May–June 1975), p. 15.

─────────────────────── **EXHIBIT 9** ───────────────────────

The Jackson Farm, II

U.S. Farming Sector Percentage Balance Sheet
Average for 1970–1972

Assets		Liabilities and Equity	
Cash and deposits	3.9%	Real estate debt	9.3%
U.S. savings bonds	1.1	Other debt	10.0
Investment in		Equity	80.7
cooperatives	2.4		
Crops	3.5		
Livestock	7.7		
Machinery and vehicles	10.6		
Household equipment			
and furnishings	3.3		
Real estate	67.5		
Total	100.0%	Total	100.0%

Source: *Economic Report of the President* (Washington, D.C.: U.S. Government Printing Office, 1974), p. 349.

EXHIBIT 10

The Jackson Farm, II

Verona Farm Credit District
Standard Financial Relationships* (based on loans granted)
Classification: Hereford Cattle

Ratio	*Standard*
Current ratio	2.42X
Acid-test ratio	1.00X
Intermediate ratio†	5.67X
Inventory turnover (regular) (COGS/EI)	1.68X
Inventory turnover (including intermediate inventory of livestock)	.80X
Debt ratio	24.0%
Debt to net worth ratio	36.5%
Interest coverage ratio	3.00X
Cash flow coverage ratio	3.20X
Gross profit margin	54.5%
Net profit margin	12.0%
Total asset turnover	0.29X
Return on assets	3.5%
Return on common stock equity	NA

---

*These standard relationships were last updated 12 months ago. They represent the composite experience of three years.

†Current and intermediate assets divided by current and intermediate debt.

NA – Not available.

QUESTIONS

1. Perform a preliminary financial ratio analysis based upon the three years of financial statements provided for The Jackson Farm. In this initial portion of your overall analysis, utilize the standard relationships computed by Dudley (Exhibit 10).

2. Expand your analysis to include consideration of information provided in Exhibits 6, 8, and 9 where useful. Draw upon any data in The Jackson Farm, Part I, that might affect this loan request.

3. Comment upon possible security arrangements for this loan. What other information might prove useful to Dudley?

4. Should Dudley grant the loan requested by Jackson?

CASE 12

Gilcrest Patio Furnishings, Inc.

Part I: Cash Budgeting and
Financial Planning

Gilcrest Patio Furnishings, Inc. (GPF), manufactures patio furniture from PVC pipe. The company was founded in 1976 as one of the first manufacturers to utilize plastic pipe products and construction. Since then, the company founder and president, Mark Gilcrest, has believed that the key to his success is his ability to translate planned company growth into forecasted financial statements. Specifically, Gilcrest had always found his banker to be receptive to his loan requests when he could demonstrate an understanding of the financial implications of his decisions. This was particularly important because the company's sales were quite seasonal and were financed by a $5 million line of credit.

Although Gilcrest did not completely understand accounting income statements and balance sheets, he had always found a forecasted cash budget to be critical. This statement helped him to understand exactly what his cash position was and where the balance was expected to be. Therefore, he had always insisted that the vice president of finance, Jeff Reilly, prepare a 12-month rolling cash budget. Reilly also prepared projected income statements and balance sheets to correspond to the cash budget. This forecast was revised throughout the year as new information was received.

In November of each year, Reilly began the preparation of the subsequent year's forecast. His objective this year was to determine if the current $5 million line of credit would be adequate to meet the financial needs of the firm in 19x1.

Reilly always started the process by asking other managers in the company to provide much of the needed information because he found that this approach built confidence in the resulting budget and forecast. It also allowed all department managers to formulate their own plans. Since each manager participated in the formulation of the budget and forecast, each felt responsible for making the actual results match the forecasts. Thus, the resulting forecast turned out to be much more accurate than a single point estimate provided by a computerized model. After receiving the managers' plans, Reilly summarized them into a large spreadsheet model that included 12 monthly cash budgets, income statements, and balance sheets.

The marketing department provided Reilly with the sales forecasts shown in Exhibit 1. Historically, the marketing department's actual results have varied 10 percent above or below their forecasts.

GPF's credit policy was 1/10, net 30. Previous experience indicated that 10 percent of the customers paid within the discount period, 42 percent paid within a month (one-month lag), and the remaining customers paid late, usually within 60 days (two-month lag). The marketing department forecasts did not include any discounts taken by customers for early payment on account.

The production department provided information of forecasted manufacturing expenses. The manufacturing process was a "level" production strategy—that is, product was produced at a level amount for the entire year. Thus, production/sales mismatches caused inventory to increase as production exceeded sales, and then to decrease as sales exceeded

---

EXHIBIT 1
Gilcrest Patio Furnishings, Inc.
Monthly Forecasted Sales

Year	Month	Sales Forecast
19x0	November	$ 4,717,372 (actual)
	December	4,832,952 (actual)
19x1	January	4,900,000
	February	5,000,000
	March	5,100,000
	April	8,200,000
	May	10,600,000
	June	10,500,000
	July	9,800,000
	August	9,200,000
	September	7,100,000
	October	5,900,000
	November	5,600,000
	December	5,200,000
19x2	January	5,300,000
	February	5,500,000

production. This permitted GPF to keep a constant number of manufacturing employees on payroll, even though monthly sales forecasts varied. In 19x1, production was estimated to run at a monthly sales level of $7,300,000, up substantially from the $6,325,000 per month produced in 19x0.

The manufacturing process was only two days long and material could be ordered and received within five days. Materials used in the manufacture of the product represented approximately half of the cost of goods sold, or 36 percent of the selling price of the product (or 36 percent of revenue). GPF's accounting department claims that 60 percent of the material bills are paid in the month in which the materials are received. The remainder of the bills are paid in the subsequent month.

The production process also requires manufacturing labor. Production labor costs represented the other half of cost of goods sold, or 36 percent of the forecasted selling price (or 36 percent of the forecasted revenue). These costs are incurred when the product is manufactured. Labor expenses are paid over two months—50 percent are paid in the month incurred and 50 percent are paid the following month.

The accounting department provided summarized monthly general, administrative, advertising, and selling expenses from the previously prepared departmental budgets. Exhibit 2 details these expenses. These expenses were assumed to be paid and expensed in the same month. GPF expensed all overhead—that is, the company did not attach overhead to the manufactured product.

The accounting department reminded Reilly that the company had a $15,000,000 mortgage outstanding with a 12.5 percent coupon rate. The company was expected to pay semiannual interest in March and September. No principal payments were expected this year. Interest expense is assumed to be accrued and paid in the same month.

The manufacturing vice president planned to upgrade the company's computerized inventory system for an estimated $3,500,000. The accountants assumed that the system would have a five-year useful life and that the company would depreciate the system using straight-line depreciation.

EXHIBIT 2
Gilcrest Patio Furnishings, Inc.

Forecasted Monthly Expenses

Expenses	Amount
General	$415,000
Administrative	230,000
Advertising	4% of revenue
Selling	7% of revenue
Other	10,000

The accountants also forecasted that the company would have to make quarterly tax payments of $100,000, payable in April, June, September, and December. Furthermore, the company is expected to maintain its dividend payments of $100,000 in February, May, August, and November.

The accounting department also provided an estimated income statement and balance sheet for the 19x0 fiscal year-end. These statements (provided in Exhibits 3 and 4) are believed to accurately reflect Gilcrest's financial position on December 31, 19x0.

Mark Gilcrest has always insisted on a minimum cash balance of $5,000,000. Company policy was to invest any excess cash in a short-term money market account. Reilly estimated that the 19x1 average pretax rate of return on such funds would be 7.5 percent. Interest income would be recognized when the cash was received.

--------------------- EXHIBIT 3 ---------------------
Gilcrest Patio Furnishings, Inc.

Income Statement (thousands)
19x0

Sales	$75,894
Less: Discounts	(76)
Cost of goods sold	(55,403)
Gross profit	$20,415
Operating expenses	
General	1,437
Administrative	2,487
Selling	5,234
Advertising	2,985
Depreciation	1,739
Other	450
Total operating expenses	$17,332
Income from operations	$3,083
Other income	150
Income before interest and taxes	$3,233
Interest expense	
Long-term interest	1,875
Short-term interest	405
Total interest expense	$2,280
Income before taxes	953
Income taxes	362
Income after taxes	$591
Common dividends	$370
Retained earnings	$221

EXHIBIT 4

Gilcrest Patio Furnishings, Inc.

Balance Sheet (thousands)
19x0

Current assets		Current liabilities	
Cash & equivalents	$7,367	Accounts payable	$1,092
Accounts receivable	6,777	Accrued labor	1,152
Inventory	5,495	Accrued taxes	185
Other current assets	141	Line of credit	2,054
Total current assets	$19,780	Other current liabilities	25
		Total current liabilities	$4,508
Fixed assets		Long-term liabilities	
Plant	19,564	Mortgage payable	15,000
Equipment	9,240	Deferred taxes	294
Accumulated depreciation	(9,552)	Other long-term debt	42
Net fixed assets	$19,252	Total long-term liabilities	$15,336
Other assets	35	Stockholders' equity	
		Common stock	1,300
Total assets	$39,067	Retained earnings	17,923
		Total equity	$19,223
		Total liabilities and equity	$39,067

GPF's line of credit agreement calls for a 2 percent risk premium over the existing prime rate, which Reilly guessed would average 8.5 percent in 19x1. Interest would be paid and expensed on the previous month's loan requirements. The loan also required a "cleanup" provision of two months—that is, for two successive months, the outstanding loan balance must be $0.

Reilly felt that he had all the information he needed to complete the forecasts, including the projected tax rate of 38 percent (34 percent federal tax and 4 percent state tax net of federal deduction).

QUESTIONS*

1. Prepare a 12-month forecasted cash budget for GPF.
2. Will the current line of credit meet GPF's financial needs for 19x1? If not, how large a line of credit will the company need?
3. Prepare 12 months of forecasted income statements and balance sheets.

*The computerized model is named "GILCRESTA.wk1."

4. What information is provided by each of the statements (cash budget, income statement, and balance sheet)? How is the information provided by each statement different?

5. Prepare an annual forecasted income statement and balance sheet for 19x1.

6. Analyze the consistency between the company's historical financial performance and it's projected financial performance. (*Hint:* Compute relevant financial ratios and percentage relationships to revenue.) Revise your forecasts to correct any discrepancies between historical relationships and forecast assumptions.

7. If you are using the computerized model, perform a sensitivity analysis on revenue. Vary revenue from − 10 percent to + 10 percent of forecast in increments of 5 percent. Obtain all monthly funds need using the data table command.

8. Is GPF's $5,000,000 minimum cash balance a reasonable amount? If not, how might a sufficient minimum cash balance be established? What do you recommend as a minimum cash balance?

9. Based on your analysis, if you were a loan officer, would you recommend making an additional loan to Gilcrest? Why or why not? If you do not recommend that all of the company's needs be financed with debt, how would you suggest that GPF restructure its finances?

CASE 13

Gilcrest Patio Furnishings, Inc.

Part II: Financial Planning

Jeff Reilly, vice president of finance for Gilcrest Patio Furnishings, Inc. (GPF), had recently completed his forecasted monthly financial statements for 19x1. The forecast indicated that the company's cash needs for that year would far exceed its current line of credit. In fact, by December 19x1, the company would still have a balance on the loan and would be in default of the "cleanup" provision.

Reilly began to think that GPF needed an infusion of long-term financing, such as long-term debt or even equity capital. In order to determine how best to solve the problem, he decided to extend the annual forecasts for four additional years. While this approach would not capture the company's seasonal borrowing needs, it would help him to understand the company's long-term requirements.

As with the 19x1 forecast, Reilly solicited information from the various other vice presidents. The marketing department estimated that annual sales would increase by 8.5 percent per year beyond 19x1. Reilly estimated that 6.0 percent of the growth would come from cost and price increases and about 2.5 percent would come from increases in unit sales.

Manufacturing estimated that higher material costs could be passed on to the consumer, so material would remain at the same percent of revenue. Labor costs, however, were expected to increase by 2 percent of revenue since overtime would be used to meet production demand.

EXHIBIT 1

Gilcrest Patio Furnishings, Inc.

Forecasted Mortgage Principal Payments

Year	Payment
19x2	$1,000,000
19x3	2,000,000
19x4	2,000,000
19x5	5,000,000

The accounting department estimated that general, administrative, and other expenses would rise with inflation, while advertising and selling expenses would continue to vary with revenue at the 19x1 rates. Furthermore, continued revenue growth would require additional plant and equipment expansion since the company was presently operating at close to plant capacity. Reilly decided to ignore these required increases for his first forecast. Thus, gross plant and equipment would be held at their 19x1 levels. Of course, depreciation would continue to accrue at the 19x1 rates.

Principal payments on the mortgage were provided as in Exhibit 1.

In order to complete the forecast, Reilly decided to maintain interest rates on both the expense and income at their 19x1 levels and to keep income tax rates at 38 percent. Since quarterly estimated taxes were assumed to exactly equal the company's tax liability, the end-of-year accrued taxes were maintained at $0. For this first forecast, dividends were maintained at the 19x1 level—$100,000 paid four times per year.

With this data in hand, Reilly began to develop the forecast model.

QUESTIONS*

1. Prepare a five-year forecast (19x1–19x5) of annual income statements and balance sheets for GPF. Use a percent of sales technique where applicable and grow the 19x1 amount by inflation where applicable.

2. Compute relevant financial ratios for the period 19x0–19x5.

3. Analyze the consistency between the historical financial performance and the forecasted financial performance. Revise your forecast to correct for any discrepancies between historical data and forecasted assumptions.

4. Estimate the annual amount of needed plant and equipment. (*Hint:* Base plant and equipment needs on maintaining the historical relationship between revenue and gross plant and equipment.)

5. If you are using the computerized model, perform a sensitivity analysis on revenue. Vary revenue from −10 percent to +10 percent of forecast in increments of 5 percent. Obtain all monthly funds need using the data table command.

*The computerized model is labeled "GILCRESTB.wk1."

6. Based on your analysis, if you were a loan officer, how would you recommend that GPF structure its needed financing?

7. If you are using the computer model, evaluate the impact of your recommendation by changing the assumption regarding debt and equity financing. What impact does your recommendation have on the company's return and risk characteristics? (*Hint:* Evaluate the impact on the financial ratios.)

CASE 14

Thompson Toys, Inc.

Part I: Cash Budgeting and
Financial Planning

Thompson Toys, Inc. (TT), is a wholesale distributor of toys, games, and hobby goods and supplies. In 20x0, the company currently employees 26 people—7 in the marketing department; 9 in the warehouse and distribution department; 7 in accounting, finance, and human resources; and 3 corporate officers.

The company was founded in 1966 by Bob Thompson. In 1975, he raised equity capital by issuing stock to family members and close associates. Subsequently, a very thin market for the stock had developed. When Thompson retired in 1989, his son John became president of the closely held business with assets of $357,292 and net income of $61,404. The company continued to grow, posting a better than 18 percent compound rate of return under John Thompson's guidance. A $500,000 bank term loan was secured in 1991 to purchase a competitor; this loan was completely repaid in three years. In 1995, a $300,000 bank line of credit was secured to finance the company's seasonal needs and a $250,000 term loan was secured for a computerized inventory system. The company's success is illustrated by the 20x0 financial statement provided in Exhibits 1 and 2.

Both Bob and John Thompson had always relied on cash budget forecasts—that is, they used the statement to know where cash balances were expected to be—but neither one had fully understood accrued accounting income statements and balance sheets.

——— EXHIBIT 1 ———
Thompson Toys, Inc.

Income Statement (thousands)
20x0

Sales	$5,748
Less: Discounts	(43)
Cost of goods sold	(3,736)
Gross profit	$1,969
Operating expenses	
General	467
Administrative	184
Selling	425
Advertising	154
Depreciation	134
Other	74
Total operating expenses	$1,438
Income from operations	$531
Other income	14
Income before interest and taxes	$545
Interest expense	
Long-term interest	21
Short-term interest	75
Total interest	$96
Income before taxes	449
Income taxes	171
Income after taxes	$278
Common dividends	$200
Retained earnings	$78

In 1992, John Thompson's eldest daughter, Morticia, joined the company after graduating from the University of Florida with a major in finance. Morticia Thompson used her computer skills to help refine the company's budgeting and financial forecasting processes. Her revisions included a 12-month rolling cash budget as well as corresponding projected income statements and balance sheets. This forecast was revised throughout the year as new information was received.

In November of each year, Morticia Thompson began to prepare the subsequent year's forecast. Her objective was to determine if the current $500,000 line of credit would be adequate to meet the financial needs of the firm in 20x1.

EXHIBIT 2
Thompson Toys, Inc.

Balance Sheet (thousands)
20x0

Current assets		Current liabilities	
Cash and equivalents	$643	Accounts payable	$130
Accounts receivable	723	Accrued taxes	22
Inventory	325	Line of credit	292
Other current assets	14	Other current liabilities	8
Total current assets	$1,705	Total current liabilities	$452
		Long-term liabilities	
Fixed assets		Long-term debt	200
Leasehold improvements	571	Deferred taxes	2
Equipment	574	Other long-term debt	9
Accumulated depreciation	(640)	Total long-term liabilities	$211
Net fixed assets	$505		
		Stockholders' equity	
Other assets	35	Common stock	450
		Retained earnings	1,132
Total assets	$2,245	Total equity	$1,582
		Total liabilities and equity	$2,245

She always initiated the process by asking other managers in the company to provide much of the needed information in order to build confidence in the resulting budget and forecast. Participating in the forecast allowed all department managers to formulate their own plans and gave them a stake in making actual results match forecasts. This approach resulted in a much more accurate forecast than a single point estimate provided by a computerized model. After receiving the managers' input, Morticia summarized their plans into a large spreadsheet model that included 12 monthly cash budgets, income statements, and balance sheets.

The marketing department provided her with the sales forecasts in Exhibit 3.

Historically, the marketing department actual results have varied 8 percent above or below their forecasts. Thompson's credit policy was 5/10, net 30. Previous experience was used to estimate when customers paid. Exhibit 4 provides estimates of the percentage of customers who paid and when they paid. The marketing department forecasts did not include any discounts taken by customers for early payment on account.

The warehouse and distribution department provided information on forecasted costs of goods sold. The ordering process was a "chase" strat-

———————————— **EXHIBIT 3** ————————————

Thompson Toys, Inc.

Monthly Forecasted Sales

Year	Month	Sales Forecast
20x0	September	$691,424 (actual)
	October	745,441 (actual)
	November	823,952 (actual)
	December	152,124 (estimated)
20x1	January	150,000
	February	150,000
	March	225,000
	April	225,000
	May	400,000
	June	525,000
	July	725,000
	August	850,000
	September	975,000
	October	975,000
	November	950,000
	December	250,000
20x2	January	125,000
	February	150,000
	March	250,000
	April	250,000

———————————— **EXHIBIT 4** ————————————

Thompson Toys, Inc.

Break Down of Customer Pay Records

When Customers Pay	% of Monthly Sales
Current month (pay within discount)	15.0%
30 days (1 month lag)	40.0
60 days (2 month lag)	25.0
90 days (3 month lag)	15.0
120 days (4 month lag)	2.0
Do not pay	3.0

egy—that is, products were purchased two months before anticipated sales. Ordering/sales matching caused inventory to increase in advance of expected sales, and then to decrease as sales forecasts decline. This permitted the company to minimize inventory carrying costs. The ordering process required a two-week lead time.

The purchasing agent estimated that the costs of products purchased for resale represented approximately 65 percent of the selling price of the product (or 65 percent of revenue). Thompson's accounting department claims that 15 percent of material bills are paid in the month in which the materials are received, 45 percent are paid on a 30-day lag, 30 percent on a 60-day lag, and the rest on a 90-day lag.

The accounting department provided summarized monthly general, administrative, advertising, and selling expenses from the previously prepared departmental budgets. Exhibit 5 details these expenses. Since TT expensed all overhead, these expenses were assumed to be paid and expensed in the same month.

The accounting department reminded Morticia Thompson that the company had a $200,000 long-term loan outstanding with a 10.5 percent coupon rate. The company was expected to pay semiannual interest in June and December. No principal payments were expected to be paid this year. Interest expense is assumed to be accrued and paid in the same month.

TT's manufacturing vice president planned to upgrade the company's computerized inventory system in July at an estimated cost of $100,000. The accountants assumed that the system would have a five-year useful life and that the company would depreciate the system using straight-line depreciation.

The accountants have also forecasted that TT would have to make quarterly tax payments of $50,000, payable in April, June, September, and December. Furthermore, the company is expected to maintain its dividend payments of $50,000 in January, April, July, and October.

Morticia Thompson thought that the company should also consider maintaining a minimum cash balance, which she initially estimated at $500,000. Company policy was to invest any excess cash in a short-term money market account. Morticia estimated that the 20x1 average pretax rate of return on such funds would be 7.5 percent.

Thompson's line of credit agreement calls for a 1 percent risk premium over the existing prime rate, which Morticia guessed would average 8.5 percent in 20x1. Interest would be paid on the previous month's loan requirements. The loan also required a one-month "cleanup" provision—that is, the loan balance must be paid in full for one month of every year.

--------------- **EXHIBIT 5** ---------------

Thompson Toys, Inc.

Forecasted Monthly Expenses

Expenses	Amount
General expenses	$41,000
Administrative expenses	16,000
Advertising expense	3% of revenue
Selling expense	7.5% of revenue
Other expenses	7,000

The projected tax rate was 38 percent (34 percent federal tax and 4 percent state tax net of federal deduction).

Morticia Thompson felt she had all the information she needed to complete the forecasts.

QUESTIONS*

1. Prepare a 12-month forecasted cash budget for Thompson Toys.

2. Will the current line of credit meet Thompson's financial needs for 20x1? If not, how large a line of credit will the company need?

3. Prepare 12 months of forecasted income statements and balance sheets.

4. What information is provided by each of the statements (cash budget, income statement, and balance sheet)? How is the information provided by each statement different?

5. Prepare an annual forecasted income statement and balance sheet for 20x1.

6. Analyze the consistency between the company's historical financial performance and its projected financial performance. (*Hint:* Compute relevant financial ratios and percentage relationships to revenue.) Revise your forecasts to correct any discrepancies between historical relationships and forecast assumptions.

7. If you are using the computerized model, perform a sensitivity analysis on revenue. Vary revenue from −10 percent to +10 percent of forecast in increments of 5 percent. Obtain all monthly funds need using the data table command.

8. Is the $500,000 minimum cash balance a reasonable amount? If not, how might a sufficient minimum cash balance be established? What minimum cash balance do you recommend?

9. Based on your analysis, if you were a loan officer, would you recommend making additional loans to Thompson Toys? Why or why not? If you do not recommend that all of the company's needs be financed with debt, how would you suggest that the company restructure its finances?

*The computerized model is labeled "THOMTOYA.wk1."

CASE 15

Thompson Toys, Inc.

Part II: Financial Forecasting and Financial Planning

Morticia Thompson, vice president of finance for Thompson Toys, Inc. (TT), had recently completed her forecasted monthly financial statements for 20x1. The forecast indicated that the company's cash needs for 20x1 would far exceed its current line of credit. In fact, by December 20x1, TT would still have a balance on the loan and would be in default of the "cleanup" provision.

Thompson began to think that TT required an infusion of long-term financing, such as long-term debt or even equity capital. To determine how best to solve the problem, she decided to extend the annual forecasts for four additional years. While this approach would not capture the company's seasonal borrowing needs, it would help her to understand the company's long-term needs.

As with the 20x1 forecast, Thompson solicited information from the various other vice presidents. The marketing department estimated that annual sales would increase by 7.5 percent per year beyond 20x1. Thompson felt that 5.0 percent of the growth would come from cost and price increases and about 2.5 percent from increases in unit sales.

Warehousing and distribution estimated that increases in costs of goods sold could be passed on to the consumer, so the cost of goods sold would continue to represent the same percent of revenue as in 20x0 and 20x1 (see Thompson Toys, Part I).

Accounting estimated that general, administrative, and other expenses would increase with inflation, while advertising and selling expenses would continue to vary with revenue at the 20x1 rates. Moreover, continued revenue growth would require additional warehouse expansion since TT was operating almost at capacity. Morticia Thompson decided to ignore these required increases for her first forecast. Thus, leasehold improvements and equipment were held at their 20x1 levels, though depreciation, of course, would continue to accrue at the annualized 20x1 rates.

The balance of $200,000 on the long-term debt was expected to be amortized in equal annual installments of $50,000 per year.

In order to complete the forecast, Thompson decided to maintain both the interest income rate and the interest expense rate at the 20x1 level. She also kept income tax rates at 38 percent. She assumed quarterly estimated taxes would exactly equal the company's tax liability, and thus the end-of-year accrued taxes would be maintained at $0. For her first forecast, she maintained dividends at the 20x1 level—$50,000 paid four times per year.

With this data in hand, she began to develop the forecast model.

QUESTIONS*

1. Prepare a five-year forecast (20x1–20x5) of annual income statements and balance sheets for Thompson Toys. Use a percent of sales technique where applicable and grow the 20x1 amount by inflation where applicable.

2. Compute relevant financial ratios for the period 20x0–20x5.

3. Analyze the consistency between the historical financial performance and the forecasted financial performance. Revise your forecast to correct for any discrepancies between historical data and forecasted assumptions.

4. Estimate the annual amount of plant and equipment needed. (*Hint:* Base plant and equipment needs on maintaining the historical relationship between revenue and gross leasehold improvements and equipment.)

5. If you are using the computerized model, perform a sensitivity analysis on revenue. Vary revenue from − 10 percent to + 10 percent of forecast in increments of 5 percent. Obtain all monthly funds need using the data table command.

6. Based on your analysis, if you were a loan officer, how would you recommend that TT structure its needed financing?

7. If you are using the computer model, evaluate the impact of your recommendation by changing the assumption regarding debt and equity financing. What impact does your recommendation have on the company's return and risk characteristics? (*Hint:* Evaluate the impact on the financial ratios.)

*The computerized model is labeled "THOMTOYB.wk1."

CASE 16

Texas Transistor

Cash Management

Victor Hosek is the assistant treasurer for Texas Transistor (TexTrans). He has been with the firm for nine years. The first six were spent within the technology ranks of the company as an electronics engineer. Hosek, in fact, took his bachelor's degree in electronics engineering from a famous Texas university noted for its excellent faculty in all phases of engineering. After two years as a senior engineer for the organization, Hosek indicated an interest in the administrative management of the firm. He spent one year as an analyst in the treasury department and has just completed his second as the assistant treasurer. During these three years, he has steeped himself in literature that focuses on the finance function of the corporate enterprise. In addition, he has attended short courses and seminars by national management and accounting associations that dealt with most phases of the financial conduct of the firm. Other cost accountants, cost analysts, financial analysts, and treasury department personnel (within TexTrans) viewed Hosek's rapid grasp of finance concepts as nothing short of phenomenal.

TexTrans is located on the outskirts of Houston, Texas. The firm began in the middle 1950s as a small manufacturer of radio and television components. By the late 1950s, the firm had expanded into the actual installation and service of complete communications systems on navigable vessels. Ships from the U.S. Navy and from the tuna industry use the intercoastal canal port facilities as a major repair yard. During the early years of the firm's activity, defense contracts typically accounted for 80 to 90 percent of annual revenues. TexTrans's management felt, however, that excessive reliance on defense contracts could lead to some very lean years with regard to business receipts. The company expanded during the 1960s into several related fields. Today TexTrans is active in the home entertainment market as well as the defense market. Transistors and integrated circuits are produced for a wide range of final products, including radios, televisions, pocket calculators, citizens band receivers, stereo equipment, and ship communications systems. Defense-related business now accounts for 25 to 30 percent of the company's annual sales. This transition to a more diversified enterprise has tended to reduce the inherent "lumpiness" of cash receipts that plagues many small firms relying on defense contracts. In the early years of TexTrans's existence, progress payments on major contracts would often be months apart as the jobs moved toward completion. Currently, the firm enjoys a reasonably stable sales pattern over its fiscal year.

Hosek has been studying the behavior of the company's daily and monthly net cash balances. Over the most recent 24 months, he observed that TexTrans's ending cash balance (by month) ranged between $165,000 and $229,000. Only twice during the period that he investigated had the daily closing cash balance even been as low as $120,000. Hosek also noted that the firm had no outstanding short-term borrowings throughout these two years. This led him to believe that TexTrans was carrying excessive cash balances; this was probably a tendency that had its roots in the period when defense contracts were the key revenue item for the company. This "first-pass" analysis gained the attention of John Knott, Hosek's boss and TexTrans's treasurer. Knott is 65 years old and due to retire on July 1 of this year. He has been TexTrans's only treasurer. Hosek would like to move into Knott's job upon the latter's retirement and feels that the treasurer's recommendation might sew it up for him. He also knows that statements relating to excess cash balances being carried by the company will have to be made very tactfully and with Knott's agreement. That bit of financial policymaking has always rested with the company treasurer. Hosek has decided that the best plan would be to present Knott with a solid analysis of the problem and convince him that a reduction in balances held for transactions purposes would be in the best interests of the firm. As all key officers own considerable stock options, potential increases in corporate profitability usually are well received by management.

Earlier this year, Hosek attended a cash management seminar in San Antonio, sponsored by the commercial bank with which TexTrans holds most of its deposits. The instructor spoke of the firm's cash balance as being "just another inventory," and suggested that the same principles that applied to the determination of an optimal stock of some raw material item might also be applied to the selection of an optimal average amount of transaction cash. Hosek really liked that presentation. He walked away from it feeling that he could put it to work. He decided to adapt the basic economic order quantity model to his cash balance problem.

To make the model "workable," it is necessary to build an estimate of the fixed costs associated with adding to or subtracting from the company's inventory of cash. As TexTrans experienced no short-term borrowings within the past two years, Hosek considered this element of the problem to be the fixed costs of liquidating a portion of the firm's portfolio of marketable securities.

In Exhibit 1, Hosek has summarized the essential activities that occur whenever liquidation of a part of the securities' portfolio takes place. In all the firm's cost analysis procedures, it is assumed that a year consists of 264 working days. An 8-hour working day is also utilized in making wage and salary cost projections. Also, minutes of labor are converted into thousandths of an hour. The assistant treasurer felt that from the information in Exhibit 1, he could make a decent estimate of the fixed cost of a security transaction (addition to the firm's cash account).

TexTrans's marketable securities portfolio is usually concentrated in three major money market instruments: (1) Treasury bills, (2) bankers' ac-

---

EXHIBIT 1

Texas Transistor

Fixed Costs Associated with Securities Liquidation

Activity	Details
1. Long-distance phone calls	Cost: $4.50
2. Assistant treasurer's time: 22 minutes	Annual salary for this position is $38,000
3. Typing of authorization letter, with three carbon copies and careful proofreading: 17 minutes	Annual salary for this position is $12,000
4. Carrying original authorization letter to treasurer, who reads and signs it: 2 minutes by same secretary as above and 2 minutes by the treasurer	Annual salary for the treasurer is $50,000
5. Movement of authorization letter just signed by the treasurer to the controller's office, followed by the opening of a new account, recording of the transaction, and proofing of the transaction: 2 minutes by same secretary as above, 10 minutes for account opening by general accountant, and 8 minutes for recording and proofing by the same general accountant	Annual salary for the general accountant is $23,000
6. Fringe benefits incurred on above times	Cost: $ 6.93
7. Brokerage fee on each transaction	Cost: $11.29

───────── EXHIBIT 2 ─────────

Texas Transistor

Selected Money Market Rates, 1976–1979
(annual yields)

Year	Prime Commercial Paper (3-month)	Bankers' Acceptances (90 days)	3-Month Treasury Bills
1976	5.24%	5.19%	4.98%
1977	5.54	5.59	5.27
1978	7.94	8.11	7.19
1979	10.97	11.04	10.07
Simple average	7.42	7.48	6.88

Source: Board of Governors of the Federal Reserve System, *Federal Reserve Bulletin* (January 1979 and 1980), p. A27.

ceptances, and (3) prime commercial paper. A young analyst who works directly for Victor Hosek supplied him with some recent rates of return on these types of securities (Exhibit 2). Hosek's intuition or feel for the market led him to believe that short-term interest rates would be closer to 1979 levels during this next year than any other levels identified in Exhibit 2. Thus, Hosek decided to use a 10.7 percent annual yield in this study as a reasonable return to expect from his firm's marketable securities portfolio. Then a review of cash flow patterns over the last 5 years, including the detailed examination of the most recent 24 months, led to a projection of a typical monthly cash outflow (or demand for cash for transactions purposes) of $1,200,000.

QUESTIONS

1. Determine the optimal cash withdrawal size from the TexTrans marketable securities portfolio during a typical month.
2. What is the total cost (in dollars) for the use of cash held for transactions purposes during the period of analysis?
3. What will be the firm's average cash balance during a typical month?
4. Assuming that fractional cash withdrawals or orders can be made, how often will an order be placed? The firm operates continually for 30 days each month.
5. If the company's cash balance at the start of a given month is $1,200,000, how much of that amount would initially be invested in securities?
6. Graph the behavior pattern of the $1,200,000 balance (already noted) over a 30-day month. In constructing your graph, round off the frequency of orders to the nearest whole day and disregard separation of the balance between cash and securities.

7. To understand the logic of the model further, provide a graph that identifies in general (a) the total cost function of holding the cash, (b) the fixed costs associated with cash transfers, and (c) the opportunity cost of earnings forgone by holding cash balances. Use dollar amounts to label the key points on the axes as they were previously computed in questions 1 and 2. Also, identify the major assumptions of this model in a cash management setting.

CASE 17

Huff Manufacturing Company

Cash Management

In March 1991, James Stricker, the financial comptroller of Huff Manufacturing, was assigned to investigate the possibility of investing some of
the company's cash balances in marketable securities. In the past, the company had left excess cash in its checking account, but management now
believed that it might be able to increase revenues by investing this cash in
short-term securities.

Stricker knew, however, that the extra return from the investment in
marketable securities would entail added costs for monitoring the firm's
checking account and for purchasing and selling securities. To develop a
policy, he would need information on the daily cash inflows and outflows
of the company, the interest rate on marketable securities, and the cost of
transferring funds between cash and marketable securities.

Stricker was interested in developing a system that would require a
minimal amount of monitoring time on his part, since his job as financial
comptroller involved a variety of other activities that kept him extremely
busy. He decided to use a "control-limit" rule to allow one of his department employees to monitor the cash balance account and initiate the appropriate transfers between cash and marketable securities.

The control-limit rule functions as follows: When the cash balance
hits the upper control limit, a specific amount is transferred into marketable securities. When cash declines to zero or to some minimally acceptable

balance, a specific amount is transferred back to cash. The cash balance, therefore, fluctuates between the upper and lower control limits. The optimal spread between the control limits depends on interest rates, transactions costs, and the variability of cash inflows and outflows.

In discussions with a money market broker, Stricker learned that interest rates on money market instruments such as certificates of deposit, bankers' acceptances, commercial paper, and Treasury securities are highly variable over time. He therefore felt that an average of past yields would be appropriate to use in estimating the yield on marketable securities. The average money market yields for the past 15 years are listed in Exhibit 1. Stricker decided to use a 365-day year to calculate a daily interest rate.

Estimating transactions costs proved particularly difficult. Besides any brokerage fee, Stricker realized that it would be extremely important to include the costs of employee time and company resources used in each transaction. He determined that the costs of buying or selling securities were approximately equal and that these costs did not vary with the size of the transaction.

In setting up a procedure for the transfer, Stricker decided to delegate the responsibility for monitoring the account to an administrative assistant and clerical tasks such as typing and filing to a secretary. As a control measure, each transaction would have to be approved by a company officer—namely, himself as comptroller. Final negotiation of the transaction would be done by an assistant comptroller, who would be responsible for

────────── **EXHIBIT 1** ──────────

Huff Manufacturing Company

Average Money Market Yields, 1976–1990
(30- to 60-day maturities)

Year	Annual Yield
1976	5.2%
1977	5.0
1978	7.3
1979	10.6
1980	12.6
1981	16.1
1982	12.2
1983	8.8
1984	9.9
1985	7.5
1986	5.9
1987	6.3
1988	7.2
1989	8.5
1990	7.8

EXHIBIT 2

Huff Manufacturing Company

Steps in the Transfer of Monies
Between Cash Accounts and Marketable Securities

Description of the Tasks	Time Spent (minutes)
1. Initiation of the transfer by the administrative assistant who monitors the cash account.	15
2. Typing of the authorization memo by a secretary.	13
3. Signature by the comptroller.	3
4. Phone call by the assistant comptroller to a money market broker to place the order. Recording of the transaction details.	30
5. Filing of the authorization.	2
6. Receipt of the broker's verification of the transaction, comparison of the completed transaction with the verbal agreement (as recorded by the assistant comptroller), and filing the memo by the secretary.	10

---

handling the portfolio of money market instruments. Exhibit 2 lists the steps involved in the transfer between marketable securities and cash, along with an estimate of the time involved for each task. Annual salaries for each position were obtained from Linda Manley of the personnel department and appear in the following table:

Position	Annual Salary
Comptroller	$70,000
Assistant comptroller	44,000
Administrative assistant	32,000
Secretary	24,000

Manley reminded Stricker that in addition to the annual salary paid to an employee, the company incurred an additional expense for fringe benefits and personnel department overhead expenses. These extra expenses were estimated at 42 percent of the annual salary. In other words, for each $10,000 earned by an employee, the company incurred an additional $4,200 annual expense for fringe benefits and overhead expense directly attributable to that employee. Thus, the total yearly expense per $10,000 of salary is $14,200. To figure the cost per hour, it was assumed that a year consisted of 240 work days of eight hours per day.

Other expenses incurred in each transaction included the brokerage and bank fees for the transaction, which totaled $15.30.

Information on the daily net cash flows for the company was obtainable from past checking account balances. The daily checking account balances for February 1991 are given in Exhibit 3.

——————— **EXHIBIT 3** ———————

Huff Manufacturing Company

Checking Account Balance
January 31, 1991–February 28, 1991

Date	End-of-Day Balance
January 31	$109,923
February 1	116,346
4	115,471
5	112,268
6	110,448
7	112,373
8	104,498
11	123,958
12	127,493
13	125,953
14	120,703
15	118,218
18	110,593
19	116,311
20	116,941
21	116,538
22	119,181
25	85,931
26	87,611
27	100,596
28	108,606

QUESTIONS

1. Determine the mean and variance of the net daily cash flows.
2. Calculate the upper control limit and return point, assuming that the lower control limit is zero. Develop a set of instructions for the administrative assistant that indicate the cash balance levels that require initiating a transaction, the type of transaction, and the dollar amount of securities to be bought or sold.
3. What is the firm's expected average cash balance under this system?
4. Notice that the return point is less than halfway between the upper and lower control limit. This means that sales of securities take place more frequently and are smaller in amount than purchases. Can you think of some reasons why it is not optimal for the firm to return to a point halfway between the upper and lower control limit?
5. Stricker would like to calculate the expected annual savings that this plan will produce. To do this, he must compare the costs of the current system with the expected costs of the new system. The costs of the new system include the opportunity cost of the average amount tied up in cash balance plus the expected transactions costs for transfers between cash and

marketable securities. The expected number of transactions per day, T, equals the following:

$$T = s^2/2z^2$$

where

s^2 = variance of net daily cash flows

z = return point

Using the expression given, how often, on average, will transactions be made? If there are 260 business days in a year, what is the expected cost of the new system? What is the expected dollar amount of annual savings from the new system?

6. How would the control limits be changed if the firm's bank required a minimum compensating balance of $20,000?

7. How would you adjust the control limits if the firm's bank imposed an average compensating balance requirement of $35,000?

8. Many banks offer interest on checking accounts. Does this mean that cash management models are useless?

9. How is your answer affected if the standard deviation of the net daily cash flows is $100,000?

CASE 18

Solt of the Earth

Accounts Receivable Marginal Analysis

In 1978, after a brief career with the Cleveland Browns, Mike "The Widowmaker" Solt was looking for a job in retailing. Little did he realize that in just a few years he, a man whose only clothes endorsement during his playing days had been for Underman briefs, would be a fashion baron. After several months of job hunting, Mike received a letter from a former fraternity brother now in the Peace Corps asking him to find sales outlets for several small Indian clothing manufacturers in the United States. Since Mike was unemployed at the time and was running desperately low on both alternative job opportunities and money, he agreed. As odd as it may seem, with the help of former Browns defensive back Larry "Mad Dog" Johnson, this was the humble beginning of Solt of the Earth Clothes.

Over the next 14 years, business expanded tremendously, and by December 1992, Mike and Larry owned three manufacturing facilities in India, one in Taiwan, and one in Hong Kong. In addition, they had a staff of 15 designers, which allowed them to keep ahead of the ever-changing fashion styles.

Although Mike and Larry proved themselves to be excellent business managers, much of their success was due to being in the right place at the right time, their popularity in the Cleveland-Columbus areas, and their personal selling abilities. Moreover, this growth of Solt of the Earth Clothes was also aided by Mike and Larry's ability to recognize their own weaknesses and seek out and take advice. Mike, a "psych" major at Ohio State, and Larry, a "poli sci" major at the University of Missouri, knew very little about the fashion world or the financial management of a major business, so they surrounded themselves with employees trained in these areas.

While Solt of the Earth had originally specialized in madras fabrics and styles that stressed the peasant and hippie looks, as time went on, the product line moved toward a more exclusive, pacesetting look. As Mike and Larry hired their own designers and upped the quality of their clothes, the role of Solt of the Earth Clothes changed from fashion follower to trendsetter.

Because of the pacesetting styles and the high-quality standards imposed by Mike and Larry, the popularity of Solt of the Earth grew at an amazing rate during the 1980s, and in 1992, sales had climbed over the $23 million mark. In spite of the higher level of sales, Mike and Larry still had considerable excess capacity in their Hong Kong plant and two of their Indian plants. To increase sales and thereby allow these production facilities to operate at closer to full capacity, Mike and Larry are in the process of evaluating five proposed new credit policies.

Currently, Solt of the Earth's credit policies are extremely stringent. They only allow sales to elite dress shops and college-town clothing stores. The purpose of these policies is to enhance Solt of the Earth's image of high quality. A brief summary of the customer requirements that must currently be met before Solt of the Earth's line can be carried is given in Exhibit 1. While the requirements for carrying Solt of the Earth's Clothes are stiff, customers are rewarded by being given exclusive territorial rights for a 15-mile radius in areas having a population of 150,000 or less. For areas having a population in excess of 150,000, only one sales outlet is allowed per 150,000 inhabitants. This exclusive territorial sales arrangement, supplemented by financial support for advertising, has created a strong relationship between Solt of the Earth and its retailers, with retailers providing

--- **EXHIBIT 1** ---

Solt of the Earth

Minimum Standards for Carrying
Solt of the Earth Clothes

1. Annual sales must have averaged $900,000 per year over the past four years.
2. No losses can have been sustained during the past five years.
3. The shops must have at least 500 square feet of selling space and/or have had annual sales of $1,200,000 during the past year.
4. The dollar value of the average investment in inventory must be at least $100,000.

prime floor space and strong promotion of the line and their exclusive right to sell it. As a result, Solt of the Earth's fashions have the image of being very exclusive, very high fashion, and very "in."

During 1993, sales of Solt of the Earth Clothes are expected to reach $25 million if the current credit policies are maintained. Of this $25 million in anticipated sales, all are expected to be made on credit. The high quality of Solt of the Earth's customers has allowed for the relatively rapid collection of these accounts receivable, and during 1993, the average collection period is expected to remain at 60 days. However, because the proposed credit policy shifts involve both a relaxation of the payment terms and an attempt to increase sales by taking on more risky customers than are currently being serviced, which will most likely cause an increase in delinquent accounts, their adoption would result in an increase in the average collection period. Moreover, the expected level of bad-debt losses ($500,000) would rise as more risky customers are acquired. While this rise is of concern to Mike and Larry, they feel that the profits from the increased sales volume may more than offset the increased bad debts. This is because the variable costs are only 78 percent of the selling price that Solt of the Earth receives on its line.

Of the five proposed credit policy changes, the first three involve rather minor relaxations of credit terms and the availability of credit to increasingly risky customers; the fourth and fifth proposed changes involve a relaxation of the current exclusive distribution policy and the sale of the Solt of the Earth line to discount stores. Although Mike and Larry have some concern that sales to discount houses and the relaxation of the exclusive distribution policy might detract from the Solt of the Earth's image, the concern is not great. As Mike says, "The Solt of the Earth line has been around long enough that sales in a few discount stores are not going to affect our image; customers will just think they are getting a great deal. After all, they will be." And Larry adds, "Since we aren't going to change the quality of the clothes we sell, there's no need to worry. We'll keep all our customers and get some new ones."

While Solt of the Earth's required rate of return on investment in accounts receivable and inventory is generally 15 percent, the return it will require on the marginal increase in investment in receivables from the proposed relaxation of credit policy is larger than this, with its size dependent on the level of risk associated with that particular policy. The required rate of return on the marginal increase in investment in receivables for each proposed credit policy is given in Exhibit 2. The current policy and the expected effects of the five proposed credit policy changes are given in Exhibit 3.

EXHIBIT 2

Solt of the Earth

Required Rate of Return on the Incremental
Increase in Investment in Receivables*

New Sales Resulting from a Credit Policy Shift from	Required Rate of Return on Incremental Sales
Present policy to policy A	17%
Policy A to policy B	19
Policy B to policy C	21
Policy C to policy D	26
Policy D to policy E	29

*Required rate of return on the *new* investment in inventory, and the increased accounts receivable associated with *original* customers changing their payment patterns = 15 percent.

EXHIBIT 3

Solt of the Earth

Expected Effect of the Proposed Credit Policy Changes

	Current Policy	Policy A	Policy B	Policy C	Policy D	Policy E
Annual sales (all credit)	$25,000,000	$27,250,000	$29,250,000	$31,000,000	$32,500,000	$33,750,000
Average collection period (assume 360-day year)						
Original (nonincremental) sales	60 days	64.29 days	70.59 days	80 days	94.74 days	120 days
New (incremental) sales		64.29 days	70.59 days	80 days	94.74 days	120 days
Bad-debt losses						
Original (nonincremental) sales*	500,000	500,000	556,250	616,250	677,500	737,500
New (incremental) sales		56,250	60,000	61,250	60,000	56,250
Average inventory (at cost)	3,150,000	3,175,000	3,200,000	3,220,000	3,240,000	3,255,000

*Here *original (nonincremental) sales* refers to the level of bad-debt losses under the previous credit policy.

QUESTIONS

1. Determine the marginal profitability from relaxing the credit policy from the present policy to policy A, from policy A to policy B, from policy B to policy C, and so forth until the marginal profitability from each possible change in credit policy is determined. (Assume a 360-day year.)

2. Basing your opinion on the analysis outlined, determine which policy should be adopted. Why should this policy be adopted?

3. How might those customers with exclusive territorial distribution rights react to the implementation of policy D or policy E? Might their possible reaction affect your decision?

CASE 19

McArthur Sales Company

Monitoring Accounts Receivable

The McArthur Sales Company was founded in 1968 by Jim McArthur to sell office equipment and supplies in the Austin, Texas, area. Jim had worked for a computer leasing company located in Dallas for six years but had wanted to start a business for some time. The opportunity arose in early 1968 when he learned that a small office equipment store in Austin was being offered for sale by the owner, who wanted to retire. After a hasty trip to Austin, Jim decided that this was his opportunity.

After 22 years of operations, McArthur Sales Company had grown from the one store at 11001 Burnet Road to a chain of eight stores with 1990 sales of approximately $2 million. In December 1990, Jim accepted an offer to sell the business to a conglomerate located in Houston.

Control of the firm was turned over to the new owners on January 1, 1991. A new top management team was brought in to run the firm, including a financial vice president (Bill Jennings). The first task faced by the new management was to analyze the firm's existing policies to determine whether any changes were warranted.

One of the first areas to be investigated was the firm's credit policies. The firm had over $178,000 invested in accounts receivable in December 1990. This represented an average collection period (based upon 1990 sales of $2,036,000) of 31.6 days.

Bonnie Heinkel, staff financial analyst, was assigned the task of analyzing the firm's collection experience and making recommendations as to needed policy corrections. The firm's most recent two years were selected as the basis for her analysis since they were both current and, in the view of management, representative of what the firm might expect in the future. In the past, the firm's management had made no explicit attempt to analyze its collections. In fact, the firm had not employed a full-time financial analyst.

As a first step in her analysis, Bonnie set out to collect monthly sales data and accounts receivable balances for each month during the previous two years. The results of that process are contained in Exhibit 1. Sales were observed to have grown from $1,687,000 in 1989 to $2,036,000 in 1990. This growth in sales was accompanied by a corresponding rise in accounts receivable from a December 1989 balance of $142,400 to a December 1990 balance of $178,800. Bonnie also noted what appeared to be a seasonal peak in sales occurring in the month of June for both years. This peak produced seasonal peaks in accounts receivable in the month of July.

The first form of analysis Bonnie decided to perform on the firm's receivables involved computation of the average collection period (ACP). The ratio is calculated as follows:

$$ACP = \frac{accounts\ receivable}{sales\ per\ day}$$

Normally, when analyzing a firm's financial statements, the accounts receivable balance is taken directly from the firm's most recent balance sheet and sales per day is calculated as the ratio of annual sales for the year ending with the date of the accounts receivable balance. However, in this instance, Bonnie felt that she should account for monthly sales in her analysis. This meant that sales per day had to be calculated using the month-end balance of accounts receivable and the corresponding sales per day for that month's sales. In an effort to check for any discrepancies in her analysis of the ACP that might arise as a result of using monthly sales to calculate sales per day, Bonnie performed similar calculations using the most recent 60 days and 90 days of sales. These calculations are presented in Exhibit 2.

An analysis of the monthly average collection period calculations in Exhibit 2 revealed the following. The 30-day calculations varied from 39.3 days for May to 59 days in September during 1989, with an average of 46.54 days. During 1989, the 60-day calculations produced a mean ACP of 46.09 days, whereas the 90-day calculations averaged 45.68 days. The results for 1990 were similar, with average monthly ACPs of 46.19, 45.76, and 45.69 days for the 30-, 60-, and 90-day calculation periods, respectively. Although the calculations varied slightly from one sales per day basis

———————— EXHIBIT 1 ————————

McArthur Sales Company

Sales and Accounts Receivable, 1989–1990
(thousands)

	1989			1990	
Month	*Sales*	*Accounts Receivable*		*Sales*	*Accounts Receivable*
January	$100	$142.4*		$106	$152.1
February	105	146.6		110	158.7
March	110	157.4		112	160.3
April	130	179.4		160	203.1
May	180	235.8		220	279.6
June	260	341.4		310	402.4
July	200	353.6		280	453.8
August	160	304.4		200	391.4
September	120	236.0		160	304.8
October	110	188.6		140	237.8
November†	108	165.8		120	195.8
December†	104	153.8		118	178.8
Total	$1,687			$2,036	

*142.4 = (.81 × 100) + (.46 × 98) + (.16 × 102).

†Sales for November and December of 1988 were $102,000 and $98,000, respectively.

———————— EXHIBIT 2 ————————

McArthur Sales Company

*Average Collection Period, 1989–1990**
(days)†

	1989			1990		
	30-Day	*60-Day*	*90-Day*	*30-Day*	*60-Day*	*90-Day*
January	42.72	43.15	42.76	43.0	43.46	43.09
February	41.88	43.12	43.50	43.3	44.08	44.58
March	42.93	43.97	41.89	42.9	43.32	44.04
April	41.4	44.85	46.84	38.1	44.83	47.90
May	39.3	45.61	50.49	38.1	44.17	51.12
June	39.4	46.58	53.98	38.9	45.57	52.46
July	53.0	46.10	49.73	48.6	46.16	50.42
August	57.1	50.73	44.18	58.7	48.93	44.58
September	59.0	50.54	44.28	57.2	50.80	42.87
October	51.4	49.24	43.56	51.0	47.56	42.77
November	46.0	45.62	44.04	49.0	45.22	41.93
December	44.4	43.57	42.96	45.5	45.04	42.57

*Average collection period is calculated as follows:

$$ACP = \frac{\text{accounts receivable}}{\text{sales per day}}$$

†Sales per day is calculated based upon the most recent 30 days' sales and the past 60 days' and 90 days'.

to another, Bonnie concluded that these differences were not particularly important. However, she was at a loss for an explanation for the observed differences. Further, the variations observed from 1989 to 1990 were so slight as to suggest no real problem. These data are summarized in Exhibit 3.

The observed variation in ACP across the calendar months of the year did, in Bonnie's estimation, pose evidence of a problem with the firm's accounts receivable policy. The average collection period varied as much as 50 percent during the year for no apparent reason. On the surface, it appeared that the firm's customers systematically slow down their payments during the months of July through October according to the 30-day ACP calculations. Similar observations were made using the 60- and 90-day calculations, although the affected months varied somewhat.

When Bonnie reported her observations to Mr. Jennings (vice president of finance), he too was puzzled by the fact that the firm's ACP varied so widely on a month-to-month basis. Bonnie noted that the swell in ACP might reflect, in part, the seasonality in firm sales and nothing more. Mr. Jennings suggested that she ask the credit department for a month-by-month breakdown on the firm's collection experience. Bonnie agreed and relayed the request to the firm's credit manager. A week later Bonnie received the collection information contained in Exhibit 4. The report contains the data for the most recent two years, as Bonnie requested.

EXHIBIT 3

McArthur Sales Company

Summary of ACP Calculations, 1989–1990

	1989	1990
30-day calculations		
Maximum	59.0 (Sept.)	58.7 (Aug.)
Minimum	39.3 (May)	38.1 (Apr.–May)
Average	46.5	46.2
60-day calculations		
Maximum	50.7 (Aug.)	50.8 (Sept.)
Minimum	43.1 (Feb.)	43.3 (Mar.)
Average	46.1	45.8
90-day calculations		
Maximum	54.0 (June)	52.5 (June)
Minimum	41.9 (Mar.)	41.9 (Nov.)
Average	45.7	45.7

EXHIBIT 4

McArthur Sales Company

Receivables Outstanding as a Percentage of Original Sales, 1989–1990 [*]

	J	F	M	A	M	J	J	A	S	O	N	D
Percentage outstanding for 1989 from sales of:												
Same month	81%	79%	80%	82%	84%	86%	89%	87%	84%	82%	80%	79%
One month before	46	48	47	48	49	51	53	54	52	50	48	47
Two months before	16	17	20	19	19	20	21	22	26	24	22	19
Percentage outstanding for 1990 from sales of:												
Same month	80	81	80	81	82	84	88	86	83	81	79	80
One month before	46	48	46	47	48	50	52	54	51	49	47	47
Two months before	18	18	19	19	20	20	21	22	25	23	22	20

[*] Bad-debt losses are negligible as all accounts are collected within three months of the sale.

QUESTIONS

1. Analyze McArthur's collection experience using the collection data provided by the firm's credit department in Exhibit 4.

2. What problems, if any, do you perceive in the use of average collection period as an instrument for monitoring a firm's collection experience? (*Hint:* Calculate sales per day for each of the three bases used and for several months over the two-year period covered by Bonnie's analysis).

3. If sales for 1991 are projected to equal $2,200,000, project the firm's accounts receivable balance for each month.

CASE 20

The Over Bearing Company

Accounts Receivable Policy

The Over Bearing Company makes bearings that it supplies to more than 30 manufacturers of small electric motors used for various industrial purposes. During the past 10 years, the Over Bearing Company has established a stable customer relationship with these manufacturing firms. Recently, however, the company has lost two of its long-term customers and has seen others take a portion of their business to a competitor. Duncan Steele, the president of Over Bearing, has become very concerned about this trend and has attempted to talk with the purchasing agents of the two firms (Reliable Electric and Humming Motors) that stopped doing business with Over Bearing. The purchasing agent for Reliable Electric told Steele that because of very high interest rates and government-induced credit rationing by commercial banks, his firm was finding it extremely difficult to pay for its purchases of bearings within the 30 days required by Over Bearing. A competitor of Over Bearing, whom this agent refused to identify, offered 60-day credit terms, so Reliable had switched its orders to this firm. The purchasing agent for Humming Motors said that because of the strong sales of its new line of energy-efficient 2-horsepower motors, Humming finds itself with plenty of cash. When another bearing company offered discounts for paying cash, Humming was in an excellent position to take advantage of the offer.

After talking to these purchasing agents, it was clear to Steele that Over Bearing's credit policy was a primary factor in the recent loss of business. Over Bearing's credit policy has long been the responsibility of the chief financial officer, James Dolt. Dolt admitted that he had never paid much attention to credit policy but left it pretty much the same as he found it when he came to Over Bearing. Steele requested that Dolt study the impact on sales of various alternative credit policies available to Over Bearing and report back to him in one week, on December 20.

Recognizing his inexperience in credit policy management, Dolt decided to seek the help of his friend, Sam Sharpe, a credit officer at the bank used by Over Bearing. He told Sharpe that Over Bearing currently offered its customers credit terms of 30 days with no cash discount option. He was able to supply Sharpe with the production and financial data shown in Exhibit 1 and the sales forecast, given the current collection policy of 30 days and no discount, shown in Exhibit 2.

Sharpe told Dolt that while his data would be very helpful, in order to make a well-informed credit policy decision, he would require additional information on the aging of delinquent accounts and on the sensitivity of Over Bearing's sales to collection policy. Dolt replied that he had been very conscientious in tracking down customers who did not pay their bills on time, and after a couple of days' work, he was able to tabulate this information in Exhibit 3.

Dolt told Sharpe that since, to his knowledge, Over Bearing had never changed its credit policy, he had no way of estimating the sensitivity of the company's sales to its collection policy. Sharpe informed him that he had on hand the results of a questionnaire sent out to the sales managers of 100 small manufacturing firms asking them such questions as: "If the typical collection policy in your industry is A, what percentage change in your sales would you forecast if your firm adopted credit policy B and other firms followed suit?" He said that the best he could do to gauge the effect of Over Bearing's collection policy on its sales would be to apply the results

─────────────── **EXHIBIT 1** ───────────────

The Over Bearing Company

*Production and Financial Data**

Price:	$5.00 per unit
Variable costs:	$3.00 per unit
Fixed costs:	$100,000 per month
Depreciation expense:	$60,000 quarterly
Marginal tax rate:	50% (taxes are paid quarterly)

*It can be assumed that production costs for a given month are paid at the beginning of the next month. Fixed costs and depreciation expense are known with certainty and have been at the levels specified for the past two years. The depreciation expense does not vary with production levels.

—————————— EXHIBIT 2 ——————————

The Over Bearing Company

Sales Forecast

State of the Industry*	Likelihood of Each State	Monthly Unit Sales
Depression	.1	78,000
Downturn	.2	88,000
Normal	.4	98,000
Upturn	.2	108,000
Boom	.1	118,000

*The state of the industry has been normal for all months in the past year, including the current month of December.

—————————— EXHIBIT 3 ——————————

The Over Bearing Company

Current Collection Policy

State of the Industry	% of Sales That Are Delinquent	% of Delinquent Sales Received		
		1 Month Late	2 Months Late	Uncollectible*
Depression	.15	.30	.30	.40
Downturn	.13	.40	.25	.35
Normal	.09	.50	.20	.30
Upturn	.05	.60	.15	.25
Boom	.02	.70	.10	.20

*One-month-late credit sales and two-month-late credit sales are received one and two months, respectively, after on-time credit sales. Uncollectible accounts are sold to a collection agency one month after the receipt of two-month-late sales for an amount that is 30 percent of the value of the sales involved.

of this questionnaire concerning various credit policies to the sales data for Over Bearing. By doing this, he was able to produce the figures shown in Exhibit 4.

Sharpe felt that these forecasts were conservative and that they would be even more dramatic if other firms in the industry had a collection policy different from Over Bearing's. He recommended using the same forecasted aging for delinquent accounts given in Exhibit 3 for all the credit policies considered. He also pointed out that, because of differences in the accuracy of the forecasts of Over Bearing's cash flow for different collection policies and because of differences in the volume of delinquent accounts, the different collection policies would expose Over Bearing to different levels of risk. To adjust for this difference in risk, he recommended that Over Bearing apply the annualized required returns on expected cash flows shown in Exhibit 5 to any investment in accounts receivable.

EXHIBIT 4

The Over Bearing Company

Possible Credit Policies*

Credit Policy: 30 days, no discount

    (See Exhibits 2 and 3)

Credit Policy: 2/10, net 30

State of Industry	Monthly Unit Sales	% of Sales Taking the Discount	% of Sales That Become Delinquent
Depression	80,000	.05	.15
Downturn	90,000	.15	.13
Normal	100,000	.25	.09
Upturn	110,000	.35	.05
Boom	120,000	.50	.02

Credit Policy: 60 days, no discount

State of Industry	Monthly Unit Sales		% of Sales That Become Delinquent
Depression	80,000		.12
Downturn	92,000		.10
Normal	104,000		.08
Upturn	116,000		.04
Boom	128,000		.02

Credit Policy: 2/10, net 60

State of Industry	Monthly Unit Sales	% of Sales Taking the Discount	% of Sales That Become Delinquent
Depression	80,000	.04	.12
Downturn	95,000	.12	.10
Normal	110,000	.22	.08
Upturn	125,000	.32	.04
Boom	140,000	.45	.02

*Discount sales are received in the month the sales are made. On-time credit sales are received one month after the sales are made for 30-day policies and two months after the sales are made for 60-day policies. The receipt of late credit sales is explained in the footnote to Exhibit 3.

    Sharpe advised Dolt that all forecasts beyond two years in the future were likely to be extremely unreliable because of the potential for rapidly changing economic conditions. For this reason, he recommended using a two-year planning horizon on any credit policy decision. Duncan Steele has announced that once it is decided which credit policy to adopt, the new policy will be put into effect on January 1 of the coming year. Sharpe's final recommendation to Dolt was to determine which of the alternative collection policies produced the highest net present value as of January 1 and to adopt that policy.

─────────────── **EXHIBIT 5** ───────────────

The Over Bearing Company

Annualized Required Returns

Credit Policy	Annualized Required Returns on Expected Cash Flows
30 days, no discount	11%
2/10, net 30	10
60 days, no discount	16
2/10, net 60	15

Dolt studied Sharpe's recommendations carefully. He did not know much about the mechanics of the proposed collection policies, the methods Sharpe had used for forecasting, or how the net present value method was going to help in the decision making. However, he did know his customers and his competition very well. Because of the wide variety of uses of electric motors, most of Over Bearing's customers have reasonably stable sales that are not sensitive to the fluctuations of business within a particular industry. On average, Over Bearing's customers are small companies whose strengths lie in their technical expertise in producing electric motors rather than in their financial and purchasing operations. Two of Over Bearing's biggest, and oldest, customers have run into severe financial difficulties caused by the shaky start of a new product line of high-horsepower motors that have experienced a high failure rate, and the financial drain from this new product line has caused them to fall behind in paying their bills.

The bearing business is highly competitive, with six or seven other firms making very similar bearings for electric motors. Even though Over Bearing has built up a loyal customer clientele through the years, the firm has always been careful to offer a competitive price for its products. The various bearing companies are widely dispersed geographically and have used differential transportation costs as a means of differentiating their product and attracting customers within a particular geographical region.

QUESTIONS

1. Compute the monthly expected dollar value of cash discount sales, credit sales, one-month-late credit sales, two-month-late credit sales, proceeds from the sale of uncollectibles, and variable costs generated by the current and the three alternative collection policies. Use Sharpe's probability estimates given in Exhibit 2.

2. Compute the monthly expected cash flow for each month, beginning in January, over a two-year horizon for the current and the three alternative collection policies. Recall that the firm has had a 30-day, no-discount policy in the past, that the past state of the industry has been normal, and

that taxes are paid quarterly. If the firm suffers a loss in any taxable month, assume that it will receive a tax rebate equal to 50 percent of the loss. Assume also that cash flows are received at the end of the relevant month (see Exhibits 3 and 4).

3. Using the discount rates given in Exhibit 5, compute the net present value as of the *beginning* of January of the expected cash flows for the current and three alternative collection policies. According to the net present value rule, which collection policy should Over Bearing accept?

4. What are the strengths and weaknesses of applying the net present value method as outlined by Sharpe to the credit policy decision faced by the Over Bearing Company?

5. What other information would it be useful for Steele to know before he makes a decision concerning the optimal credit policy? How would this information be used in the decision-making process?

CASE 21

Neeley Beverage, Inc.

Inventory Management

Neeley Beverage, Inc., is a soft drink distributor serving the northeastern United States, having been in this business for the past 30 years. Started by Justin Neeley, the firm has prospered during this time span, but a recessionary period that began 12 months ago has resulted in a moderate reduction in sales. As indicated in Exhibit 1, the company has encountered a substantial increase in sales volume during the most recent five years, with the only downturn occurring in the last year.

Neeley has been quite proud of the company's growth pattern. However, he has also become aware of numerous difficulties resulting from the rapid growth and is particularly disenchanted with his ability to maintain adequate control of the firm's operations. The need for change has been so extensive that Neeley has been unable to continue a personal involvement in all decisions. One such specific area of concern has been in inventory management. With the growth in revenues, a concurrent increase in inventories has been observed, and Neeley questions the advisability of the large surge in inventory stocks. John Williams, the production manager, takes great pride in not being out of stock when orders are received. Yet Neeley feels strongly that the base inventory is excessive, although he has no way of supporting his intuitive judgment. Neeley wants a quantitative method of analysis that could be used in determining the best inventory level for future planning periods. With such a technique, he states, he could

———————————— **EXHIBIT 1** ————————————

Neeley Beverage, Inc.

Financial Data, 1988–1992*

	1988	1989	1990	1991	1992
Sales	$987,000	$1,210,000	$1,460,000	$1,790,000	$1,705,000
Earnings before interest and taxes	59,220	95,071	172,545	173,550	164,280
Inventory†	393,000	484,000	768,421	895,000	920,700
Current assets	393,000	714,400	1,012,000	1,275,700	1,310,000
Total assets	493,500	864,285	1,327,272	1,704,762	1,794,737

*The asset items are year-end figures.

†The makeup of the inventory is 60 percent finished goods and 40 percent raw material and work-in-process.

relegate the decision-making process to the quantitative analysis and therefore not have to be faced with a decision regarding inventory management.

In an effort to investigate feasible methods for examining the company's inventory policies, Neeley has visited the president of Management Consultants, Inc., by whom you are employed. The president has, in turn, assigned the effort to you, the express purpose being to develop an appropriate inventory model for Neeley Beverage, Inc.

In visiting the corporate site, you have examined the corporation's records and interviewed the appropriate personnel, with the following discoveries:

1. The firm's sales tend to be moderately cyclical between quarters, with 70 percent of sales being distributed evenly throughout the second and third quarters. Furthermore, the remaining two quarters generally prove approximately equivalent in revenues. The marketing department projects the 1993 sales to be $1,860,000.

2. Neeley's products comprise three lines, but College Delight accounts for 85 percent of the total sales and, in turn, a like percentage of inventory. The remaining two product lines are relatively new and represent no real problem in terms of inventory management.

3. The drinks are sold only to retail outlets (no vending machine sales) in a package containing six no-refund containers. The selling price is 75 cents.

4. In reviewing the cost of producing and packaging the six-drink assembly, you observe the following makeup:
Material	$0.30
Labor	0.18
Container	0.06
Allocation of overhead	0.03

5. In the production process, management has experimented with several production plans—for example, producing in accordance with sales level for the respective quarter. However, after such investigations, the corporate personnel consider the best production schedule to be one in which the production level remains constant throughout the year.

6. The production process involves three separate stages: (1) production of drink content, (2) manufacturing the containers, and (3) filling, sealing, and packaging the containers. Each procedure requires a machinery setup involving seven hours, five hours, and six hours, respectively. The labor rate for the individuals performing the setups is $4.75, regardless of the process. In addition to the labor involved, several materials are essential in initializing the manufacturing stage. After careful inquiry, you determine the cost by process to be as follows:

Mixture setup	$48.
Container setup	17.
Packaging setup	24.

7. The 1992 inventory balance as noted in Exhibit 1 represents the current inventory position. As seen, the majority of the inventory (60 percent) is in the "finished goods" category, which, in fact, is the area of concern on the part of Neeley.

8. Although the finished goods of the College Delight drink are considered excessive, no criterion has been developed for justifying a given base level. In talking with the responsible personnel, you discover two preferences. First, as a result of pressure from the bank to improve the organization's profitability, Neeley is more aware of efficient asset utilization. Although no plan has been instigated, the financial officer has investigated the financial position of similar businesses. For instance, the average inventory turnover of like firms, as recorded in the I.R.S. *Industrial Financial Ratios* is 4.63 times.[1] Typically, the inventory comprises 55 percent finished goods, and 45 percent work-in-process and raw materials. In a second approach to the base inventory question, Neeley, as opposed to Williams, who prefers never to have a stockout, indicates that a 10 percent probability of being out of finished goods inventory should be defined as acceptable. A review of the past variation in finished goods of College Delight over time shows a standard deviation of $146,725. Regardless of which criterion is to be applied, an immediate adjustment would simply not be feasible; rather, the modification in inventory would be a target to be achieved by year-end.

9. Other costs relating to inventory management include (a) monthly insurance premiums per $1,000 equaling $1.83, with inventory being insured at 80 percent of cost of production; (b) storage facilities rented at a monthly cost of 10 cents per square yard, with each yard providing space for 90 containers; (c) depreciation of equipment relating to inventory maintenance at a fixed sum

---

[1] The inventory turnover ratio is expressed in terms of sales and the ending inventory balance.

of $1,400; and (d) personnel costs of $45,467 in 1992 varying directly with the average amount of inventory.

10. The firm's opportunity cost for funds is 10 percent.

QUESTIONS

1. Most economic-order-quantity (EOQ) models are presented in terms of the optimal order quantity for *raw materials*, while the present case is addressing the issue of the optimal *production* level. What are the similarities and differences between the two applications?

2. Based first upon the target inventory turnover standard (4.63 times) and then upon the acceptable probability of being out of stock (10 percent), determine the appropriate year-end finished goods inventory level for the College Delight drink.

3. In light of the year-end target inventory for College Delight, how many units should be produced within the forthcoming planning horizon of one year?

4. Calculate the "economic order quantity" for the production level of College Delight drinks.

5. How many times would production be scheduled during the year?

6. What would be the approximate inventory level for College Delight at the conclusion of each quarter? Do these figures offer any indication as to a potential problem area by having a year-end target as opposed to, say, a quarterly inventory goal?

7. As best as can be determined from the data given in the case, compute the average unit and dollar inventory for the 1992 College Delight finished goods inventory. Also, from your calculations of the quarterly inventory balances in question 6, compute an expected average inventory level (units and dollars) for 1993. With the foregoing data, and assuming that production was scheduled eight times during 1992, determine the annual benefits accruing to the firm as a result of adopting the proposed EOQ model.

8. Will the model do as Neeley believes—that is, eliminate the need for human judgment in the final inventory management decision?

CASE 22

Davidson Tractor and Implement Company

Capital Budgeting: Introductory

Jack Murray felt especially good as he strolled toward the mahogany-paneled meeting room of the Davidson Tractor and Implement Company (DTI). That room was the focal point of the fourth floor of the DTI central administrative office building located in Des Moines, Iowa. Every Monday at 9:00 A.M. the key officers of the firm held what was referred to as "the management meeting." During this meeting, the major decisions and policies that would have far-reaching effects on the company's future direction were made and formulated. Major capital expenditure proposals were approved, rejected, or returned to the originating financial analyst for further development at the "horrible Monday" sessions, as they were sarcastically, and often accurately, referred to by those who made formal presentations before the top-level management group. Murray had witnessed several employees, who were part of DTI's financial management training program, leave the firm because they were unable to stand the strain of the penetrating questions and comments typically posed by the management group at the weekly sessions. Murray, however, thrived upon such intense personal contact and looked forward to each subsequent presentation. With those recurring sessions, he improved his technique of orally presenting well-researched financial data.

The main reason that Murray had selected DTI as his initial place of employment upon attaining his undergraduate business degree from a major midwestern university was the firm's well-structured financial management training program. It consisted of two years of rotating job assignments wherein a basically talented individual could actually receive the equivalent of six to eight years of normal work experience. The training directors of DTI were fond of noting the difference between six years' experience one time and one year's experience six times. The financial management training program, of course, was designed to produce the former. It was composed of six benchmark assignments in the areas of (1) payroll accounting, (2) data processing, (3) general accounting, (4) cost accounting, (5) cost analysis, and (6) financial analysis. The participant in the program filled an actual vacancy in the area for a specific period of time; this prevented "do-nothing" assignments. When the area supervisor felt that the trainee had made sufficient progress, it was recommended to the training director that the individual be transferred to the next higher assignment in the program. A more specific identification of program content is found in Exhibit 1. Rarely was the sequence of job assignments violated. This was because the work in the financial analysis department of the firm was considered the most important and to operate effectively in that area required a thorough knowledge of the company's financial control system. This was achieved through completion of the previous five assignments.

Murray had performed in an outstanding manner during his training program and was to be assigned to a final tractor assembly plant about 20 miles east of Windsor, Ontario, Canada, within a month. At the Branton Assembly Plant, he would be financial analysis supervisor, a responsible position for a man just about to turn 26 years of age. The vast majority of those who did complete the rigorous two-year internship within the financial organization of DTI did not automatically move into supervisory positions but usually became floor leaders where the analysis work of about six to eight individuals was coordinated through a single senior analyst.

Today, Murray would make a presentation to the management group of DTI dealing with mutually exclusive capital expenditure possibilities. DTI owns and operates the Cuyahoga Falls Transmission and Axle Plant, located a few miles north of Akron, Ohio. This full-scale production facility manufactures more than 50 percent of the transmissions and axles used in the complete line of tractors and harvesting equipment offered by DTI to the agribusiness industry. Because of the extensive machining processes performed on the steel parts that become part of the final transmission and axle assembly, a very large amount of steel shavings and other more bulky steel scrap is generated at this location. The steel scrap is sold as a by-product of the manufacturing operation to various firms involved in the recycling process from which come several grades and types of usable steel. The scrap is classified as either rough or fine. The essential difference is that the fine scrap brings a considerably higher price in the marketplace than the rough material. Both the rough and fine steel scrap are prepared

—————————————— **EXHIBIT 1** ——————————————

Davidson Tractor and Implement Company

Financial Training Program

Assignment and Description	Duration (months)
1. *Payroll Accounting.* Prepare, issue, and validate weekly and biweekly hourly and salary checks; perform overtime analysis by department and plant; prepare fringe benefit cost analysis by department and plant.	3
2. *Data Processing.* Learn to operate all equipment; run jobs and deliver reports on a timely basis; write a few minor programs designed in conjunction with the cost accounting section.	4
3. *General Accounting.* Learn all procedures relating to accounts receivable and payable, including authorization procedure that controls the printing of checks on the computer facility; prepare aging of accounts receivable report; participate in most phases of corporate cash management, including the investment of excess cash and determination of minimum balance requirements at the firm's several deposit accounts.	4
4. *Cost Accounting.* Participate in the annual setting of cost standards on all parts and assemblies used in the firm's manufacturing process; maintain data processing master file on all cost changes resulting in variances from the established standard; prepare the gross profit report by product line.	4
5. *Cost Analysis.* Perform as a cost analyst responsible for controlling and analyzing all cost levels associated with a major plant in the DTI organization; explain unusual cost overruns; prepare a monthly cost forecast for a major plant and explain significant deviations from last month's forecast.	4
6. *Financial Analysis.* Analyze and make recommendations on major capital expenditure proposals ($250,000 initial cash outlay and over); project net profit and cash flow (monthly and annually) by product line and plant; explain deviations from forecast.	5

for sale through a grinding and compressing procedure done by large machines called chip crushers. The selling prices and operating costs of the chip crushers, however, differ according to whether rough or fine scrap is being processed.

For the past two weeks, Jack Murray had gathered the financial data necessary to making an economically efficient choice between two models of chip crushers manufactured by Lamsden-Sexton, Inc. The higher-cost model was identified by the code letters CCH (used in the production of fine scrap); the lower-cost machine was noted by the code letters CCL (used in the production of rough scrap). Murray was to make a recommendation as to whether DTI should invest in CCH or CCL. It has previously been determined that one of the two chip crushers would be purchased.

As he entered the executive committee room, Murray immediately noticed one individual seated at the discussion table whom he had not expected to see in Des Moines this Monday. That was Alex Longwood, sales manager for the Cuyahoga Falls Transmission and Axle Plant. Robert Lacy, the plant manager, was there, as anticipated, but Longwood's presence puzzled Murray. He had an instant notion that the reason behind Longwood's materialization at the DTI central office would not be favorable to the analysis he was about to give the firm's officers and invited guests. Murray reflected upon his trip to Ohio some 10 days before and his final meeting with Lacy and Longwood. Although they had been most helpful in supplying him with needed information related to the purchase of either CCH or CCL, he somehow sensed that they were hoping that his ultimate capital expenditure analysis would favor the purchase of CCL.

The investment outlay associated with CCH has been computed to be $480,000 versus a $400,000 outlay required for CCL. These estimates are firm quotes provided by Lamsden-Sexton, Inc., which would install the machine at no added cost. All the investment outlay is to be depreciated on a straight-line basis toward a zero estimated salvage value, over a 20-year economic life. In conjunction with the sales staff of Lamsden-Sexton, Inc., and the industrial engineering group located at the Transmission and Axle Plant, Murray has estimated that annual operating costs associated with CCH would be $480,000 and that for CCL would be $250,000. These costs are projected at a constant level over each of the next 20 years.

Alex Longwood supplied Jack Murray with the 20-year estimate of scrap revenues tied to each chip crusher. The fine scrap is expected to produce $800,000 per year in added sales, while the rough scrap is expected to add $500,000 annually to the sales total for DTI. Murray had these sales estimates checked by the central office marketing staff; that group felt that the figures generated at the Ohio plant were reasonable. The DTI central office marketing people did impress upon Murray that the final sales outlet for the rough and fine steel scrap was largely concentrated in the Cleveland, Ohio, vicinity, less than an hour's drive from the Transmission and Axle Plant. Thus, the Ohio marketing group was considered expert on scrap revenue projections because of its proximity to the several buyers of the material.

For the past decade, it has been established financial policy at DTI to evaluate possible capital expenditures using discounted cash flow techniques. As an additional information item, the payback period is also computed. The corporate tax rate used for these analyses is 50 percent.

Murray's evaluation of the chip crusher project was the initial item on the agenda at this Monday's management meeting. He briefly described the nature of the project to the group; then he introduced William Clay, a sales representative from Lamsden-Sexton, Inc. Clay discussed the differing sales prices for CCH and CCL. He impressed upon the group that the investment cost of each machine was a firm quote, including installation fees, so long as a purchase agreement was signed by both parties within the next 30 days. Murray then turned on the overhead slide projector and presented the key financial data and assumptions leading to his ultimate recommendation. His calculations reflected the fact that the office of the financial vice president had issued a memorandum instructing the financial analysts to use a 14 percent cost of capital in all their capital expenditure analyses during the next quarter of the year. Exhibits 2, 3, and 4 form the main elements of Murray's presentation.

Murray began by referring to Exhibit 2 and explaining the assumptions and company policies inherent in it. His objective here was to highlight clearly the uncertainties associated with the projection of net cash flows tied to each chip crusher. This was done by stating who was responsible within the DTI organization for supplying the key estimates displayed in Exhibit 2. The sales revenues, as mentioned earlier, were estimated by Alex Longwood's department at the Ohio plant. Again, the operating cost inputs were the joint effort of Lamsden-Sexton representatives and the Ohio plant's industrial engineering department. The tax rate and depreciation method used in derivation of the cash flows were set by company policy. For each of the next 20 years, the net cash flows associated with the more expensive chip crusher were estimated at $172,000; the less costly machine was expected to generate cash flows of $135,000 per year over the same period.

--- EXHIBIT 2 ---

Davidson Tractor and Implement Company

Chip Crusher Project: Cash Flow Projections

	CCH	CCL
Annual scrap revenues (net)	$800,000	$500,000
Less: Change in operating costs	480,000	250,000
Less: Change in depreciation	24,000	20,000
Change in taxable income	$296,000	$230,000
Less: Change in tax @ 50%	148,000	115,000
Change in after-tax profits	$148,000	$115,000
Plus: Change in depreciation	24,000	20,000
Change in annual net cash flow (assumed constant for each of next 20 years)	$172,000	$135,000

EXHIBIT 3

Davidson Tractor and Implement Company

Chip Crusher Project: Internal Rates of Return

Part A: Analysis of CCH

Change in Annual Net Cash Flow	20-Year Annuity Factor at 35% and 36%	Present Value at 35% and 36%
$172,000	2.8501 (35%)	$490,217 (35%)
172,000	2.7718 (36%)	476,750 (36%)

$$\text{Interpolation: } \frac{\$490,217 - \$480,000}{\$490,217 - \$476,750} = \frac{\$10,217}{\$13,467} = .76$$

The internal rate of return is, therefore, 35.76%.

Part B: Analysis of CCL

Change in Annual Net Cash Flow	20-Year Annuity Factor at 33% and 34%	Present Value at 33% and 34%
$135,000	3.0202 (33%)	$407,727 (33%)
135,000	2.9327 (34%)	395,915 (34%)

$$\text{Interpolation: } \frac{\$407,727 - \$400,000}{\$407,727 - \$395,915} = \frac{\$ 7,727}{\$11,812} = .65$$

The internal rate of return is, therefore, 33.65%.

Next, Murray focused the group's attention upon Exhibits 3 and 4. These tabulations contained the various measures of investment worth favored by the DTI organization. Murray pointed out that all the time-adjusted evaluation methods that he had calculated (internal rate of return, net present value, and profitability index) favored investment in machine CCH, the more costly of the mutually exclusive alternatives. Even the payback period of CCH was expected to be faster than that of CCL. While observing that both projects were profitable if considered independently of each other, Murray reminded the group that only one could be purchased. He concluded that it made economic sense to spend the extra $80,000 and acquire CCH.

"Jack, do your revenue figures take into consideration the fact that DTI would generate some scrap sales regardless of whether we bought either machine?"

That question came from Daniel Jenkins, vice president of marketing. Murray had anticipated it. "Yes," he replied. "I used the term 'net' in the exhibit where the scrap figures are estimated to indicate that only the ex-

─────────────── **EXHIBIT 4** ───────────────

Davidson Tractor and Implement Company

Chip Crusher Project: Net Present Values,
Profitability Indexes, and Payback Periods

Part A: Analysis of CCH

Change in Annual Net Cash Flow	20-Year Annuity Factor at 14%	Present Value at 14%
$172,000	6.6231	$1,139,173
	Less: Investment outlay	480,000
	Net present value	$ 659,173

$$\text{Profitability index} = \frac{\$1,139,173}{\$\ 480,000} = 2.37$$

$$\text{Payback period} = \frac{\$480,000}{\$172,000} = 2.79 \text{ years*}$$

Part B: Analysis of CCL

Change in Annual Net Cash Flow	20-Year Annuity Factor at 14%	Present Value at 14%
$135,000	6.6231	$ 894,119
	Less: Investment outlay	400,000
	Net present value	$ 494,119

$$\text{Profitability index} = \frac{\$894,119}{\$400,000} = 2.24$$

$$\text{Payback period} = \frac{\$400,000}{\$135,000} = 2.96 \text{ years}$$

*Can be computed directly as projected net cash flows are even throughout economic life of the project.

cess above what DTI would generate without any new machine purchase has been analyzed."

"Fine," replied Jenkins. Then he continued, "Over the weekend Bob Lacy and Alex Longwood called me to discuss some new information that I think will have to be incorporated into your computations. Since Alex is better versed on the material than I am, I've asked him to make a few comments to you and the rest of the management group."

Horrible Monday, Murray thought to himself, here it comes.

Longwood began. "Since Jack visited our plant a little over a week ago to gather inputs to this analysis, we have had to reassess the sales estimates supplied to him. New contracts let out and agreed upon during the past week with the several dealers in the Cleveland area who buy our processed scrap all indicate that future revenues of the type being discussed today will be lower than we had anticipated."

"Low enough to affect Jack's final recommendation to buy CCH?" asked Ronald Davidson, president of DTI.

"We're not sure," Bob Lacy answered. "We would like Jack to incorporate the newer sales estimates into his evaluation procedure and then discuss the implications with this group."

Murray looked at Lacy and Longwood. "What are the new sales figures?" he asked.

Longwood flipped through a file folder in front of him and began, "For CCH we believe that $750,000 per year is more accurate, and for CCL we recommend use of $480,000 per year as the revenue projection." Longwood went on. "If this should alter the conclusion from your initial analysis, we have a proposal in the wings back in Cuyahoga Falls that promises an internal rate of return of around 17 to 18 percent on an $80,000 required investment outlay."

All of a sudden, things appeared clearer to Jack Murray. Lacy and Longwood were opting for the lower-priced chip crusher in hopes of gaining use of the $80,000 price differential for investment in another project at their own plant.

Ronald Davidson turned to Jenkins and asked, "Do you think the new sales figures are firm enough to warrant Jack's running through his analysis again?"

"Yes."

"All right," said Davidson, "Jack, I want you to rework your computations and report back to this group immediately after lunch, at 1:00 P.M."

QUESTIONS

1. Compute all measures of investment worth (internal rate of return, net present value, profitability index, and payback period) originally calculated by Murray, but reflect the new sales projections in your analysis.

2. Is the solution as straightforward as it was when Murray made his initial presentation to the DTI management group?

3. Which chip crusher (CCH or CCL) would you recommend that DTI purchase?

CASE 23

Danforth & Donnalley Laundry Products Company

Capital Budgeting:
Relevant Cash Flows

On April 14, 1993, at 3:00 P.M., James Danforth, president of Danforth & Donnalley (D&D) Laundry Products Company, called to order a meeting of the financial directors. The purpose of the meeting was to make a capital budgeting decision with respect to the introduction and production of a new product, a liquid detergent called Blast.

   D&D was formed in 1975 with the merger of Danforth Chemical Company, headquartered in Seattle, Washington, producers of Lift-Off detergent, the leading laundry detergent on the West Coast; and Donnalley Home Products Company, headquartered in Detroit, Michigan, makers of Wave detergent, a major midwestern laundry product. As a result of the merger, D&D was producing and marketing two major product lines. Although these products were in direct competition, they were not without product differentiation: Lift-Off was a low-suds, concentrated powder, while Wave was a more traditional powder detergent. Each line brought with it considerable brand loyalty, and by 1993, sales from the two detergent lines had increased tenfold from their 1975 levels, with both products now being sold nationally.

   In the face of increased competition and technological innovation, D&D had spent large amounts of time and money over the past four years researching and developing a new, highly concentrated liquid laundry detergent. D&D's new detergent, which they called Blast, had many obvious advantages over the conventional powdered products. It was felt that with Blast the consumer would benefit in three major areas. Blast was so highly concentrated that only 2 ounces was needed to do an average load of laundry as compared with 8 to 12 ounces of powdered detergent. Moreover, because it was a liquid, it was possible to pour Blast directly on stains and hard-to-wash spots, eliminating the need for a presoak and giving Blast cleaning abilities that powders could not possibly match. And finally, Blast would be packaged in a lightweight, unbreakable plastic bottle with a sure-grip handle, making it much easier to use and more convenient to store than the bulky boxes of powdered detergents with which it would compete.

The meeting was attended by James Danforth, president of D&D; Jim Donnalley, director of the board; Guy Rainey, vice president in charge of new products; Urban McDonald, controller; and Steve Gasper, a newcomer to D&D's financial staff, who was invited by McDonald to sit in on the meeting. Danforth called the meeting to order, gave a brief statement of its purpose, and immediately gave the floor to Guy Rainey.

Rainey opened with a presentation of the cost and cash flow analysis for the new product. To keep things clear, he passed out copies of the projected cash flows to those present (see Exhibits 1 and 2). In support of this information, he provided some insight into how these calculations were determined. Rainey proposed that the initial cost for Blast included $500,000 for the test marketing, which was conducted in the Detroit area

———————— EXHIBIT 1 ————————
D&D Laundry Products Company

Annual Cash Flows from the Acceptance of Blast
(including those flows resulting from sales
diverted from the existing product lines)

Year	Cash Flows
1	$280,000
2	280,000
3	280,000
4	280,000
5	280,000
6	350,000
7	350,000
8	350,000
9	350,000
10	350,000
11	250,000
12	250,000
13	250,000
14	250,000
15	250,000

EXHIBIT 2

D&D Laundry Products Company

Annual Cash Flows from the Acceptance of Blast
(not including those flows resulting from
sales diverted from the existing product lines)

Year	Cash Flows
1	$250,000
2	250,000
3	250,000
4	250,000
5	250,000
6	315,000
7	315,000
8	315,000
9	315,000
10	315,000
11	225,000
12	225,000
13	225,000
14	225,000
15	225,000

and completed in the previous June, and $2 million for new specialized equipment and packaging facilities. The estimated life for the facilities was 15 years, after which they would have no salvage value. This 15-year estimated life assumption coincides with company policy set by Donnalley not to consider cash flows occurring more than 15 years into the future, as estimates that far ahead "tend to become little more than blind guesses."

Rainey cautioned against taking the annual cash flows shown in Exhibit 1 at face value since portions of these cash flows actually are a result of sales that had been diverted from Lift-Off and Wave. For this reason, Rainey also produced the annual cash flows shown in Exhibit 2, which had been adjusted to include only those cash flows incremental to the company as a whole.

At this point, discussion opened between Donnalley and McDonald, and it was concluded that the opportunity cost on funds is 10 percent. Gasper then questioned the fact that no costs were included in the proposed cash budget for plant facilities, which would be needed to produce the new product.

Rainey replied that, at the present time, Lift-Off's production facilities were being utilized at only 55 percent of capacity, and since these facilities were suitable for use in the production of Blast, no new plant facilities other than the specialized equipment and packaging facilities previously mentioned need be acquired for the production of the new product line. It was estimated that full production of Blast would only require 10 percent of the plant capacity.

McDonald then asked if there had been any consideration of increased working capital needs to operate the investment project. Rainey answered that there had and that this project would require $200,000 of additional working capital; however, as this money would never leave the firm and would always be in liquid form, it was not considered an outflow and, hence, was not included in the calculations.

Donnalley argued that this project should be charged something for its use of the current excess plant facilities. His reasoning was that if an outside firm tried to rent this space from D&D, it would be charged somewhere in the neighborhood of $2 million, and since this project would compete with other current projects, it should be treated as an outside project and charged as such. However, he went on to acknowledge that D&D has a strict policy forbidding the renting or leasing out of any of its production facilities. If they didn't charge for facilities, he concluded, the firm might end up accepting projects that under normal circumstances would be rejected.

From here, the discussion continued, centering on the questions of what to do about the "lost contribution from other projects," the test marketing costs, and the working capital.

QUESTIONS

1. If you were in Steve Gasper's place, would you argue to include the cost from market testing as a cash outflow?

2. What would your opinion be as to how to deal with the question of working capital?

3. Would you suggest that the product be charged for the use of excess production facilities and building? Would this opinion change under the hypothetical assumption that needed production facilities for the current line of powdered detergents were at 55 percent of capacity and expected to grow at a rate of 20 percent a year and maximum production capacity was 100 percent? What would be the present value of this cash flow given the fact that the currently proposed new plant would involve cash outflows of $5 million in three years (assuming that acceptance of the Blast project would not affect the size of the proposed outlay, only the timing, and that the new plant and facilities would be operable indefinitely). (*Hint:* Assume that the introduction of Blast would only move the need for a new plant ahead by one year, that the cash outflow would remain at $5 million regardless of when incurred, and that the plant would operate indefinitely.)

4. Would you suggest that the cash flows resulting from erosion of sales from current laundry detergent products be included as a cash inflow?

If there was a chance that competition would introduce a similar product were D&D to fail to introduce Blast, would this affect your answer?

5. If debt is used to finance this project, should the interest payments associated with this new debt be considered cash flows?

6. What are the NPV, IRR, and PI of this project, including cash flows resulting from lost sales from existing product lines? What are the NPV, IRR, and PI of this project excluding these flows? Under the assumption that there is a good chance that competition will introduce a similar product if D&D doesn't, would you accept or reject this project?

CASE 24

Lamar Ironworks, Inc.

Capital Budgeting:
Relevant Cash Flows

In the spring of 1972, Lamar Ironworks, Inc., embarked on a program to develop a new laser-powered welding process. Nine years and $2.6 million later, Lamar is now on the verge of patenting what it feels will be a revolutionary development in welding technology. Lamar's management team believes that the potential applications of the technology are virtually unlimited. The use of laser welding will make possible microwelding procedures that heretofore have required very costly and much less reliable electrical arc welding techniques. To develop the process commercially, Lamar estimates that an investment of another $10 million will be required in machinery and equipment.[1] In addition, to market the new laser welding equipment, Lamar estimates that it will need to invest $2.2 million in inventories and accounts receivable.

Lamar faces a dilemma in marketing the new laser welders in that it presently manufactures and sells the arc welders that the laser welders will replace. However, Lamar feels that within one or two years, at most, a competitor for its laser welder will be marketed. Thus, the estimated lost arc

---

[1]Lamar uses straight-line depreciation and zero salvage values for tax purposes. The machinery and equipment purchased for the laser welder project have a 10-year recovery period (in accordance with the Economic Recovery Act of 1981) for tax purposes but are expected to remain productive for 15 years or more.

welder operating income (earnings before interest and taxes) of $200,000 per year will occur whether or not Lamar markets its laser welder. Estimated after-tax income figures for the laser welder investment (net of the income lost due to reduced arc welder sales) over the next 15 years are found in Exhibit 1. Lamar restricts its investment analyses to 15 years because of the uncertainties associated with longer projections. In addition, Lamar has made preliminary arrangements with a life insurance company to borrow $4 million at 14 percent interest. The loan would require semi-annual interest payments of $280,000, with the full principal amount due at the end of the term of the loan. The remainder of the funds needed to finance the project would be raised using owner funds. Because of Lamar's past profitability and conservative financing strategy, the firm has up to $15 million of retained owner funds that are available to help finance the project. Lamar's management feels that, given the planned financing of the Laser project and the risks involved, a 20 percent after-tax rate of return should be used to evaluate the investment of Lamar stockholder funds in the project.

--------------------------------- **EXHIBIT 1** ---------------------------------

Lamar Ironworks, Inc.

After-Tax Net Income for the Laser Welder

Year	EBIT*	Interest†	EBT‡	Estimated Net Income§
1	$2,411,852	$560,000	$1,851,852	$1,000,000
2	2,411,852	560,000	1,851,852	1,000,000
3	2,411,852	560,000	1,851,852	1,000,000
4	2,411,852	560,000	1,851,852	1,000,000
5	2,411,852	560,000	1,851,852	1,000,000
6	2,782,222	560,000	2,222,222	1,200,000
7	2,782,222	560,000	2,222,222	1,200,000
8	2,782,222	560,000	2,222,222	1,200,000
9	2,782,222	560,000	2,222,222	1,200,000
10	2,782,222	560,000	2,222,222	1,200,000
11	3,152,593	560,000	2,592,593	1,400,000
12	3,152,593	560,000	2,592,593	1,400,000
13	3,152,593	560,000	2,592,593	1,400,000
14	3,152,593	560,000	2,592,593	1,400,000
15	3,152,593	560,000	2,592,593	1,400,000

*Estimated earnings before interest and taxes for the laser welder project. This figure is net of the $200,000 per year in EBIT Lamar estimates it will lose owing to reduced arc welder sales resulting from the sale of laser welders. In addition, these figures reflect the added depreciation expense (cost recovery) from the $10 million in machinery and equipment that must be purchased.

†Interest on a $4 million, 14 percent loan that Lamar plans to use to help finance the project.

‡Earnings before taxes.

§Lamar's marginal tax rate is 46 percent.

Under the provisions of the Economic Recovery Act of 1981, Lamar will receive a 10 percent investment tax credit on any new machinery and equipment it acquires to produce the new laser welder. In addition, Lamar will pay taxes at a rate of 46 percent on any added income from the laser project.

QUESTIONS

1. What is the required investment needed to make the laser welder commercially viable? How should the $2.6 million of research and development costs impact the project's initial cost?

2. What are the annual after-tax cash flows for the laser project? How should the lost arc welder sales affect the laser project cash flows?

3. What required rate of return should be used in evaluating the laser welder project?

4. Should the laser welder be commercially developed? How would your analysis be affected if Lamar had the opportunity to sell its patent to the laser welder? What is the minimum price that Lamar should consider accepting were it to sell the Laser patent?

CASE 25

Benefits Monthly, Inc.

Capital Budgeting: Relevant Cash Flows and Decision Criteria

In the spring of 19x1, Tom Abner, president of Benefits Monthly, Inc. (BMI), was considering the development of a new division in North Carolina.

Currently, BMI sells a bundled benefits package called a "cafeteria plan" to companies, which purchase the plan on behalf of their employees. The package permits employees to choose from a variety of prepaid company benefits such as the traditional medical insurance and the more non-traditional benefits such as child care, car insurance, homeowners' insurance, prepaid dental and/or prepaid legal insurance. Companies favor these plans over traditional insurance plans because they can specify the dollar amount to be spent per employee, and thus contain benefit costs. Employees, or subscribers, then "spend" these allocated dollars by choosing the type of benefits they most need. This contrasts with traditional plans in which the company specifies both the type of benefit and its provider.

BMI does not actually provide each of the insurance products it offers. Instead, it subcontracts with individual providers. For example, a law firm contracted to provide legal services would receive a fee each month for each of the subscribers or plan participants who selected this benefit and in return would render legal services to the subscribers on a "free" or reduced-cost basis. The fees paid by BMI to the law firm would come from funds received from BMI's corporate or individual clients.

BMI was founded 18 years ago in California by Tom and Jerry Abner, two brothers who had 22 years of combined experience in the insurance industry. They started BMI to expand their insurance brokerage business. The business had expanded rapidly and in 19x0 was fully developed in 14 states concentrated along the East and West Coasts. Each state had been developed as a separate division since all states required separate filings with their respective insurance commissions. BMI had regional offices on both coasts—in San Francisco in the West and in Baltimore in the East.

Each division was free to develop its own providers of the prepaid benefits—for example, prepaid dental services were provided by dentists in the local communities. Each subscriber was free to select his or her provider for each of the services purchased. The providers then received a monthly fee for each subscriber in their base. On average, benefit providers were paid 55 percent of the monthly revenue received by BMI on behalf of their subscribers.

The sales force was "local" to the state and salespeople were paid a percentage of the monthly revenue received from each of their "client" companies, organizations, or individual subscribers. BMI considered the sales force to be contracted services. Each salesperson maintained his or her own business and paid his or her own expenses. In a state where the business was well established, BMI divisions paid, on average, 15 percent of revenue as commissions. A "new" division, however, typically paid 20 percent of revenue to its sales force in order to quickly develop the business. When the business reached maturity, usually after seven or eight years, the overall sales commission decreased to 15 percent of revenue as more of the business was developed as large cases. (Large cases typically paid lower commissions or were "sold" by salaried BMI employees.)

BMI provided consolidated services to its subscriber base, sales force, and providers at each of its regional offices. BMI's chief financial officer, Marilyn Schnider, estimated that the East Coast (Baltimore) regional office expended 10 percent of regional revenue managing the subscriber base, processing the monthly paperwork and checks, and providing services to the subscribers, sales force, and providers.

In addition, each division gave local support to its subscriber base, sales force, and providers. This support was provided through fixed operating costs, such as answering telephone requests for information about services and mailing printed brochures to subscribers.

As Tom Abner evaluated the prospects for a North Carolina division, he speculated that the new division would require approximately $135,000 in start-up costs. Start-up costs would include a variety of expenses in 19x0, such as filing fees paid to state insurance commissions, lease expenses for office space, recruiting fees and salaries for employees hired prior to the development of the business, and recruiting fees for the providers and sales force. In addition, the new division would require $10,000 in legal fees, $10,000 in new office computers, $5,000 in telephone systems, and

$10,000 in moving expenses. Marilyn Schnider informed Tom Abner that the accounting firm would insist that most of these costs be capitalized and amortized over 5 years for tax purposes and 10 years for accounting purposes. In her opinion, only the moving costs could be considered expenses during the start-up year of operation. All other costs would have to be capitalized.

The state of North Carolina required that $500,000 be permanently escrowed with a bank. BMI would be permitted to receive the interest on the investment; the rate of interest currently quoted by North Carolina National Bank was 5.5 percent (pretax).

Tom Abner asked Schnider to provide him with additional projections for the first five years of operation of the start-up division. Her response to his memo included the following:

> The North Carolina division is expected to parallel the company's overall average monthly contract price of $14.38. The new division is expected to produce an annual average of 7,000 contracts per month during the first year of operations. Thereafter, the revenue is expected to grow at 5 percent due to inflation (price increases) and 15 percent due to real growth in the number of average contracts per month for the next five years. Thereafter, real growth should slow to 10 percent for five years, followed by 5 percent for five years, and finally, a constant rate of 3 percent. The new revenues are expected to require additional investments in net working capital (current assets minus current liabilities). The additional cash flow is expected to parallel that of other divisions: 9 percent per dollar of additional revenue.

> Our best estimate is that approximately 1,000 of the new divisions's first-year contracts will be cannibalized from the Virginia Division. The average monthly price for these contracts is $14.38. Sales from this region were forecasted to grow at 5 percent due to inflation and 10 percent due to real growth without the North Carolina Division. These sales are assumed to pay 55 percent providers' fees, 15 percent commissions, and 10 percent management in the Virginia Division. The Virginia Division's fixed operating costs will probably not decline as a result of the lost revenue.

> The expenses for the North Carolina Division are expected to reflect those of other new divisions—$175,000 in fixed operating expenses initially, with increases paralleling inflation.

> With respect to the appropriate required rate of return, our current cost of capital is approximately 15 percent. Usually we require an additional risk premium of 2.5 percent for start-up operations, since such projects carry with them more uncertainty. This rate is substantially above the rate of interest that our $500,000 escrowed funds will earn. Thus, we should require an additional "opportunity" cost from this project.

> As you know, the current tax laws require a 37.5 percent marginal federal and state rate (including the federal deduction for state taxes).

As Tom Abner detailed the cash flow calculations, he realized that he needed to make an assumption regarding the divisional value at the appropriate horizon. Historically, companies similar to BMI have sold at market price-earnings ratios of 12.2, at market price–cash flow ratios of 8.7, and at market price–book of business of .4 (the book of business is defined as the annual revenue that would be received if all subscribers remained in force). He wondered how he might incorporate this information into his analysis.

QUESTIONS*

1. Prepare an analysis of the investment in the North Carolina Division. Compute all marginal cash flows. How might the terminal value of the division be computed?

2. Compute the net present value using both the company's cost of capital and the risk-adjusted discount rate. Which of these values is more accurate? Why?

3. Compute the divisional internal rate of return and the modified internal rate of return. Which of these rates is more accurate? Why?

4. Compute the divisional payback and accounting rate of return. What information do these numbers give you? Should this information be considered in Tom Abner's analysis?

5. Should BMI invest in the North Carolina Division? Support your position.

*The spreadsheet model is named "BMI.wk1."

CASE 26

Harding Plastic
Molding Company

Capital Budgeting: Ranking Problems

On January 11, 1993, the finance committee of Harding Plastic Molding Company (HPMC) met to consider eight capital budgeting projects. Present at the meeting were Robert L. Harding, president and founder; Susan Jorgensen, comptroller; and Chris Woelk, head of research and development. Over the past five years, this committee has met every month to consider and make a final judgment on all proposed capital outlays brought up for review during the period.

Harding Plastic Molding Company was founded in 1972 by Robert L. Harding to produce plastic parts and molding for the Detroit automakers. For the first 10 years of operations, HPMC has worked solely as a subcontractor for the automakers, but since then the company has made strong efforts to diversify in order to avoid the cyclical problems faced by the auto industry. By 1988, this diversification attempt had led HPMC into the production of over 1,000 different items, including kitchen utensils, camera housings, and phonographic and recording equipment. It had also led to an increase in sales of 500 percent during the 1982–1992 period. As this dramatic increase in sales was paralleled by a corresponding increase in production volume, HPMC was forced, in late 1991, to expand production facilities. This plant and equipment expansion involved capital expenditures of approximately $10.5 million and resulted in an increase of production capacity of about 40 percent. Because of this increased production capacity, HPMC has made a concerted effort to attract new business and, consequently, has recently entered into contracts with a large toy firm and a major discount department store chain. Still, non–auto-related business represents only 32 percent of HPMC's overall business. Thus, HPMC has continued to solicit nonautomotive business, and as a result of this effort and its internal research and development, the firm has four sets of mutually exclusive projects to consider at this month's finance committee meeting.

Over the past 10 years, HPMC's capital budgeting approach has evolved into a somewhat elaborate procedure in which new proposals are categorized into three areas: profit, research and development, and safety. Projects falling into the profit or research and development area are evaluated using present value techniques, assuming a 10 percent opportunity rate; those falling into the safety classification are evaluated in a more subjective framework. Besides the requirement that research and development projects receive favorable results from the present value criteria, a total dollar limit is assigned to projects of this category—typically about $750,000 per year. This limitation was imposed by Harding primarily because of the limited availability of quality researchers in the plastics industry. He felt that if more funds than this were allocated, "we simply couldn't find the manpower to administer them properly." The benefits derived from safety projects, on the other hand, are not measured in terms of cash flows; hence, present value methods are not used in their evaluation. Evaluating safety projects is a pragmatically difficult task requiring quantifying the benefits from these projects into dollar terms. Thus, safety projects are subjectively evaluated by a management-worker committee with a limited budget. All eight projects to be evaluated in January are classified as profit projects.

The first set of projects listed on the meeting's agenda for examination involve the utilization of HPMC's precision equipment. Project A calls for the production of vacuum containers for thermos bottles produced for a large discount hardware chain. The containers would be manufactured in five different size and color combinations. This project would be carried out over a three-year period, for which HPMC would be guaranteed a minimum return plus a percentage of the sales. Project B involves the manufacture of inexpensive photographic equipment for a national photography outlet. Although HPMC currently has excess plant capacity, each of these projects would utilize precision equipment whose excess capacity is limited. Thus, adopting either project would tie up all precision facilities. In addition, the purchase of new equipment would be both prohibitively expensive and involve a time delay of approximately two years, thus making projects A and B mutually exclusive. (The cash flows associated with projects A and B are given in Exhibit 1.)

——————— **EXHIBIT 1** ———————

Harding Plastic Molding Company

Cash Flows

Year	Project A	Project B
0	$-75,000	$-75,000
1	10,000	43,000
2	30,000	43,000
3	100,000	43,000

——————— **EXHIBIT 2** ———————

Harding Plastic Molding Company

Cash Flows

Year	Project C	Project D
0	$-8,000	$-20,000
1	11,000	25,000

The second set of projects involves the renting of computer facilities over a one-year period to aid in customer billing and perhaps inventory control. Project C entails the evaluation of a customer billing system proposed by Advanced Computer Corporation. Under this system, all the bookkeeping and billing presently being done by HPMC's accounting department would now be done by Advanced. In addition to saving bookkeeping costs, Advanced would provide a more efficient billing system and do a credit analysis of delinquent customers, which could be used in the future for in-depth credit analysis. Project D is proposed by International Computer Corporation and includes a billing system similar to that offered by Advanced, as well as an inventory control system that will keep track of all raw materials and parts in stock and reorder when necessary, thereby reducing the likelihood of material stockouts, which has become more and more frequent over the past three years. (The cash flows for projects C and D are given in Exhibit 2.)

The third decision that faces the financial directors of HPMC involves a newly developed and patented process for molding hard plastics. HPMC can either manufacture and market the equipment necessary to mold such plastics or it can sell the patent rights to Polyplastics, Inc., the world's largest producer of plastics products. (The cash flows for projects E and F are shown in Exhibit 3.) At present, the process has not been fully tested, and if HPMC is going to market it itself, it will be necessary to complete this testing and begin production of plant facilities immediately. On the other hand, the selling of these patent rights to Polyplastics would involve only

─────── EXHIBIT 3 ───────

Harding Plastic Molding Company

Cash Flows

Year	Project E	Project F
0	$-30,000	$-271,500
1	210,000	100,000
2		100,000
3		100,000
4		100,000
5		100,000
6		100,000
7		100,000
8		100,000
9		100,000
10		100,000

minor testing and refinements, which could be completed within the year. Thus, a decision between the two courses of action is necessary immediately.

The final set of projects up for consideration concerns the replacement of some of the machinery. HPMC can go into one of two directions: Project G suggests the purchase and installation of moderately priced, extremely efficient equipment with an expected life of 5 years; while project H advocates the purchase of a similarly priced, although less efficient, machine with a life expectancy of 10 years. (The cash flows for these alternatives are shown in Exhibit 4.)

As the meeting opened, debate immediately centered on the most appropriate method for evaluating all the projects. Harding suggested that since the projects to be considered were mutually exclusive, perhaps their usual capital budgeting criteria of net present value was inappropriate. He felt that, in examining these projects, they should be more concerned with relative profitability of some measure of yield. Both Jorgensen and Woelk agreed with Harding's point of view, with Jorgensen advocating a profitability index approach and Woelk preferring to use the internal rate of return. Jorgensen argued that the use of the profitability index would provide a benefit-cost ratio, directly implying relative profitability, so that they would merely need to rank the projects and select those with the highest profitability index. Woelk suggested that the calculation of an internal rate of return would also give a measure of profitability and perhaps be somewhat easier to interpret. To settle the issue, Harding suggested that they calculate all three measures, as they would undoubtedly yield the same ranking.

————— EXHIBIT 4 —————
Harding Plastic Molding Company

Cash Flows

Year	Project G	Project H
0	$-500,000	$-500,000
1	225,000	150,000
2	225,000	150,000
3	225,000	150,000
4	225,000	150,000
5	225,000	150,000
6		150,000
7		150,000
8		150,000
9		150,000
10		150,000

From here the discussion turned to an appropriate approach to the problem of differing lives among mutually exclusive projects E and F, and G and H. Woelk argued that there really was no problem here, that since all the cash flows from these projects could be determined, any of the discounted cash flow methods of capital budgeting would work well. Jorgensen agreed that this was true, but felt that some compensation should be made for the fact that the projects being considered did not have equal lives.

QUESTIONS

1. Was Harding correct in stating that the NPV, PI, and IRR necessarily will yield the same ranking order? Under what situations might the NPV, PI, and IRR methods provide different rankings? Why is this possible?

2. What are the NPV, PI, and IRR for projects A and B? What has caused the ranking conflicts? Should project A or B be chosen? Might your answer change if project B is a typical project in the plastic molding industry? For example, if projects for HPMC generally yield approximately 12 percent, is it logical to assume that the IRR for project B of approximately 33 percent is a correct calculation for ranking purposes? (*Hint:* Examine the reinvestment assumption rate.)

3. What are the NPV, PI, and IRR for projects C and D? Should project C or D be chosen? Does your answer change if these projects are considered under a capital constraint? What return on the marginal $12,000 not employed in project C is necessary to make one indifferent to choosing one project over the other under a capital rationing situation?

4. What are the NPV, PI, and IRR for projects E and F? Are these projects

comparable even though they have unequal lives? Why? Which project should be chosen? Assume that these projects are not considered under a capital constraint.

5. What are the NPV, PI, and IRR for projects G and H? Are these projects comparable even though they have unequal lives? Why? Which project should be chosen? Assume that these projects are not considered under a capital constraint.

CASE 27

Ron Willingham Courses, Inc.

Capital Budgeting: Basic Difficulties

Ron Willingham Courses, Inc., founded by Ron Willingham in 1972, has dealt primarily in personal and professional motivational courses, particularly for corporate employees. Willingham and his associates have developed several programs that have proved successful among the individuals completing the courses.

At the present time, extensive thought and consideration are being committed to a new program to be used by banks and/or savings and loan institutions as a client service. The course material, entitled the MONY Plan, is addressed to the need and strategy for managing an individual's personal resources. James Williams, the executive vice president of Ron Willingham, has identified a strong potential market for such courses among both business executives actively involved in the management of large amounts of corporate funds and persons having little experience in the proper management of money. In visiting with the executives of various financial institutions, Williams has received several commitments to purchase the course. However, he is reluctant to initiate the sales campaign before the completion of an investigation into the impact of several strategies upon the profitability of the firm. Specifically, questions still remain concerning the expected life of the instructional material and the marketing strategy.

In analyzing the prospects of the investment, Willingham and Williams consider the basic product to have an expected life of approximately five years (plan A). However, this estimate could be significantly lengthened, either through conducting an extensive marketing campaign in subsequent years (plan B) or by undertaking a major revision in the course package in the fifth year (plan C). The options under consideration may be summarized as follows:

Plan A:　The first strategy requires an investment at the present time totaling $300,000. This amount would provide the necessary funds for production equipment ($250,000) as well as working capital requirements of ($50,000). The working capital portion of the investment may be liquidated upon the termination of the course. The expected life of the project is five years.

Plan B:　The second alternative would permit an increase in the expected life of the course to 10 years. Based upon experience with prior investments of a similar type, the firm's management considers the chances of extending a project's life to be quite sensitive to increased efforts in the area of customer awareness in the latter years of the program. Thus, the extension of the product life would come from an intensive marketing campaign in years 6 through 10. The capital investment would be similar to the amount under plan A in that the same capital expenditure would be made ($250,000); however, $100,000 of working capital would have to be maintained, as opposed to only $50,000 for plan A.

Plan C:　The final analysis to be performed relates to a two-phase investment in which the initial investment of $350,000 is committed (including $100,000 of working capital), but $200,000 must also be expended on equipment at the conclusion of the fifth year. This investment would result in substantive modifications and improvements in the program. While time is of the essence in going to the market, within the next few years several major improvements in educational equipment are expected. Such a two-phase investment would allow the firm to reap the benefits of these developments.

To sum up, the management is considering two basic approaches for promoting MONY Plan: (1) a concentrated effort whose intent is to saturate the market during a five-year period (plan A); (2) an extended investment in MONY Plan, with the prolonged life being the result of a marketing campaign in years 6 through 10 (plan B) or a major revamping of the course structure in the fifth year (plan C).

The estimates of the annual receipts and operations expenses for the three plans are given in Exhibit 1.

─────── **EXHIBIT 1** ───────

Ron Willingham Courses, Inc.

*Estimated Annual Receipts
and Operational Expense*

Sales

Year	Plan A	Plan B	Plan C
1	$100,000	$ 75,000	$ 75,000
2	300,000	125,000	125,000
3	450,000	200,000	200,000
4	450,000	280,000	280,000
5	450,000	350,000	350,000
6		400,000	475,000
7		425,000	500,000
8		475,000	500,000
9		450,000	500,000
10		250,000	500,000

Marketing Expenses per Year

Year(s)	Plan A	Plan B	Plan C
1–5	$35,000	$25,000	$25,000
6–7		50,000	25,000
8–9		70,000	25,000
10		25,000	25,000

These additional data are thought to bear on the decision:

1. The production of the material will require the use of a portion of an existing plant not included in the capital investment figures quoted in Exhibit 1. This part of the plant, which represents excess floor space, could be considered to have a book value of $150,000 and a corresponding annual depreciation of $10,000 per year. However, this segment of the plant could not be used otherwise owing to the floor plan of the building.

2. Cost of goods sold of similar programs has generally been a variable cost approximating 60 percent of sales.

3. Administrative expenses for the company will be $10,000 annually, which has been the level of administration expenses for the past year. However, only $4,000 of this amount will be allocated via the cost accounting system to the new plan.

4. The bank has agreed to finance $100,000 of the investment at an interest rate of 10 percent, with the interest being payable yearly, and the principal coming due at the end of the project life.

5. The company's tax rate is 40 percent and it uses straight-line depreciation (no salvage) for all expenditures.

QUESTIONS

1. Determine the costs of the three alternatives.
2. Compute the annual after-tax cash flows for the three plans.
3. Compute the net present value, the profitability index, and the internal rate of return for each plan, assuming a cost of capital of 10 percent.
4. Which course of action should be taken by the firm? Explain.

CASE 28

Fly-by-Night Airlines

Capital Budgeting: Replacement Decision

Fly-by-Night Airlines is a major commercial air carrier offering passenger service between most large cities in the United States. One of its more profitable routes is between Los Angeles and New York. Competition on this route is intense, and James "Red" Baron, supervisor of transcontinental operations for Fly-by-Night, is considering upgrading the quality of the fleet of aircraft used on the Los Angeles–New York run.

As it has in the past, Fly-by-Night plans to purchase all its planes from Puddle Jumper Aircraft Company. Puddle Jumper markets three aircraft: (1) the old reliable PJ-1, for the last 10 years the workhorse of the airline industry; (2) the soon-to-be-introduced PJ-2, currently in the test flight stage; and (3) the technologically advanced PJ-3, still in the design stage. Although the PJ-2 and PJ-3 will not be available for service until sometime in the future, Puddle Jumper is now taking contingency orders for these planes. If Fly-by-Night is to have any hope for prompt delivery, it must order the planes today, even though it will not take delivery or pay for them until sometime in the future. Fly-by-Night is very interested in the newer models because they are more fuel efficient and less polluting, require less maintenance, and are much quieter than the old PJ-1.

Fly-by-Night currently uses five PJ-1 planes to service its Los Angeles–New York route. These planes were purchased 10 years ago for a cost of $15 million per plane; each is being depreciated on a straight-line basis to a salvage value of zero over a 25-year economic life from the date of purchase. Each PJ-1 plane could be sold currently at a market value of $8 million. This market price for the PJ-1 is expected to drop to $5 million by the end of third year and to $3 million by the end of the sixth year.

Red Baron is considering replacing the PJ-1 planes with either the PJ-2 or the PJ-3. The PJ-2 will be available for delivery in three years and could generate its first cash flow from commercial service in the fourth year. The PJ-3 will be available for delivery in six years and could generate its first cash flow in the seventh year.

To assist him in making this decision, Baron wants to know the net present values of three different investment options. For all options, he is using a 15-year planning horizon. Under option A, the firm will continue to use the PJ-1s for three more years, replace them with the PJ-2s at the end of the third year, and use these PJ-2s for the remainder of the hori-zon—12 years. Option B is the same as option A, except that rather than continuing to use the PJ-2s for the remainder of the horizon, these planes will be replaced at the end of the sixth year by the PJ-3s, which will then be used for the remainder of the horizon—9 years. Under option C, the firm will continue to use its current fleet of PJ-1s for 6 years, replace them with PJ-3s at the end of the sixth year, and use these PJ-3s for the remain-der of the horizon—9 years.

The purchase price for a PJ-2 three years from now will be $20 mil-lion. This cost will be depreciated on a straight-line basis over 12 years to a salvage value of $8 million. The PJ-2 is expected to have a market value in the sixth year of $18 million. Six years from now, when the PJ-3 becomes available, it will cost $30 million per plane and will be depreciated on a straight-line basis over nine years to a salvage value of $12 million.

EXHIBIT 1

Fly-by-Night Airlines

Operating Data on Puddle Jumper Planes
(expected value per plane)

	PJ-1	PJ-2	PJ-3
1. Fuel consumption (gallons/flight between L.A. and N.Y.)	4,000	3,000	2,000
2. Maintenance time (maintenance days/year)	40	30	20
3. Upgrading costs* (dollars/year of operation)	100,000	50,000	16,666.67
4. Capacity per plane	200	250	350

*Includes expenses for noise and pollution reduction, safety improvements, etc. The figures for the PJ-2 apply to the end of year 4, and those for the PJ-3 to the end of year 7.

EXHIBIT 2

Fly-by-Night Airlines

Economic Data for Airline Industry

1. Fuel costs will be $0.55 per gallon by year-end and will grow at a constant expected annual rate of 9% per year.
2. For all planes: by year-end maintenance costs will be $60,000 per day the plane is in maintenance. Maintenance costs will grow at a constant expected annual rate of 5% per year.
3. Upgrading costs will grow at a constant expected annual rate of 8% per year for each plane.

Economic Data for Los Angeles–New York Route*

Plane

1. Passenger load factor
   .95 (drops to .92 after the PJ-2   PJ-1
       or PJ-3 is introduced by the
       manufacturer)
   .90
   .82   PJ-2
                        PJ-3

$$\text{Passenger load factor} = \frac{\text{average number of passengers per flight}}{\text{passenger capacity of plane}}$$

2. Number of one-way flights
   Los Angeles–New York per year†
   300   PJ-1
   320   PJ-2
   335   PJ-3
3. The average price of a one-way ticket between Los Angeles and New York will be $400 by year-end and is expected to grow at a constant annual rate of 4%. The ticket price remains the same regardless of which plane is used.
4. Personnel and administrative expenses (e.g., pilot, flight attendant, ticket agent salaries) are currently, and are expected to continue to be, 85% of ticket revenues.

---

*All figures for which growth rates are not specified are assumed to remain constant over time.

†The differences in number of flights per year are due to differences in time spent on maintenance and upgrading.

To assist him in making this decision, Baron has obtained the data shown in Exhibits 1 and 2 from aerospace engineers at Puddle Jumper and from transportation economists at Fly-by-Night.

The passenger load factors come from a careful analysis of future demand and supply conditions and the degree of competition on the Los Angeles–New York route. Fly-by-Night's transportation economists feel that it is quite likely that the major competitors serving this route will eventually all convert to the newer aircraft and that, to remain competitive, Fly-by-Night will eventually have to do the same. They are uncertain whether the PJ-2 or PJ-3 will become the more popular plane, but they feel that correctly guessing which plane will gain long-run acceptance by the flying public may be the key to any change in market share on this route. The future price of fuel is likely to be the key determinant of the future relative efficiency of these two planes. In general, however, the economists believe it will be very difficult for firms operating the Los Angeles–New York run to change their market share substantially in the future.

Baron has made a list of other information that he feels is relevant to this decision. First, to retain a license for the Los Angeles–New York route, airlines are required by a federal government regulatory agency to allocate enough aircraft to the route to service a minimum of 300,000 passengers per year. Second, since both the PJ-2 and PJ-3 aircraft have not yet been used in commercial service, their cost and operating figures are likely to be more uncertain than those for the PJ-1—at least until the bugs are eliminated. For this reason, Baron has decided to use a larger risk-adjusted discount rate or cost of capital for the expected cash flows generated by the PJ-2 and PJ-3 planes. His choices of discount rates are:

Plane	Appropriate Cost of Capital
PJ-1	10%
PJ-2	12
PJ-3	15

Baron has decided to discount all purchase costs or salvage values at 15 percent. Finally, the firm's marginal tax rate is 50 percent.

QUESTIONS

1. If Fly-by-Night decides to upgrade its fleet by using the PJ-2 exclusively, how many PJ-2 planes will it need to buy to meet the federal government regulation requiring that an airline serving the Los Angeles–New York route have the *capability* of carrying a minimum of 300,000 passengers per year? If the company decides to use the PJ-3 exclusively, how many PJ-3 planes will it need to buy to meet this federal regulation? (Notice that the actual number of passengers that Fly-by-Night expects to carry is slightly higher if it uses the PJ-3 or PJ-2 than it presently carries using the PJ-1. The reason is that the larger-capacity planes will allow it to eliminate some of the overbooking problems it now faces with the PJ-1 during holiday periods. However, management feels that Fly-by-Night cannot significantly increase its ridership by buying increased capacity.)

2. Compute the ticket revenues that would be generated for Fly-by-Night in each year over the 15-year horizon under options A, B, and C.

3. Compute the total operating costs that would be generated in each year over the 15-year horizon under options A, B, and C. Operating costs include fuel, maintenance, upgrading, and personnel expenditures.

4. Compute the net cash flow for each year for each option. If the firm suffers a loss in any year in its Los Angeles–New York operations, assume that it has other income in that year from which the loss can be deducted for tax purposes.

5. Compute the net present value for each option.

6. Comment on what you think are the strengths and weaknesses of the way Red Baron has chosen to analyze this replacement decision. What assumptions is he implicitly making in his analysis? Would you have done anything differently? If so, what?

CASE 29

Simpson and Selph, Ltd.

Capital Budgeting: Replacement Decision
with Cost of Capital

Brian Douglas, a corporate financial analyst for Simpson and Selph, Ltd. (SS), was charged with evaluating the replacement of a carpet-binding machine. Simpson and Selph is a small carpet manufacturing company located in Macon, Georgia. The machine to be replaced was purchased five years ago for $350,000 and was depreciated for five years using the accelerated cost recovery schedule (ACRS) depreciation rates. The carpet binder currently has no book value and, if replaced, must be scrapped at a cost of $50,000. If not replaced, the production department estimates that the machine's production capacity over the next several years will decline as it experiences increasing downtime. Since the company can sell all the carpet it can produce on the machine, downtime translates into lost revenue. The vice president for operations estimates that the carpet binder will produce carpet worth $600,000 in 19x6. Beginning in 19x7, the revenue from the machine is estimated to decline by 3 percent per year. The carpet binder can be nursed along to a useful life of five more years. Fixed costs associated with this machine are estimated to remain at $150,000 for each of the five years and variable costs are estimated at 40 percent of revenue for each of the five years.

SS is considering two alternative replacement machines. The first is the same brand as the old machine, a Harley. The new Harley will cost $250,000, with an additional cost of $10,000 for installation. The accounting department plans on depreciating the full cost over five years using straight-line depreciation. The new Harley will have the same production capacity as the old one. Thus, in the first year of operation, 19x6, the Harley will produce $600,000 in revenue. In each of the following four years of operation, it will increase revenue by the rate of inflation—estimated at 4.5 percent per year.

The new Harley will have a different cost structure from the old machine. Fixed costs will only be $100,000 (excluding depreciation) for each year and variable costs are estimated at 41 percent of revenue per year. At the end of five years, the engineers estimate that the machine will be worth $100,000.

The alternative machine under consideration, a Davidson, will cost $325,000, with $15,000 installation costs. This machine is assumed to have a tax life of five years. The accounting department will depreciate the Davidson using straight-line depreciation. This machine will increase production capacity in 19x6 to $650,000 and the marketing department estimates that all produced carpet can be sold. For the remaining four years, revenue will increase by inflation. Fixed costs, $125,000 per year, will be higher than for the Harley, but variable costs are estimated to decline to 36 percent of revenue owing to reduced waste of material. At the end of five years, the Davidson is likely to be worth $125,000.

Since both new machines will increase revenue, an investment in net working capital must be considered. The new Harley will require a $30,000 investment in net working capital in 19x5 and the Davidson will require a $50,000 investment in the same year. Douglas estimates that this working capital investment can be recovered in the final year of operation.

The company's current capital structure (Exhibit 1) approximates its target capital structure.

The company's long-term debt is rated Aa and currently yields 11 percent. The company's common stock currently sells for $42.625. New common could be issued at a 5 percent discount, including float. Next year's dividends are expected to be $4. Exhibit 2 shows dividends for the past five years.

EXHIBIT 1

Simpson and Selph, Ltd.

Capital Structure

Source	Amount
Long-term debt	$32,000,000
Common equity at par	6,400,000
Additional paid-in capital	3,200,000
Retained earnings	22,400,000

—— **EXHIBIT 2** ——

Simpson and Selph, Ltd.

Historical Dividends

Year	Dividend
19x5	$3.75
19x4	3.50
19x3	3.25
19x2	3.10
19x1	3.00

Value Line gives SS stock a beta of 1.2. The same service also forecasts the 90-day Treasury bill rate at 6.4 percent and the 5-year Treasury note at 7.8 percent. The Standard and Poor's Index of 500 stocks is expected to yield 15 percent for the next several years.

QUESTIONS*

1. Compute the net present value, profitability index, internal rate of return, modified internal rate of return, and payback for each of the alternative machines. Which project would you recommend? Why?

2. Compute the net present value, profitability index, internal rate of return, modified internal rate of return, and payback for the marginal cash flows associated with the two alternative machines. Which project would you recommend? Why?

3. Assume that the cash flows associated with the Davidson machine are more risky than those for the company's average project and thus require a 2 percent higher discount rate. Further assume that the cash flows associated with the new Harley are less risky than those for the average company project. Which project would you recommend? Why?

*The spreadsheet is named "SIMPSON.wk1."

CASE 30

Chapman Coal Corporation

Capital Budgeting:
The Risk-Adjusted Rate
of Return and Certainty-
Equivalent Approaches

On December 31, 1989, the Chapman Coal Corporation was investigating the feasibility of two mutually exclusive projects. The first prospective investment involved a strip mining operation in eastern Tennessee. The second investment also involved the extraction of coal, but this expenditure would be an underground site in southwestern Virginia.

For the past several months, Gene Graham had been involved in the development of revenue and expense projections for the two projects. In his analysis, sufficient data existed from prior investments to provide relatively accurate cost data. After having drawn upon this information, Graham made the following projections as to investment costs for each operation:

	Strip Mining	Underground Mining
Leasehold investment	$ 400,000	$ 300,000
Equipment	3,000,000	1,500,000
Additional working capital requirements	200,000	200,000
Total	$3,600,000	$2,000,000

With respect to these figures, experience suggests that a 10-year life may be expected on either of the two prospective investments, with the practice being to expense the leasehold investments on a straight-line basis over the life. Furthermore, the equipment would be depreciated over the same life on a straight-line basis. However, the projected salvage value for the strip mining operation would be $600,000, while the equipment for the underground plant could be expected to have a residual value of $150,000. The exigency for incremental working capital as a result of the investment would arise at the time of the investment but could be released upon the termination of the project with only a negligible chance of the full amount not being recovered.

In addition to the cost estimates, the engineers, using studies of the subsurface formations, were able to make projections as to the revenues that could be generated from the two fields. Based upon their studies, expected earnings after taxes for the two investments would be as follows:

	Years	Annual Expected Earnings after Taxes
Strip mining	1-4	$400,000
	5-7	220,000
	8-10	100,000
Underground mining	1-4	360,000
	5-7	230,000
	8-10	130,000

Upon receiving this information, Graham questioned the reliability of the anticipated earnings. In response, David Hughes, head of the engineering staff at Chapman Coal, informed him that both projects would have to be considered more risky than the firm's typical investment. Furthermore, the personnel conducting the analysis indicated that the expected cash flows from the underground mining operation were subject to considerably more uncertainty than those from the strip mining. In fact, Hughes considered the extraction of coal through the underground facility to be twice as risky as the strip mining alternative. For this reason, he recommended that the strip mining project be discounted at a 10 percent rate, while the underground mining proposal be analyzed with a 20 percent criterion. Graham questioned Hughes's logic since the company's cost of capital had been computed to be 8 percent. He believed that this figure better reflected the stockholders' required rate of return and for that reason should be used as the discount rate for both projects.

In support of his position concerning the riskiness of the two proposed investments, Hughes developed some in-depth worksheets for Graham that suggested other possible returns depending upon the amount of coal actually extracted from the mines. As a summary measurement of the possible deviations from the expected values, the engineering staff further calculated the standard deviation of the returns. These calculations are as follows:

	Years	Standard Deviation of Earnings after Taxes
Strip mining	1-4	$340,000
	5-7	250,000
	8-10	190,000
Underground mining	1-4	315,000
	5-7	276,500
	8-10	236,000

In addition to the standard deviation of these reported earnings, the engineering personnel estimated the standard deviation relating to the salvage value of each project to be $300,000 for the strip mining facility and $135,000 for the underground mining equipment.

In reviewing the engineering department's work, Graham was quite pleased with the results. However, a question remained in his mind as to the soundness of employing the various discount rates suggested by Hughes. Graham had been particularly interested in this question even before the two projects in question had been brought before him. As an alternative to adjusting the discount rate for dissimilar investments in terms of risk, he had been conducting some informal seminars with top management in hopes of discerning their attitude toward risk. From these sessions, he was able to specify the relationship between the level of risk and the willingness of management to accept such uncertainty, as reflected by "certainty-equivalent factors." The results of these meetings are depicted in Exhibit 1. With this information, Graham felt that a better approach would be to adjust the cash flows by the appropriate certainty-equivalent factors and to discount these adjusted flows at the firm's cost of capital. However, Hughes was of the opinion that the risk-free rate, which is currently 6 percent, would be more appropriate for such an analysis. At this point, the investigation was temporarily halted until the questions could be resolved.

——————— EXHIBIT 1 ———————

Chapman Coal Corporation

Management's Risk-Return Profile

Coefficient of Variation*	Certainty-Equivalent Factor†
.5	.95
.6	.93
.7	.91
.8	.88
.9	.85
1.0	.82
1.1	.78
1.2	.74
1.3	.70
1.4	.64
1.5	.58
1.6	.52
1.7	.43
1.8	.33
1.9	.15

*The coefficient of variation is a relative measure of dispersion, calculated by dividing the standard deviation by the expected value.

†The factor states the amount management would accept for certain in lieu of $1 expected return.

QUESTIONS

1. Given both the expected values of returns and a measure of the risk accompanying these returns for two mutually exclusive projects, can an individual determine the better investment to accept? ("Better" is defined as the investment that is identified as unequivocably preferable for any decision maker.)

2. Specifically define the "certainty-equivalent factor." How does it differ from the probability of an event occurring?

3. Using Exhibit 1, graph the relationship between risk and the certainty-equivalent factor. Would the company's management be considered risk seeking, risk neutral, or risk averting? Explain your answer.

4. a. Calculate the net present value for each investment employing (i) the certainty-equivalent approach and (ii) the risk-adjusted rate of return method.

    b. Are the results of the certainty-equivalent methodology and the risk-adjusted rate approach consistent—that is, do both techniques indicate acceptance of the same project? If an inconsistency does exist, explain the reason(s) why.

5. Under what condition(s) should the decision maker use the risk-adjusted discount rate or an adjustment of cash flows by a certainty-equivalent factor as opposed to simply discounting the expected cash flows by the cost of capital?

6.   a. Compute the necessary expected cash flows of an "average-risk" asset that would be deemed equivalently acceptable to management as the underground mining operation when examined by the risk-adjusted rate of return.

      b. Set up the solution (but do not solve) for determining the risk-adjusted rate of return that would provide results identical to those for certainty-equivalent approach for the strip mining project.

CASE 31

Central Florida
Computer Company

Capital Budgeting: Risk-Adjusted
Discount Rates

Central Florida Computer Company (CFCC), a leading manufacturer of IBM look-alike computers, is considering the installation of a new production line to manufacture clones of IBM computers. Mike Stoltz, the newest financial analyst, is evaluating the proposal in the spring of 19x0, with anticipated investments occurring late in 19x0 and revenue beginning to be received by January 1, 19x1. If a "go" decision is made, the proposed assembly line will be housed in Casselberry, Florida. The proposed portion of the plant was identified last year by an outside consultant at a cost of $60,000. At the moment, a portion of this plant is vacant. The 10,500 square feet required for the assembly line represents 25 percent of the entire plant. The plant originally cost $1,450,000 12 years ago and is being depreciated over 20 years. While there are no plans for the building, warehouse space currently leases for $11 per square foot per year.

CFCC must spend $1.1 million on equipment for the line, plus $10,000 in shipping and installation costs. The equipment manufacturer is willing to guarantee these expenses, so CFCC's management is certain of these cash flows. The machines are expected to have a five-year economic life. For tax purposes, they are classified as special manufacturing tools, and hence fall into a three-year MACRS depreciation schedule. (This schedule requires percentage depreciations of 33 percent, 45 percent, 15 percent, and 7 percent for each of the four years, respectively.)

CFCC's marketing department feels that sales for the division will depend upon the state of the economy. Exhibit 1 details the marketing department's sales estimates.

The marketing department expects that unit sales will be flat over the five-year life of the assembly line, but prices, and hence revenues, are expected to increase with inflation by 6 percent per year over the life of the line. The initial selling price is expected to be $1,500 per unit.

The engineering department expects that fixed costs (excluding depreciation) will be a constant $70,000 per year and that variable component costs (parts assembled to manufacture the computers) and labor costs will be 45 percent of revenues. The department is virtually certain of both of these estimates. CFCC's marginal tax rate during the period is expected to remain at 38 percent.

The new assembly line will require an increase in the level of CFCC's raw material inventories, finished goods inventory, and accounts receivable. The expected increase in current assets will be somewhat offset by a corresponding increase in current liabilities. The resulting increase in net working capital will require an investment of $30,000 in 19x0 prior to 19x1 sales. Beginning in 19x1, additional annual increases in net working capital will be required; they will vary directly with annual changes in revenue at a rate of 11.25 cents per dollar of marginal revenue. Thus, the working capital investment in 19x1 will be 11.25 cents per dollar of 19x2 revenue increase over the 19x1 revenue level. All of the working capital investments will be recoverable at the end of the project's life.

At the end of the line's operating life, the line will be closed down. CFCC expects to turn the plant square footage over to another project. The assembly line machinery, on the other hand, will be sold for its estimated salvage value. The engineers have provided the estimates of terminal value before taxes (Exhibit 2).

CFCC's stock is traded on the over-the-counter market at $30 per share, with an estimated beta of 1.5. Analysts expect that the company will pay $2 in dividends per share in 19x1; dividends have grown 9 percent annually for the past 10 years. Currently, Treasury securities yield 7 percent and the Standard & Poor's 500 Index is expected to return 14 percent

--------------------- **EXHIBIT 1** ---------------------

Central Florida Computer Company

Sales Forecasts

State of Economy	Probability	Sales (Units)
Recession	.35	300
Slow growth	.40	400
Strong growth	.25	500

--- EXHIBIT 2 ---

Central Florida Computer Company

Forecasts of Terminal Value

State of Economy	Probability	Selling Price
Recession	.35	$100,000
Slow growth	.40	400,000
Strong growth	.25	900,000

--- EXHIBIT 3 ---

Central Florida Computer Company

Capital Structure

Source	Amount
Long-term debt	$3,500,000
Capital stock paid in	1,000,000
Retained earnings	4,000,000

annually for the next several years. CFCC borrows from the local bank at 11 percent.

CFCC's operating committee has always maintained the company's book value capital structure at what it believes is the company's optimal or target capital structure. Exhibit 3 provides the company's current capital structure.

QUESTIONS*

1. Assuming that this project has the same risk characteristics as the company's "average" project, estimate the projected cash flows and calculate the expected net present value, profitability index, internal rate of return, modified internal rate of return, payback period, and accounting rate of return. Assume that the company uses a 12 percent discount rate for its "average" project. Would you recommend the project? Why or why not?

2. Compute the company's current cost of capital. How does this information affect your recommendation?

3. Perform a scenario analysis on the project. Estimate the probability that the project will have a negative net present value at the company's cost of capital.

4. Assume that the analyst concludes that this project is significantly more risky than the "average" project. Management believes that the discount rate for such risky projects should be increased by 2 percent in order to

*The spreadsheet model is named "CFCC.wk1."

compensate for the risk. How would this information affect your recommendation?

5. If the economy is weak, one option might be to abandon the project at the end of 19x1. The machinery, with much less wear, might then sell for $850,000. Compute the necessary calculations. How does this information affect your recommendation?

6. Perform a sensitivity analysis on the sales and salvage value assumptions—that is, fix the salvage value at the most likely value and estimate the effect of a value 70, 80, 90, 100, 110, 120, and 130 percent of the most likely sales assumption. Now hold sales at its most likely value and examine the effect of a value 70, 80, 90, 100, 110, 120, and 130 percent of the most likely salvage value assumption. Graph the results on the same axis. How do you interpret this information?

7. Use a two-variable data table to examine the effects of varying both sales and salvage value assumptions as a percent of their most likely value. Be sure that your data points reflect the stated distributions. Summarize the resulting sample observations in a frequency table. Compute the probability of each occurrence. Compute and graph the cumulative density function. How do you interpret this information? How does this information affect your recommendation?

CASE 32

University City Lounge

Capital Budgeting:
Probability Distributions

Richard James operates University City Lounge (UCL) as a small corporation in the college community of Claremont, Pennsylvania, about 65 miles north of Pittsburgh. Although it is primarily a university-oriented city, Claremont has a diversified and sound industrial base. In fact, the town's older residents like to boast that the community has never suffered a depression. James founded UCL five years ago in the downtown section of the city; it serves largely as the main retail outlet for the 10,000 students of Claremont State University. As other shopowners left the downtown area to move to newly constructed shopping centers on the outskirts of the city, James expanded his restaurant and lounge into the vacated adjacent spaces. He enjoys a profitable operation. The net income from the business has grown by about 10 percent each year since its inception. James owns all the stock of UCL.

James is 28 years old, a Navy veteran, and a high school graduate. The firm has no outstanding contractual debt. A one-year note that was taken at a local commercial bank to launch the business was repaid on a timely basis. James maintains good personal relations with several local bankers who frequent his restaurant and lounge operation; all of them are impressed with his hard work at the business.

The restaurant and lounge are organized to appeal to high school students, college students, and, in general, young adults. This is accomplished through the maintenance of three separate environments within the space rented by James. The center of the business is a short-order food and drink service. The menu is brief and includes hot dogs, hamburgers, pizza, sliced beef sandwiches, fried shrimp, soft drinks, and beer. The room that houses this aspect of the business contains ten tables that seat four persons each and five large booths that hold six persons each. Waitresses are employed to serve customers only in this area of UCL.

A separate game room to the left (with respect to the entrance) of the main eating area contains two air hockey tables, six pinball machines, and two bar-sized pool tables. There are five tables that seat 20 customers in total in the game room, so that food and drink are readily consumed in the area. The appeal of this aspect of the UCL operation is centered largely within the high school crowd; even so, a surprisingly large number of Claremont State students find the atmosphere and diversions of the game room pleasantly relaxing.

The third area within UCL is situated to the right of the central dining space and serves as a television viewing lounge. The room is spacious, easily holding the 10 tables (seating 40 people) that are placed there. Until today, a secondhand 21-inch (diagonally measured) color television set was utilized as an entertainment vehicle in the lounge. The set was placed on a viewing stand built into the wall above the small bar in the room. The bar houses the hardware needed to serve beer and soft drinks in the TV lounge. Fifteen bar stools rim the edge of the bar and are considered the choice viewing areas for the major sporting events that are always tuned in by Richard James. Next to the fundamental operation of the business, James enjoys a good ball game on his color set more than just about anything.

This afternoon, the eight-year-old set failed to operate properly, for the third time in as many weeks. The disgruntled owner of UCL decided to replace the erratic set before he lost too many of his regular TV lounge patrons. Anyway, prior to this problem, James had been dissatisfied with the volume of business in the lounge area. He knew that an additional 6 tables and 24 chairs could be placed comfortably in the viewing room, should the level of sales warrant it. So he retired to his small office to examine some material on available television mechanisms that he had been collecting for the last six months.

Rather quickly, James was able to narrow his choice of possible investments to two mutually exclusive entertainment systems. He definitely would purchase either (1) a conventional color set with a 25-inch (diagonally measured) screen or (2) a product called Video-Projector, which offers a 24-square-foot (6 feet high by 4 feet wide) viewing area along with an extremely clear image. The Video-Projector is several times more costly than the conventional set, so James found analysis of this potential acquisition to be anything but easy. He immediately called Daniel Ruggins, the certified public accountant who handles all James's tax matters and also serves as his financial advisor. Ruggins has dealt with UCL during the entire five years that it has been open and is quite familiar with the firm's revenue and cost structure. Upon arriving at UCL, Ruggins met with James and began to develop the data necessary for making an effective choice between the two television systems.

First, they discussed the investment outlay required for each project. The conventional set costs $700 delivered and installed. James thought that the higher level of sales coming from this asset purchase could be achieved only if added inventory in the form of more food, drink, and utensils were kept on hand. The value of this inventory buildup was put at $200.

The Video-Projector could be purchased for $3,800, including setup costs. James decided that to maximize sales revenue during peak hours in the lounge area, this alternative would entail more seating capacity. He would add 6 tables at a unit cost of $30 and 24 chairs at a unit cost of $10. The additional inventory associated with this asset choice was valued at $300. Both Ruggins and James agreed that the inventory buildup for either project would be considered a permanent addition to the asset structure of the firm. This meant that the funds tied up by the inventory rise would not be freed when the television project expired; rather, some other vehicle for maintaining the higher sales level would be found.

The assets of UCL were always depreciated using the straight-line method. A five-year time horizon was decided upon as the relevant period for the analysis. This was because James envisioned that by that time either he would be ready to construct his own building, allowing him to operate a more sophisticated type of eating establishment, or he would completely remodel his leased facilities and accomplish the same purpose. This longer-run business and career objective meant that the bulk of UCL's assets would be sold five years from now. Because of rather rough treatment in the lounge, the salvage value on both sets was placed at zero. Likewise, no scrap value was placed on the tables and chairs that would be purchased as part of the Video-Projector alternative.

At this point, James and Ruggins directed their attention toward development of the expected benefits from each of the prospective investments. The seating capacities for each room of the operation were summarized for review. These figures are contained in Exhibit 1. Upon review of these data, James and Ruggins felt totally comfortable with the estimates of no new seats being needed for the conventional set alternative and 24 being necessary to exploit fully the novelty aspect of the Video-Projector. While at most times the restaurant appeared to be 70 percent full, an average day's business would draw about 218 customers into the UCL. The relationship of customers to total seats was referred to as the "current seating factor" (CSF) by Ruggins. He had observed that the CSF of 1.5 times was rather stable over the years for this company. Because of this stability,

---
EXHIBIT 1
University City Lounge

Room Seating Capacities

	Main Dining Area	Game Room	TV Lounge
Current seats	70	20	55
Average number of excess seats	14	4	25
Additional seats needed for conventional set project	0	0	0
Additional seats needed for Video-Projector project	0	0	24

Total current capacity: 145 seats

Total capacity with Video-Projector project: 169 seats

---

he readily used the CSF as a forecasting statistic. Even if the TV lounge area were replaced with ordinary dining space, James felt certain that the CSF of 1.5 could be maintained. The benefits of the imminent purchase, then, would be projected above this base level of business activity.

Noting that the students of Claremont State often complained about the bland flavoring of institutional food, James operated UCL on all 365 days of the year. As a popular alternative dining establishment, UCL found it profitable to maintain such extended hours. Sunday often turned out to be a high-volume day, largely because of the telecasting of pro football games and also because an Alleghany County ordinance permitted beer sales on any day of the week.

To place the derivation of revenue estimates into an orderly perspective, Ruggins directed James's attention to Exhibits 2 and 3.

Last year, UCL earned $24,371 after taxes. The "other expenses" line item shown in the condensed income statement includes a $14,000 annual salary (drawn on a biweekly basis) earned by James as the operating manager. The cost of goods sold, which amounted to 52.4 percent of the $358,000 in net sales, is primarily a variable expense. The other expenses (38 percent of last year's sales) are mainly fixed. Ruggins stated that he thought the use of 52 percent would accurately reflect the cash operating costs occasioned by any sales increases brought on by the television system project. Depreciation charges would be computed separately from this 52 percent of sales factor.

The average tax rate experienced last year by UCL was 29.1 percent. James felt that application of a 29 percent rate for the five-year projection

—————————————— EXHIBIT 2 ——————————————

University City Lounge

Condensed Income Statement for Last Year

	Amount	% of Total
Net sales	$358,000	100.0%
Cost of goods sold	187,592	52.4
Gross profit	$170,408	47.6
Other expenses	136,040	38.0
Profit before taxes	$ 34,368	9.6
Taxes	9,997	2.8
Net profit	$ 24,371	6.8

—————————————— EXHIBIT 3 ——————————————

University City Lounge

Sales Analysis by Customer

A. Current seating factor × current capacity = normal number of customers per day

                        1.5 × 145 = 218

B. Annual sales / annual operating days = normal sales per day

       358,000 / 365 = $981 per day

C. Normal sales per day / number of customers per day = average sales per customer

            981 / 218 = $4.50

needed in this analysis was reasonable. Ruggins differed, explaining that the adequate growth in income achieved by UCL in the past should continue as long as the local university expanded. This rising income would raise UCL's average tax rate. The C.P.A. suggested using a 34 percent tax rate for the capital expenditure analysis.

James told Ruggins that he hoped the purchase of the conventional set would bring in one additional customer every day of the year. Ruggins called that estimate overly optimistic and proceeded to demonstrate that assertion to his client. He drew upon the calculations contained in Exhibit 3, which show that a typical customer spends $4.50 on each visit to UCL.

One net new customer every operating day translates into an annual sales gain of $1,643 (Exhibit 4). Ruggins told James that as a roundhouse guess (without actually working through the figures), he felt that the incremental cash flows from that large a sales increase would result in an internal rate of return of about 75 percent.

"No new ordinary set will give you that high a return, Rick."

—————————— EXHIBIT 4 ——————————

University City Lounge

Projected Sales Increase from
One Additional Customer per Day

A. New customers per day × annual operating days = equivalent new
annual
customers
1 × 365 = 365
B. Equivalent new annual customers × average sales = projected
per customer   sales increase
365 × \$4.50 = \$1,643

—————————— EXHIBIT 5 ——————————

University City Lounge

Projected New Customers per Day
Conventional Set Project

*New Customers per Day**	*Probability of Occurrence**
.15	.10
.20	.20
.33	.40
.40	.20
.60	.10

*Assumed to be the same for each year of the investment horizon.

"I'm convinced," James replied.

After a few more intense hours of questions and concentration, the two men arrived at some projections in which they had confidence. In Exhibit 5, information relates to the conventional set option. At the most, James could now foresee a net increase of six-tenths of a new customer per day during each year of the project's useful life, and that possibility was given only a 10 percent chance of occurring.

The estimates dealing with the Video-Projector differ materially from the conventional set projections. A 24-square-foot viewing screen has proven to be an extraordinarily popular attraction in eating establishments located in other university-dominated locales. The device projects the red, green, and blue colors forming the image onto the curved screen from a control panel located 12 feet from it. Advertisements claimed that the picture is so precise the viewer can see the "grain on the bat" or the "laces on the ball." James strongly felt that these distinguishing features of the Video-Projector would attract large crowds to the TV lounge for sporting events and better-than-average movies. More optimism, then, characterized the forecast tied to this option. Ruggins cautioned that any other res-

————————— **EXHIBIT 6** —————————

University City Lounge

Projected New Customers per Day
Video-Projector Project

Years	New Customers per Day	Probability of Occurrence
1–2	1.00	.20
	2.00	.60
	3.80	.20
3–5	.85	.30
	1.70	.40
	3.20	.30

taurant in town could also buy the same device. Exhibit 6 tabulates their final assessment related to this possible purchase.

With this work accomplished, Ruggins returned to his office to begin a detailed analysis of the mutually exclusive investment opportunities. Before leaving, he and James had arrived at a consensus on two other points. First, James could invest in essentially risk-free Treasury securities of comparable maturity to the life of the television project and earn an after-tax return of 5 percent. Second, during the investment horizon, the average sales per customer level of $4.50 would be assumed to remain constant.

QUESTIONS

1. Compute the expected net present value and profitability index for each project.
2. Compute the standard deviation about the expected net present value for each project.
3. Compute and graph the cumulative distribution of the profitability index for each project. Use the following cumulative probabilities:

.10	.60
.20	.70
.30	.80
.40	.90
.50	.95

4. Which system do you recommend that James purchase?

CASE 33

Little New Orleans
Amusement Park

Capital Budgeting: Simulation from
Probability Distributions

Jennifer Lawson owns and operates the Little New Orleans Amusement Park in Hamilton, Ohio, a small town in the suburbs of Cincinnati. The park was opened 12 years ago with the proceeds of Lawson's inheritance from her great-aunt, Lucy Bea Bowling of Shreveport, Louisiana. In Aunt Lucy's memory, the park had a New Orleans French Quarter theme. The park's buildings and grounds were decorated to reflect the ambience and character of Bourbon Street and the bayou, and several alleys were filled with assorted Cajun gift shops, restaurants, snack bars, jazz clubs, and thrill rides. The rides included several roller coasters, Ferris wheels, and scramblers, as well as a parachute drop and a water flume for the more adventurous. Children's rides included a carousel, bumper cars, and boat rides.

Currently, the park encompassed 145 acres, with 58 acres left for development. During the past five years, management had added two thrill rides, a jazz club, and several gift shops and snack bars as attendance at the park had doubled. Park revenues and net income had grown at, respectively, 17.6 and 14.4 percent compounded annually during the past 10 years.

Park revenue was generated from three divisions: (1) park usage, (2) gifts, and (3) concessions. Expenses in the gift and concession divisions were a combination of fixed and variable. Fixed expenses included salaries, costumes, training, utilities, and taxes. Variable expenses in the gift division represented the costs of the purchased products, which averaged 65 percent of revenue. In the concession division, food expenses were variable at 75 percent of revenue. Exhibit 1 gives selected income data for each of the divisions for the last year. Corresponding balance sheet information is provided in Exhibit 2.

Lawson was considering the addition of a scary ride for adults and children over 12 years of age. She had hired Park Consultants, a design team, to select the equipment and create the scenery and sets that would surround the waiting area, entrance, ride route, and exit area. The design team had narrowed the choice to two mutually exclusive designs. One, called "The Voodoo Queen Escape," would be a roller coaster ride where passengers try to escape the evil powers of the Voodoo Queen. The alternative design, "The Bayou Voodoo Princess," would be a boat thrill ride through decorations reflecting the swamps of Louisiana. This ride was con-

--- EXHIBIT 1 ---

Little New Orleans Amusement Park

Selected Income Data for Current Year

	Company	Park	Gift	Concession
Sales	$50,315	$9,792	$21,231	$19,292
Cost of goods sold	28,270	0	13,800	14,469
Gross profit	22,045	9,792	7,431	4,823
Other expenses	7,968	4,896	1,589	1,483
Earnings before taxes	14,077	4,896	5,842	3,340
Taxes	5,350			
Net income	8,727			

--- EXHIBIT 2 ---

Little New Orleans Amusement Park

Selected Balance Sheet Data for Current Year

	Company	Park	Gift	Concession
Assets				
Cash	$23,513	$20,562	$1,524	$1,427
Accounts receivable	2,123	0	2,123	0
Inventory	4,149	0	3,185	965
Net fixed assets	28,502	22,521	2,123	3,858
Total assets	$58,287	$43,083	$8,955	$6,250
Liabilities and Equity				
Current liabilities	$18,119	$2,448	$7,695	$7,976
Long-term debt	20,000			
Owners' equity	20,169			
Total liabilities and equity	$58,288			

sidered to be very innovative and an exciting addition to the park, while the Queen Escape was similar to the average roller coaster. Lawson definitely intended to develop one of the rides, but her decision was complicated by the cost differential between the two—the Voodoo Princess would cost more than three times as much as the Queen Escape.

She called John Hanson, a university finance professor who had taught her basic finance class when she was in the college of business. Although she had not fully grasped all the concepts that Professor Hanson had tried to teach her, she had come away from his course with an appreciation for the need to gather certain information before making a financial decision. Consequently, she frequently contacted Hanson when she needed financial advice and he had always been able to help her frame the decision, information, and analysis.

First, Lawson and Hanson asked Park Consultants to estimate the investment outlays required for each of the rides. The Queen Escape was relatively easy to evaluate: its total cost was estimated to be $1,925,000, including design, building, and installation. The investment for the Voodoo Princess was more difficult to measure; however, the best estimate was $6,576,000. Lawson anticipated that this amount might vary by as much as 10 percent.

The amusement park always depreciated assets using a straight-line method over a five-year horizon. Because of the daily use of this equipment, the salvage value of both rides was assumed to be a dismantle-and-demolition expense of $200,000, with no value of the equipment assumed.

Estimation of the benefits associated with each ride was more difficult. Each ride would seat 50 patrons per trip. On average, a ride would last six minutes, with two minutes to load and two minutes to unload between rides. Thus, each ride would make 60 trips per day in an average 10-hour day. Lawson hoped that the purchase of the Voodoo Escape would bring in 1,000 additional customers every day of the year. Hanson called her estimate overly optimistic, and to demonstrate why, he drew on the calculations in Exhibit 3, which shows that a typical patron spends $25.95 on each visit to the park.

One thousand new customers every operating day translates into annual revenue of $9,471,750 (see Exhibit 4). Hanson told Lawson that the incremental cash flows from that large an attendance increase would result in an internal rate of return well beyond a reasonable level for one ride.

After several hours of research and discussion, the two friends arrived at projections reflecting the probable average number of new patrons per day who would be attracted to the park by the Queen Escape ride. The estimates of the number of new patrons who would be attracted to the park each day by the Voodoo Princess ride differed significantly. As other parks developed new water rides, patrons would become blasé about Little New Orleans' new water ride and the number of new patrons would decline. Exhibits 5 and 6 detail the probabilities of new patrons for each project.

EXHIBIT 3

New Orleans Amusement Park

Revenue Analysis by Customer

A. Revolutions per day × ride utilization per revolution = average number of patrons per day
      60 × 88.53 = 5,312

B. Annual revenue / annual operating days = average revenue per day
      $50,315,250 / 365 = $137,850

C. Average revenue per day / number of patrons per day = average revenue per patron
      $137,850 / 5,312 = $25.95

D. Average cost of park admittance in current year = $5.05 based on $5.95 for adults and $3.95 for children

E. Current year average amount spent in gifts/person = $10.95

F. Current year average amount spent in concession/person = $9.95

EXHIBIT 4

New Orleans Amusement Park

Projected Revenue Increase from
1,000 Additional Patrons per Day

A. New patrons per day × annual operating days = equivalent new annual patrons
      1,000 × 365 = 365,000 patrons

B. Equivalent annual patrons × average revenue per patron = projected revenue increase
      365,000 × $25.95 = $9,471,750

EXHIBIT 5

New Orleans Amusement Park

The Voodoo Queen Escape Ride
Projected New Patrons per Day

Year	New Patrons/Day	Probability of Occurrence
1–5	200	.10
	340	.20
	390	.40
	560	.20
	670	.10

————————————— **EXHIBIT 6** —————————————

New Orleans Amusement Park

The Voodoo Princess Ride
Projected New Patrons per Day

Year	New Patrons/Day	Probability of Occurrence
1–2	750	.20
	1,000	.60
	1,500	.20

Year	New Patrons/Day	Probability of Occurrence
3–5	750	.30
	1,600	.40
	3,000	.30

Hanson asked Lawson to forecast the expenses associated with each of the new rides. She indicated that two crews would be hired to manage the rides and that the total cost of $700,000 per year to manage the rides would be fixed and should remain constant over the forecast period. She estimated that all other costs would be variable (products for the gift shop, food for the restaurants and snack bars). Hanson was able to use the information in Exhibit 3 to estimate the variable cost of goods sold at 56.18 percent of revenue.

Lawson also felt that both rides would require investments in net working capital. In the first year of operation, the Queen Escape would require an estimated $200,000 in net working capital, while the Voodoo Princess would require an estimated $300,000.

Taxes were forecasted to remain at 38 percent over the entire period.

With the forecast parameters completed, Hanson returned to his office to begin the analysis. Before he left, he and Lawson had agreed that the alternative investments she might consider were risk-free Treasury securities. Securities of a similar time horizon to the rides were currently earning 8.02 percent.

QUESTIONS*

1. Compute the expected cash flows, net present values, profitability index, and internal rate of return for each project. Which project do you recommend? Why?

2. Compute the standard deviation about the expected net present value of each project. How does this information affect your recommendation?

*The spreadsheet model is named "NOAMUSE.wk1".

3. Compute the coefficient of variation for each ride. How does this information affect your recommendation?

4. If you are using the spreadsheet model, run the simulation on the disk with 250 observations. Describe how the models work. Interpret the results of the models.

5. Which project do you recommend? Why?

CASE 34

Grubstake Mining Company

*Capital Budgeting: Multiperiod Capital
Asset Pricing Model*

For the last 30 years, the Grubstake Mining Company has been run by the
Grub brothers, Bud and LaVerne. When the company went public 10 years
ago, Bud and LaVerne became majority stockholders and president and
chairman, respectively. The company's stock is closely held among the
Grub brothers and their friends, many of whom, like the Grubs, have large
proportions of their wealth invested in Grubstake.

 The company's principal line of business is coal mining, although in
the last two years it was diversified into lumber and land-based oil exploration and drilling. Grubstake also owns several inactive gold and silver
mines in Colorado and Wyoming. The recent dramatic rise in gold and
silver prices has prompted Edward Giles, a Grubstake vice president for-
merly in charge of all gold and silver mine operations, to attempt to per-
suade the brothers to reopen some of the old mines. The most promising
of these alternatives is the old Dry Gulch Silver Mine in Schick, Wyoming,
which was last operated eight years ago and has the largest known reserves
of silver of all the inactive mines. Giles told Bud Grub that he thought it
would cost about $1.5 million to renovate the Dry Gulch mine, which would
then be capable of producing a $2 million cash flow over the next two years,
giving it a less than two-year payback period. Bud Grub agreed to form a
committee to investigate in more detail the profitability of reopening the

Dry Gulch Mine. The committee comprised the following five members, with their general responsibilities indicated:

Member	Responsibility	Age
Edward Giles	Chairman	59
John O'Toole	Mine renovation	42
Gabriel Hayes	Mine operations	68
Bill Bunker	Distribution	61
J. Philburt Wyngate III	Finance	31

Each committee member has spent the last month assembling information related to his area of responsibility, and the committee is scheduled to meet in three days to exchange and analyze this information and formulate a recommendation to the Grub brothers. A decision on reopening the Dry Gulch Mine will be made on June 1, with a target date of September 1 for resuming mining operations.

Three of the committee members, Giles, Hayes, and Bunker, used to work in the old silver mining operations and it is well known that they would like very much to see the old mines reopen. O'Toole is experienced in coal mining operations but has little experience with silver mining and considers it a very risky business. Wyngate knows nothing whatsoever about any kind of mining, although he has followed the gold and silver futures markets very carefully.

Giles, the committee chairman, has received preliminary reports from each of the committee members. John O'Toole, who was put in charge of estimating the cost of reopening the mine, has assembled the following figures:

Date Action Taken	Action	Estimated Cost
June	Clean-up of main shafts	$110,000
July	Restructuring of shaft supports	180,000
June	Rewiring of mine electrical system	150,000
July	Repair of railroad tracks	130,000
July	Overhaul of mining equipment	270,000
August	Purchase of new mining equipment	350,000
August	Hiring cost of new laborers	120,000
June	Repair of roads into the mine	140,000

O'Toole also forecasts that in August, one month before the mine would begin operation, the company would have to make an initial investment of $150,000 in spare parts. While he points out that these costs are only estimates, he feels they will prove to be quite accurate, provided the renovation process begins on June 1, as scheduled. (All figures here and later should be taken as end-of-the-month figures.) O'Toole estimates that the company would have to incur these costs every two years because of the wear and tear on equipment and the opening of new mine shafts over time.

The rewiring, track repair, and new mining equipment costs would generate monthly depreciation expenses using the straight-line method over a 2-year or 24-month life with a zero salvage value. All other mine renovation expenses would not be depreciated. Finally, none of the initial investment in inventory would be recovered at the end of the planning horizon.

Hayes, having been the supervisor of the Dry Gulch Mine when it last operated, is quite familiar with the mine's operations. If the mine is re-opened, the plan is to operate it at full capacity for five days a week with one eight-hour shift. Given this plan, Hayes estimates that the total operating costs (including labor, materials, and any additional equipment) of running the mine so as to process the maximum amount of ore possible would be $100,000 per month. He cautions that this figure may vary somewhat depending on the density of the rock encountered and other factors, but he feels that total operating costs should be pretty constant at $100,000 a month.

In mining, there is always the danger of an accident that will seriously affect the costs of operation. Hayes has recommended that the company acquire insurance against any additional costs or lost output that might be incurred through a natural mining accident at Dry Gulch Mine. The monthly cost of this insurance is $5,000.

In his report, Hayes cautions that although operating costs to process ore can be forecast with a reasonable degree of certainty, output of pure silver from a given quantity of ore is very difficult to forecast. Because of the uncertainty of the location and richness of the veins of silver, the same level of mining operations in each month can produce vastly different outputs of pure silver from month to month. Using historical data taken from the years in which the mine previously operated, Hayes estimates that the random monthly output of silver will conform to the probability distribution in Exhibit 1.

Bill Bunker will be responsible for getting the silver ingots to the spot market for immediate sale. At first, in personal conversation with Giles, he proposed selling the silver directly to some Texas oilmen who, it was ru-

─────────── **EXHIBIT 1** ───────────

Dry Gulch Mine
Grubstake Mining Company

Monthly Random Silver Output

Pure Silver Output (troy ounces)	Probability
8,000	.2
12,000	.6
16,000	.2

mored, were buying large quantities of silver, but Giles told him that he thought the Grub brothers would prefer to market the silver through more conventional channels. This suggestion led Bunker to draw up plans for shipping the silver by rail to Chicago, where it can be sold to various spot market dealers who will inventory it in various warehouses in the area. He feels quite certain that the shipping and insurance costs of using this market will be 75 cents per troy ounce of silver.

The responsibility for determining the ultimate profitability of any investment in reopening the Dry Gulch Mine has fallen on the shoulders of J. Philburt Wyngate III. Wyngate was hired by the Grubstake Mining Company two years ago as part of an effort to recruit recent M.B.A.s to help modernize the company's corporate finance section. The understanding was that he would supply Grubstake with the latest techniques in financial planning and control. Grubstake's recent decision to expand into the lumber and oil markets depended heavily on his capital budgeting analysis. Since those investments have been very successful, Wyngate is currently held in high regard by the Grub brothers.

Wyngate and his staff are running a little behind in preparing the full report for the committee, but Wyngate has given Chairman Giles a brief written description of his approach to determining the profitability of reopening the mine (see Exhibit 2).

EXHIBIT 2

Grubstake Mining Company

Memo written by J. Philburt Wyngate III

We feel that this committee should base its decision on reopening the Dry Gulch Mine on whether or not that decision increases the wealth of the stockholders of Grubstake Mining. To predict the impact that this decision will have on the market value of our stockholders' common stock, we need to estimate expected future cash flows and the appropriate risk-adjusted discount rates for computing the net present value of those cash flows.

We recommend forecasting monthly cash flows for two years. The two-year horizon was selected because we feel it is difficult to forecast accurately beyond this date and because the Grub brothers would never authorize reopening the mine if it were not expected to "pay off in two years." In addition, since Mr. O'Toole projects that new renovation expenses must be incurred every two years, the mine investment has a natural two-year repetitive cycle. Thus, the profitability of the mine will depend on the profitability of the two-year cycle of operations.

To facilitate the estimation of expected future cash flows, the finance section has formulated the following forecasted probability distribution for silver prices for each month in the first year of operation of the mine, beginning in September (cash flows are assumed to be received at the end of the month):

Spot Price for Silver This Year (dollars per troy ounce)	Probability
5	.3
25	.4
45	.3

We have arrived at the following probability distribution for silver prices for each month in the *following* year:

Spot Price for Silver Next Year (dollars per troy ounce)	Probability
5	.2
15	.6
25	.2

For both years, we feel that these random changes in silver prices will be independent over time and independent of the random output of silver from the Dry Gulch Mine.

We believe that the so-called capital asset pricing model is the most appropriate model to use in this case for determining the risk-adjusted discount rates. The strengths of the capital asset pricing model are: (1) it recognizes that the expected cash flows should be discounted at a rate commensurate with the risk of the cash flow; (2) it requires a minimum amount of information about forecasted probability distributions; and (3) as long as the estimates are accurate, this model will always give the theoretically correct answer for the market value of the project.

The capital asset pricing model we will use to compute the net present value (NPV) of reopening the Dry Gulch Mine is

$$NPV = \sum_{t=0}^{T} \frac{E(X_t)}{\prod_{k=0}^{t} [1 + E(R_{tk})]}$$

T = project's life in months

$E(X_t)$ = expected cash flow for the project in the tth month

$E(R_{tk})$ = required rate of return in month k on a security that is a claim on the cash flow received in month t. This number is the correct risk-adjusted discount rate in month k for the expected cash flow in month t.

Π = product operator (e.g., $\prod_{i=0}^{n} a_i = a_0 \cdot a_1 \cdot a_2 \cdots a_n$)

The risk-adjusted discount rate is computed using the following formula:

$$E(R_{tk}) = R_{Fk} + [E(R_{mk}) - R_{Fk}](\text{beta})_{tk} \tag{1}$$

where

R_{Fk} = the monthly riskless rate of interest in month k

R_{mk} = the monthly random rate of return in month k on a market index, such as the Standard & Poor's 500 Index

$(\text{beta})_{tk} = \dfrac{\text{cov}(R_{tk}, R_{mk})}{\text{var}(R_{mk})}$ = the covariance between the rate of return in the kth month on a security that is a claim on the cash flow received in month t and the rate of return in the kth month on the market index, all divided by the variance of the monthly return on the market index. This number measures the risk of the cash flow.

As a proxy for a security that is a claim on the cash flow from the Dry Gulch Silver Mine, we propose using futures contracts in silver. For example, a September futures contract in silver is a security that if purchased today would entitle its owner to delivery of 5,000 troy ounces of silver at the end of September. We propose using the required rate of return in month k on this security as our proxy for $E(R_{tk})$, the appropriate discount rate in month k for the expected cash flow received in the month of September (the tth month).

Thus, t denotes the time the futures contract matures or delivers and k denotes the index that runs from the current month to month t. To compute the appropriate risk-adjusted discount rate using formula (1), we need to forecast the joint returns on futures contracts and the market index. First, we consider futures contracts that deliver in the first year. We forecast that the joint distribution of monthly returns on these futures contracts and the market index will be the same in each month of this year as given:

Monthly Rate of Return for This Year on All Silver Futures That Deliver This Year	Monthly Rate of Return on the Market Index for This Year	Joint Probability
−.008	.004	.1
.000	.005	.2
.008	.007	.4
.016	.009	.2
.024	.010	.1

These distributions can be used with formula (1) to determine the appropriate monthly discount rates for expected monthly cash flows from the mine that are received this year.

Next, we consider futures contracts that deliver in the next year. We forecast that the joint distribution of monthly returns on these futures contracts and the market index will be the same in each month of *this* year as given:

Monthly Rate of Return for This Year on All Silver Futures That Deliver Next Year	Monthly Rate of Return on the Market Index for This Year	Joint Probability
−.010	.004	.1
.000	.005	.2
.005	.007	.4
.015	.009	.2
.020	.010	.1

These distributions can be used with formula (1) to determine the appropriate monthly discount rates for *this* year to be applied to expected monthly cash flows that are received *next* year.

Finally, still considering futures contracts that deliver in the next year, we want to make forecasts similar to those just given, but for returns in the *next* rather than this year. These forecasts for next year are as given:

Monthly Rate of Return for Next *Year* *on All Silver Futures That* *Deliver* Next *Year*	*Monthly Rate of Return on* *the Market Index for* Next *Year*	*Joint* *Probability*
−.016	−.004	.1
−.010	.000	.2
.004	.004	.4
.020	.008	.2
.050	.012	.1

We are forecasting a monthly rate of return on riskless assets of .4 percent during the first year of operation of the mine and .2 percent during the following year (i.e., .004 and .002 in decimals).

Operation of the mine will generate a tax-deductible expense in the form of a depletion allowance. We have computed the allowance to be $2 per troy ounce of silver produced. To simplify our tax computations, we are assuming that Grubstake pays its taxes monthly at the marginal rate of 50 percent.

In the past, our firm has been fortunate to be able to finance its investments exclusively with internally generated funds. This practice will continue in the future.

The finance section is currently working on the computation of the value to our firm of the decision to reopen the mine.

QUESTIONS

1. Using information gathered by the various committee members and Wyngate's preliminary report (Exhibit 2) describing the methods he intends to use in computing the net present value of reopening the mine, compute the solutions that you think Wyngate will obtain for each of the following:
   a. The monthly after-tax initial costs to renovate the mine for each of the three months June through August.
   b. The expected monthly after-tax cash flows from the Dry Gulch Mine over the 24 months from September of the current year to September of the second year.
   c. The monthly risk-adjusted discount rates that are associated with each of the monthly expected cash flows in (b).
   d. The net present value (from the capital asset pricing model as specified by Wyngate) of the decision to open the mine.
2. How do you rate Wyngate's understanding of the capital asset pricing model—in particular, his understanding of the model's strengths and weaknesses, its assumptions, and its applicability to the decision about reopening the mine?
3. If you were chairing Giles's committee and received the information provided by the other committee members, what decision concerning the future of the Dry Gulch Mine would you recommend to the Grub brothers? How would you support your recommendation?

CASE 35

Reflex Energy Company, Inc.

Capital Budgeting and the CAPM

The Reflex Energy Company was founded in 1985 by Cliff Richardson and Melonie Moss. The company holds patents for the design and manufacture of small-capacity electric generators used by cogenerators in the production of electric power. Richardson and Moss developed the base technology for the Department of Defense while they were faculty members in the department of electrical engineering at the University of Texas at Austin. The primary feature of their patent is that it makes it economically feasible for relatively small firms to become generators of their own electrical power.

Except for several successful experiments, the technology has not yet had a commercial application. However, in the spring of 1987, Reflex Energy was approached by a small chemical processing plant near Dallas (Casey Chemicals, Inc.) with the idea of constructing and operating a cogeneration plant on their plant site. The primary owner of the plant, Al Niece, estimates that one of Reflex's small generators could provide 90 percent of the plant's electrical power needs during the generator's two-year life.

The cogeneration plant would be project-financed,[1] with Reflex

---

[1]See the appendix to this case for a description of project financing of electric power cogeneration facilities.

building, owning, and operating the power plant on-site for the next two years. To help finance the project, Casey has agreed to make a nonrecourse loan to Reflex for $3 million at a below-market rate of 8 percent. This rate compares favorably with the current market rate on a similar loan, which is 10 percent. The loan would be taken down immediately, with interest paid annually and the principal amount due at the end of two years.

Estimated gross revenues from the plant will be $7 million per year for each of the next two years, after which time the project will be terminated. Operating expenses are estimated to equal two-thirds of the estimated revenues, and the entire project is expected to cost Reflex Energy $4 million. Reflex will depreciate the cost of the project over two years using straight-line depreciation. Finally, Reflex has sufficient operating loss carry-forwards that it does not expect to pay taxes on the profits from this particular venture. Consequently, the firm plans to ignore taxes in its analysis.

Reflex Energy's equity was offered to the public for the first time in 1987, and its price has been relatively volatile over its short history. In fact, the company's chief financial officer, Jessica Heggen, recently observed that the firm's beta coefficient (a measure of systematic risk based on the covariation of the company's stock price changes with those of the market for all stocks) was 2.40. This number was among the highest for all reported stocks. Heggen did not really understand why the beta was so high but suspected that it reflected the highly volatile nature of the firm's prior research contract work. However, when she sat down to evaluate the required rate of return for the Casey project, she was very uncomfortable using the company's beta as the basis for her analysis for the following reasons: (1) the proposed project involves the construction and operation of an electrical power plant, whereas the firm's prior business had been exclusively contract research; and (2) three-fourths of the proposed investment would be financed by borrowing, whereas the firm had previously relied on about 40 percent debt financing. Both of these factors led Heggen to reevaluate the project's systematic risk. The first step in this analysis involved collecting the following data on three utility companies that she considered to be roughly comparable in their "riskiness" to the proposed project. These beta coefficients and the debt to equity ratios for the proxy firms are found in Exhibit 1.

In addition, Heggen plans to use a risk-free borrowing rate of 10 percent and a market risk premium of 6 to 8 percent.[2]

---

[2]The market risk premium is the difference between the expected rate of return for the market portfolio and the risk-free rate of interest. The range of estimates used here reflects the results of a major study of historical returns.

──────── **EXHIBIT 1** ────────

Reflex Energy Company

Proxy Firm Betas and Leverage Ratios

Firm	Debt to Equity Ratio	Equity Beta
A	0.9	0.5
B	1.0	1.0
C	1.8	1.5

QUESTIONS

1. Estimate the beta for the investment project (i.e., its asset or project beta).
2. What rate of return do you think Reflex should require for the project based on the capital asset pricing model?
3. Using the capital asset pricing model, what "equity" rate of return should Reflex require?
4. What is the project's net present value using no debt financing? What is the net present value using the proposed financing mix?
5. Should the project be undertaken? Discuss.

CASE 35

Appendix

An Overview of Project Financing[1]

In a project financing, an individual venture stands alone as an independent entity, and its nature is such that it has a clearly defined life span. Cash flows are paid out to the owners as they are earned—rather than reinvested in new projects under the same management—and the legal entity set up to establish the project has a finite life. There need not be any debt involved in such an arrangement (for example, many R&D limited partnerships are all-equity, but are clearly finite-lived, project-oriented entities). When there is debt, however, the creditors have recourse only to the assets and cash flows of the project itself; they do not have further recourse to the owners. The use of debt in a project financing is thus comparable to the issuance of revenue bonds by a municipality, for which payments are restricted to the proceeds from a particular set of user fees or tax revenues,[2] and a project's viability as an independent financial entity likewise depends on the substance behind the projected revenue stream.

---

[1] This appendix relies on a paper written by Andrew Chen, John Kensinger, and John Martin, "Integration without Merger: Project Financing," Working paper, University of Texas, (March 1991).

[2] When the revenues to be derived from a new municipal project offer more stability than the general revenues of a municipality, the cost of capital can be reduced by isolating the project from the general pool. Given the political hurdles to overcome in making a project happen, the ability to point to a low cost of capital can be a selling point (theoretically, the low-risk project will reduce the municipality's overall cost of capital).

Far from being a johnny-come-lately gimmick that has yet to stand the test of time, venture-by-venture financing of finite-lived projects has ancient roots and, in fact, was the rule in commerce until the nineteenth century.[3] Project financing did not die with the industrial revolution, but continued to be used through the years by European financiers for separately accountable ventures such as overseas mineral exploration projects.

It is becoming increasingly common for corporations to establish individual projects as separate, finite-lived entities.[4] Project financing is being used extensively to fund not only real estate development and oil and gas exploration, but also independent electric power generation facilities, factories, and research and development efforts. Yet there has been little analysis of project financing in the academic literature, and what descriptive material is available is sparse and sometimes contradictory. Nonetheless, during the 1980s, a vigorous market in the private placement of limited-recourse project financing has confronted financial managers in several industries with need to decide between making project financing arrangements, and raising the funds for a project on the parent's own account.[5]

The common thread running through project financings is that they reflect a community of interests among a group of independent entities. Thus, project financing offers a finite-lived alternative to merger. Selecting project financing versus internal financing is a more radical choice than most financial decisions, however, because it involves an alternative organizational form that is fundamentally different from the traditional corporation in two significant ways: (1) the legal entity that gives the project substance is finite-lived, with its identity defined by that specific project; and (2) as a result, the cash flows generated by the project (including depreciation/depletion) are paid directly to the investors, who make the reinvestment decisions themselves. Unlike in the traditional integrated corporation, management does not have the "first option" in deciding how to reinvest the project's cash flows.

[3]See Kensinger and Martin, "Project Financing: Raising Money the Old-Fashioned Way," *Journal of Applied Corporate Finance 1* (Fall 1988): 69–81, for a summary of the early history of project financing and the reasons for its period of quiescence.

[4]From January 1, 1981 through February 28, 1990, underwriters have announced over $43.9 billion worth of project financings—an amount of financing equivalent to the formation of a new company in the upper echelon of the Fortune 500. The average of $835 million in announced project financings per month during 1988 and 1989 compares with an average of $30.2 billion per month of new securities (both debt and equity) issued by all U.S. corporations (*sources:* IDD Information Services, Inc., U.S. Securities and Exchange Commission, and the Board of Governors of the Federal Reserve System). Given that many project financings are not advertised by their underwriters, it is evident that project financing deserves to be taken seriously.

[5]Project financing has become widespread among companies in oil and gas production, refining, gas transmission, chemicals, food processing, and textiles.

The Public Utility Regulatory Policy Act (PURPA) of 1978 (which requires utilities to purchase electricity from independent, federally licensed generating facilities) provided the stimulus for a dramatic increase in the number of project financings for electric cogeneration facilities. Specifically designed to encourage the formation of joint ventures and partnerships for cogeneration and renewable fuels facilities, the law was subjected to numerous challenges by special-interest groups until it was finally upheld by the U.S. Supreme Court in 1982. From that point, project financing for electric power generation projects grew rapidly. With this catalyst, specialized project financing groups developed within several investment banking firms, commercial banks, and institutional investors. Then, in August 1988, General Electric Capital Corporation announced the formation of a new industrial project financing group. Since its formation, it has become GE's fastest-growing unit and has arranged project financing to build the nation's largest beverage can production plant as well as several newsprint plants.

Exhibit 2 reveals not only a steady growth in project financing over the past decade, but also an increasing diversity of activities financed in this manner. In addition, it shows how the average size of projects has increased significantly as the project financing sector has matured. The dip in activity during 1986 and 1987 was due, at least in part, to the significant changes in the income tax laws enacted in 1986. The vigorous recovery in 1988 and 1989 suggests that adjustments have been made without long-term harm to the genre.

In the case of independent power production projects, project financing has quickly come to dominate the whole field. This arena therefore offers fruitful opportunities for testing hypotheses about the use of project financing.

This field represents a unique set of "cookie cutter" projects that closely resemble one another. They use established technologies, are highly automated, and require a minimal staff to operate. Moreover, operating costs are generally stabilized via five-year or longer fixed-price operating contracts. Their output of electricity and steam can clearly be categorized as commodities, which uniformly are sold under long-term (20 years or more in common) fixed-price contracts issued by the local utility, which buys the electricity, and the site owner, which buys the steam for use in its production processes.

EXHIBIT 2

Project Financings Announced January 1, 1981 through December 31, 1989

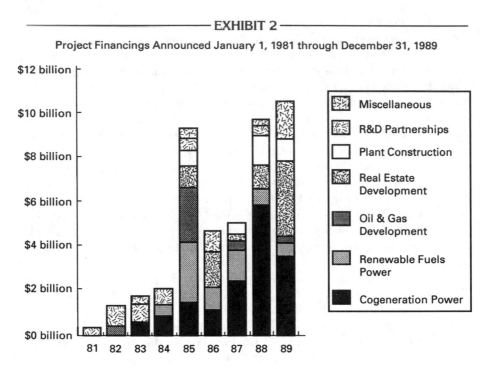

Mean Average Project Size

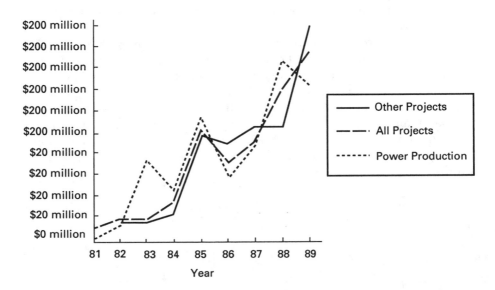

CASE 36

Connally Oil Company

Valuation

In 1970, Ed Connally, a long-time businessman in Dallas, Texas, established a new firm for the purpose of exploring for oil and gas in the West Texas area. During the next 18 years (1970–1988), he drilled for oil and/or gas over 200 times, completing 110 successful wells. Connally generally invested only a small amount in each drilling venture, relying on partners to put up most of the money.

In 1988, a serious illness required Connally to sharply curtail his drilling activities. However, he continued to operate the production division of the firm, with his wife becoming increasingly involved in the company's management. By 1990, Connally had totally removed himself from the business and his wife, Virginia, had assumed the position of company president. In this role, she became the primary decision maker in operating the existing oil and gas leases. Then, in 1992, she decided that the firm was requiring more time than she wanted to devote to its continued operations. However, the Connallys were reluctant to sell a business that they had spent so many years developing. They first attempted to locate a manager with experience in oil and gas exploration who also would be compatible with the Connally family. Their efforts were essentially unsuccessful. After several discouraging interviews with prospective managers, they decided to consider selling the company.

Connally first visited with Marcus Mann, a local public accountant, for suggestions on how to sell the firm. Mann reviewed the corporation's most recent financial statements, which are presented in Exhibits 1 and 2. Since the principal income for the firm comes from oil and gas income, he suggested an appraisal of the oil properties by a petroleum engineer. He offered to arrange an appointment with Jack Selers, who owned a petroleum consulting firm. The meeting was scheduled for the next day.

In the meeting with Selers, Connally presented data regarding the present oil wells that were being operated. Selers, in turn, offered his services to estimate the future production that would come from the well locations as well as the amount of income that could be realized over the life of the wells. After an extended visit, Connally decided to use Selers for the appraisal. Selers indicated that he could have his report ready in one month. They tentatively set their next meeting for five weeks later.

While waiting for the Selers report, Connally thought he should initiate contacts with prospective buyers. He went by to visit an old friend, Robert Mulstand, who served as the vice president and trust officer for the Securities Bank and had helped to sell firms for several different estates managed by the bank. Mulstand recommended that Connally consider mailing out a notice to prospective purchasers advising them that Connally Oil Company would be for sale. A stated date would be established for accepting bids to purchase the firm. Mulstand also explained that the bank had a list of individuals who might be interested in such an investment. However, until the study had been completed by Selers, Mulstand did not envision much that could be done, other than simply preparing a mailing list for bid invitations. Connally asked Mulstand to prepare the list, and as quickly as the Selers report was completed, he would be back with Mulstand to develop the materials for the mailing. Connally postponed any further action regarding the sale of the company until after his meeting with Selers.

Several weeks later, Selers called Connally and indicated that he had finished his evaluation. They agreed to meet the next day, at which time Selers presented an in-depth report on the estimated oil and gas reserves. He also had converted these numbers into projected dollar revenues. Using historical cost data and adjusting for inflation, Selers then projected cash expenses in operating the wells, as well as depreciation and depletion.[1] A summary of Selers's report appears in Exhibits 3 and 4. Exhibit 3 is the cover letter accompanying the report and highlighting the overall conclusions as well as the assumptions made in preparing the report. Exhibit 4 sets forth revenues and expenses estimated for each year.

With this information in hand, Connally returned to Mulstand to fi-

---

[1]Depletion is similar to depreciation in that it represents an operating expense that does not require a cash outflow. Just as depreciation is an allocation of the cost of equipment over its life, depletion is an effort to allocate the cost of an oil lease over the life of the lease.

--- **EXHIBIT 1** ---

Connally Oil Company, Inc.

Balance Sheet

Assets

Current assets	Amount
Cash and marketable securities	$400,600
Accounts receivable	78,900
Total current assets	$479,500
Investments	
Land cost, prune farm	6,800
California, prune farm	29,800
Allowance for depreciation, prune farm	(14,000)
Oil and gas leases	141,200
Reserve for depletion leases	(140,700)
Medical building	270,541
Allowance for depreciation	(82,446)
Land, medical building	18,427
Total investments	$229,622
Fixed assets	
Oil field equipment	44,100
Allowance for depreciation	(19,000)
Oil well equipment	611,307
Allowance for depreciation, lease equipment	(473,956)
Office furniture and equipment	24,425
Allowance for depreciation, furniture and equipment	(22,337)
Auto equipment	10,471
Allowance for depreciation, auto equipment	(3,757)
Total fixed assets	$171,253
Other assets	
Inventory, equipment	90,700
Total assets	$971,075

Liabilities and Equity

Current liabilities	$155,700
Equity	
Par value	73,800
Paid-in capital	10,500
Retained earnings	731,075
Total equity	$815,375
Total liabilities and equity	$971,075

--- **EXHIBIT 2** ---

Connally Oil Company, Inc.

Income Statement for the Six Months Ended September 30, 1992

Oil & Gas Division	Year to Date
Gross oil income	$179,922
Expenses, oil division	
Production expenses	63,200
Depletion expenses	21,300
Depreciation, lease equipment	20,100
Operating expenses	28,000
Total oil expenses	132,600
Net income, oil division	47,322

Farm Division	
Gross farm income	4,700
Farm expenses	
Operating expenses	1,700
Depreciation	400
Total farm expenses	2,100
Net income, farm division	2,600

Medical Building Division	
Gross medical building income	28,250
Medical building expenses	
Cash operating expenses	9,000
Depreciation expense	8,700
Total medical building expenses	17,700
Net income, medical building	10,550
Net income, all divisions	$60,472

nalize an announcement regarding the planned sale of Connally Oil Company. After several meetings, Connally and Mulstand completed the announcement of the pending sale. This document is provided in Exhibit 5.

The announcement was mailed on October 1, instructing bids to be made within 45 days. A number of bids were received, with four being of particular interest to Connally. Excerpts from these bids are as follows:

1. Bidder: Roy M. Tong Company
   Terms: (a) Tong is willing to purchase all the stock of Connally Oil Company, Inc., if all debts and obligations have been paid or otherwise provided for by other parties.
   (b) Purchase price for the stock and the terms of the agreement shall be as follows:
   (1) $1,050,000 cash at closing.
   (2) $160,000 cash out of 75 percent of the after-tax income of

---
EXHIBIT 3

Connally Oil Company, Inc.

Jack D. Selers
Petroleum Consultant:
Midland, Texas 79701

August 30, 1992

Mr. Ed Connally
P.O. Box 3218
Dallas, Texas 73218

Dear Mr. Connally:

At your request, I have made an engineering study and evaluation to determine the future net oil and gas reserves and future net income attributable to Connally Oil Company's interest in various oil and gas properties located in West Texas. The effective date of this report is July 1, 1992.

The estimated future net oil and its reserves are 297,600 barrels of oil and 768,000 thousand cubic feet of gas. The future net income generated by the production of these reserves will be $3,100,000. Future net income is income attributable to Connally's net revenue interest after deduction of direct operating expenses and production and ad valorem taxes. No provision was made for deduction of federal income taxes.

There are 56 leases contained in the evaluation. All but 3 of the leases are located in the Spraberry Trend Area. Connally Oil Company operated 48 of the leases, containing 58 wells. The other 8 leases are operated by another company, but Connally Company owns an interest in the investments.

Future oil and gas reserves, operating expenses, and future net income for each individual lease are shown. Leases are listed by operator and in the field in which they are located. The future cash flow for all leases is also shown.

Initial oil prices used were those currently in effect and were escalated 8 percent per year to a maximum of $25.75 per barrel. Current operating expenses were escalated 8 percent per year as long as oil prices increased. Gas prices were held constant.

Copies of records, work papers, and well data are retained in my files and will be made available for discussion with you or other authorized parties at your convenience.

Very truly yours,

Jack D. Selers
Petroleum Consultant

JDS:bm

─────── EXHIBIT 4 ───────

Connally Oil Company, Inc.

Oil and Gas Properties
July 1, 1992
Prepared by Jack Selers

Year	Revenue	Operating Costs	Depletion	Depreciation	Net Income
1993	$238,187	$ 66,685	$35,727	$36,000	$ 99,775
1994	462,658	138,353	64,772	36,000	223,522
1995	461,549	149,035	60,001	36,000	216,513
1996	451,344	160,248	54,161	—	236,935
1997	442,179	172,367	48,639	—	221,173
1998	424,036	177,102	42,403	—	204,531
1999	392,893	167,071	35,360	—	190,462
2000	380,397	169,525	30,431	—	180,441
2001	341,085	157,969	23,876	—	159,240
2002	304,482	151,961	18,268	—	134,253
2003	274,772	145,934	13,738	—	115,100
2004	252,229	144,488	10,089	—	97,652
2005	224,979	136,788	6,749	—	81,442
2006	195,554	125,081	3,844	—	66,629
2007	158,006	103,230	1,580	—	53,196
Remaining	595,515	423,523	—	—	171,992

Connally Oil Company, Inc., after Tong is repaid from the after-tax income of Connally Oil Company, Inc., $1,050,000 down payment plus interest ("New York Bank Big Loan Prime Rate") on said down payment, plus $2,500-a-month overhead for supervision charges to the Tong Tulsa offices accrual from the date of closing.

(3) All cash of Connally Oil Company, Inc., will be disbursed as dividends before closing of the purchase.

2. Bidder: Petroleum Exploration Company
   Terms: (a) Petroleum Exploration Company (PEC) hereby submits a cash offer of $1,225,121 for all the interests in the wells and all related interests in the leases and all associated lease and well equipment, including material or equipment related to the operation.

   (b) The offer is subject to the negotiation and execution of a purchase agreement covering the following major points:

   (1) PEC can legally market the production under terms and conditions no less favorable than those under which you were marketing on September 1, 1992.

   (2) PEC shall be entitled to review the applicable gas contracts, with the terms being acceptable to PEC.

   (3) PEC shall have the right and opportunity, subject to operator's approval, to inspect the property and to witness or con-

———————————— EXHIBIT 5 ————————————

Connally Oil Company, Inc.

Announcement for Bid Invitations
of Connally Oil Company
Securities Bank, Dallas, Texas

The owners of substantially all the outstanding shares of common stock of Connally Oil Company, Dallas, Texas, have elected to sell their stock. The Trust Department of Securities Bank, Dallas, Texas, has been authorized to invite you and other selected parties to evaluate the offering and enter into negotiations for the purchase of the Connally Oil Company stock.

The principal assets of the company consist of oil and gas properties. Future oil and gas reserves as of July 1, 1992 were estimated to be approximately 297,600 barrels of oil and 768,000 Mcf gas. An estimate as to future net income generated by the production of these reserves is approximately $3,100,000. This figure is exclusive of the company's share of salvable equipment. The estimate of future net income is derived from incomes attributable to Connally Oil Company's net revenue interest after deduction of direct operating expenses and production and ad valorem taxes. No provision is made for federal income taxes.

There are 56 leases contained in the evaluation. All but 3 of the leases are located in the Spraberry Trend area. Connally Oil Company operates 48 of the leases, containing 58 wells. The other 8 leases are nonoperated. The company owns an average of approximately 16 percent working interest in all these leases.

In addition to oil and gas properties, Connally Oil Company owns three real estate properties:

1. Medical office building
2. Prune, walnut, and olive farm, 11.1 acres
3. Equipment yard and warehouse shed, Stanton, Texas

Connally Oil Company estimates the value of these real estate holdings to be approximately $300,000.

Enclosed is an engineering study and evaluation on the oil and gas properties. This report, effective date July 1, 1992, has been prepared by Jack D. Selers, registered petroleum engineer, Midland, Texas. In addition, we are furnishing financial statements prepared by Condler and Company, certified public accountants, Dallas, Texas. These statements are as of September 30, 1992 fiscal year-end for Connally Oil Company.

If you wish to record your interest in making an offer for all the outstanding shares of Connally Oil Company, please communicate with the undersigned, Vice President and Trust Officer, Securities Bank, Dallas, Texas. It would be appreciated if you would include banking references in your communication. The bid should be received within 45 days of the receipt of the letter.

Yours very truly,

Robert E. Mulstand
Vice President and Trust Officer
Securities Bank

duct any well tests it may deem necessary, and the test results must be acceptable to PEC.

3.   Bidder: Petro Company of Texas

Terms: (a) Based on the information you have furnished us, including data submitted with your letter of October 1, 1992, Petro Company of Texas offers $1,607,555 cash for all the outstanding shares of stock of Connally Oil Company, Inc.

(b) This offer is based on financial statements furnished by Connally Oil Company, Inc., for periods through September 30, 1992. However, it is understood that the medical office building at 702–704 Hickory Street in Dallas, Texas, and the prune, walnut, and olive farm at Corning, California, shall remain with the original stockholders. Further, subsequent to the data of said statements, there shall be no payment or liability incurred for bonuses to employees and representatives, dividends to stockholders, salary increases or employment contracts, or distributions of company funds or properties except for payment of existing company obligations and payments required to be made in the course of routine operations. Such properties will be operated to the time of closing in a normal and routine manner with no unusual expenditures or amount of production.

(c) Our attorneys shall have the right to review the Connally Oil Company files prior to closing to satisfy themselves that the company has good title to substantially all the interests described in the informational data that you have furnished us. In this connection, it is anticipated that the closing will take place in your office no later than December 31, 1992. All files and records of Connally Oil Company will be delivered to us promptly after closing.

(d) Although you have made no requirement that the employees of Connally Oil Company be retained and no commitment to that effect is hereby intended, we anticipate a need for substantially all the field personnel and some of the members of the office staff.

4.   Bidder: Colorado Minerals Company

Terms: (a) Colorado Minerals Company will issue 275,000 shares of its authorized common stock to the owners of all the issued and outstanding shares of Connally Oil Company, Inc., subject to the terms and conditions of a definitive agreement acceptable to and executed by the selling stockholders of Connally Oil Company, Inc., and Colorado Minerals Company as purchaser. Additionally, Colorado will, if desired by the selling stockholders of Connally Oil Company, agree to repurchase all of the shares issued as aforesaid at $6 per share within 60 days after Notice Date (to be defined) provided, however, that Colorado shall retain the exclusive option and right to repurchase 175,000 of such shares at $9 per share within 60 days after Notice Date (to be defined). The rights relating to this covenant will be subject to an antidilution provision relating to stock splits and/or stock dividends.

(b) Alternatively, Colorado will pay the sum of U.S. $1,401,000 for all the issued and outstanding stock of Connally Oil Company, Inc.

QUESTIONS

1. Calculate what you believe is a "fair" value for Connally Oil Company's stock. (There is no single right answer). Assume that your required rate of return is 12 percent and that your marginal tax rate is 40 percent. Also assume that cash flows received from oil and gas leases after 2007 are received in 2012.

2. Which offer do you believe is best for Connally? Consider Connally's situation (retirement age, health, etc.) in making a choice. Would you accept this offer? Why?

CASE 37

The Bonneau Company[1]

Acquisition and Valuation

When Ed Bonneau reflects back on the early days of starting his own business, he remembers clearly the event that prompted his "going on his own." The day had started routinely enough, but ended in what at the time felt like a disaster. Bonneau went to work on that fateful day in 1965 preparing in his mind what calls he would make; he went home wondering how he would tell his wife, Barbara, that he had lost his job.

As a sales representative for a sunglass company, Bonneau had done relatively well during the two preceding years. Previously, he had worked for several years in sales for a cosmetics company; before that, he had gone into the restaurant business—unsuccessfully, he is always quick to say. Then, in 1963, he went to work for a sunglass firm as a sales representative. He enjoyed the work and made an acceptable income for the time, but the business was highly seasonal and he was essentially idle five months of the year.

Although Bonneau enjoyed the free time his first year on the job, he knew that he would not be satisfied with the arrangement long-term, especially since he had a growing family and needed a higher income. During

---

[1]The Bonneau Company, founded by Ed and Barbara Bonneau, is located in the Dallas–Fort Worth area. While many of the facts of the case are true, the numbers have been altered for the purposes of confidentiality.

that first year, he thought of starting his own company to market other products during the slow months. He approached his boss about being allowed to work with other products during the slow times, and even asked if they could work together, but received a less than encouraging response. In Bonneau's words, "He did not see me as a manager."

Shortly after Bonneau arrived at work on that memorable day in 1965, he again raised the issue, since he saw no sense in giving full time to a job that he believed only required part time. Abruptly, he was told to empty his sample case, since his services would no longer be needed by the firm. On the way home, Bonneau stopped at a restaurant at the regional Addison airport (in the northwest Dallas area) to have some coffee and to take a few minutes to gather his thoughts on what he should do and how he should tell his wife what had happened. He remembers thinking, "I just gave up the best job I have ever had."

Within a few days, the Bonneaus had decided to develop their own sunglass business. Bonneau thought he could sell at least 50 percent of what he had been selling with his former employer, but would now receive the entire profits for himself. So the decision was made to make the Bonneau Company a full-time affair.

THE EARLY HISTORY

With only $1,000 to invest personally, the Bonneaus' first problem was to find the seed capital to finance their venture. Bonneau decided to call on Floyd Teutsch, a personal friend and banker from his hometown. Teutsch loaned them $10,000, and later agreed to co-sign on a $25,000 note. With this money in hand, the Bonneaus drove to New York from Dallas (with the children in the backseat) to purchase some inventory. Searching through the Yellow Pages and walking along Fifth Avenue, they identified retailers who sold sunglasses and called on several to see if they were interested in selling their inventory. On the third day, they found a retailer who wanted to liquidate his entire inventory. They agreed to send him a cashier check for $16,000, after which he would ship the inventory to Texas. They returned home and leased an 11-by-80 square-foot storefront close to their home.

In the first full year, Bonneau had hoped to do $100,000 in business; the actual sales were $156,000. Over the following six years, sales grew at an annual compound rate exceeding 70 percent, and in 1972, sales were $4 million. The firm then began distributing its product through chain drugstores, and by the end of the 1970s, sales had grown to $12 million.

During those years, the major players in the sunglass industry were Foster Grant and a joint venture between Polaroid and American Optical. Polaroid entered the sunglass industry in the early 1970s and at its peak in the field achieved $50 million in annual sales, making it the largest company in the history of the industry. Bonneau was understandably concerned that a "major" was becoming a key competitor. As it turned out, however, American Optical and Polaroid eventually divorced and Bonneau was able to buy the remaining inventory.

EXTERNAL GROWTH

In addition to pursuing internal growth, the Bonneau Company seized several opportunities to acquire other companies, either as ongoing firms or simply for their assets, typically in the form of inventories and/or receivables. Renauld was an acquisition of the first type, and the purchase of Polaroid's inventories was an acquisition of the second type. The most significant acquisition, however, was Pennsylvania Optical.

One of the problems that continued to nag the Bonneau Company was the seasonality of the sunglass industry. In the early and mid-1980s, Bonneau became increasingly aware that nonprescription reading glasses were coming into the marketplace. He recalls, "We were interested in finding product lines that were not overly seasonal, as were sunglasses. So we began looking at reading glasses as an opportunity. We had tried to carry some reading glasses as one of our product lines, but had never been successful. We then heard that Pennsylvania Optical, a firm that specialized in reading glasses, could be purchased."

Pennsylvania Optical was a 98-year-old firm in Reading, Pennsylvania, that in recent years had been a subsidiary of a larger firm. In a matter of five years, it had been acquired three times. In none of these sales had Pennsylvania Optical been the primary part of the transaction; it just happened to be a subsidiary of the firm being acquired and thus changed hands more by default than by intent. As a result, the company went through a five-year period of near-dormancy. Bonneau thought that it was amazing the firm managed to stay alive. Its sales force had been reduced significantly and management had ceased being aggressive in its strategies. Once again, its parent company was seeking to divest Pennsylvania Optical.

When Brad McDonald, the sales vice president for the Bonneau Company, heard that Pennsylvania Optical was for sale but there were no takers, he arranged to meet with Penn Op's management and reported the results of the meeting to Bonneau. Although Bonneau was not initially excited about the possible purchase, he sensed McDonald's enthusiasm and agreed to a meeting. He, McDonald, and Ken Dortch, Bonneau's vice president for finance, went to Reading to meet with the Penn Op management. While there, they visited with the mergers and acquisitions group at Mellen Bank, since on his earlier visit, McDonald had tentatively arranged to have the banking group represent the Bonneau Company if the deal went forward. Mellen's retainer was strictly on the come, as were most fee arrangements of merger and acquisition departments at that time. After the visit, the Bonneau group came to see more clearly the synergy that could be achieved between reading glasses and sunglasses, especially since they often retailed in the same stores. Another favorable consideration was that Penn Op's customers included several mass merchandisers the Bonneau Company wanted for customers, including Wal-Mart, K Mart, and Woolworth.

After looking at the numbers, Bonneau and his people began trying to negotiate the purchase, but, unable to reach an agreement, soon terminated the negotiations. Then, about one week later, the prospects of the sale were resurrected during a telephone conservation between Bonneau and the Pennsylvania Optical chairman of the board. The final arrangements were made and the purchase was consummated.

The asking price for Penn Op was $6 million. Remembering the negotiation process, Bonneau commented, "I still don't know what they really expected to receive for the business. We had a consultant value the company. We also tried to think about what the firm was worth to us. We offered a cash price of $5 million, plus the assumption of the firm's pension liability of about $1 million. They accepted our offer."

At the time of the acquisition, Pennsylvania Optical had $6 million in annual sales. Bonneau merged the sales forces, making the combined staff responsible for marketing all the product lines, both sunglasses and reading glasses. This immediately enhanced the distribution and selling of Pennsylvania Optical products. Within three years, sales for Penn Op had doubled and the business was once again profitable and thriving.

THE BONNEAU FINANCIAL POSITION

The Bonneau Company had by 1990 experienced 25 years of successful operations in the sunglass industry and had become a significant player in the mid-price range of that industry. With few exceptions, the firm's sales growth had been uninterrupted over the years, with sales reaching $46 million in 1990.

Asked about the firm's sustainable competitive advantage, Bonneau explained that they did not, in his opinion, have any cost advantage. Rather, "it is an advantage of staying power and being here for 25 years. . . . We have a broad marketing appeal, and we can service a wide range of customers who have a lot of different needs, whether it be men's glasses, women's glasses, sporting glasses, fashion glasses, or polarized lenses."

The Bonneau Company's 1989 and 1990 financial statements are presented in Exhibit 1. These statements combine all the firm's operations, both for the Bonneau Company and for Pennsylvania Optical.

─────────────── **EXHIBIT 1** ───────────────

The Bonneau Company
Financial Statements
(thousands)

Balance Sheet

Assets

	1990	1989
Cash	$290	$575
Accounts receivable	9,335	9,115
Inventory	7,820	8,005
Prepaid expenses	650	585
Total current assets	$18,095	$18,280
Long-term receivables	$3,000	$425
Plant and equipment	$4,265	$3,935
Less: accumulated depreciation	2,655	2,225
Net plant and equipment	$1,610	$1,710
Other assets	350	795
Total assets	$23,055	$21,210

Liabilities and Equity

	1990	1989
Short-term bank notes	$5,445	$5,120
Accounts payable	1,820	1,450
Accrued liabilities	2,045	1,685
Other current liabilities	635	740
Total current liabilities	$9,945	$8,995
Pension liability	1,075	1,075
Long-term debt	1,000	1,425
Total long-term liabilities	$2,075	$2,500
Total liabilities	$12,020	$11,495
Common stock		
Par value	$15	$15
Paid-in capital	70	70
Retained earnings	10,950	9,630
Total equity	$11,035	$9,715
Total debt and equity	$23,055	$21,210

Income Statement

	1990	1989
Sales	$46,545	$44,950
Cost of goods sold	22,545	23,100
Gross profit	$24,000	$21,850
Operating expenses	20,275	18,740
Operating income	$3,725	$3,110
Interest income	185	185
Earnings before interest and taxes	$3,910	$3,295
Interest expense	1,280	1,215
Earnings before taxes	$2,630	$2,080
Estimated tax provisions	1,155	705
Net income	$1,475	$1,375
Dividends	155	505
Change in retained earnings	$1,320	$870

A NEW OPPORTUNITY: THE FOSTER GRANT CORPORATION

The most recent event of significance for the Bonneau Company is the contemplated acquisition of the Foster Grant Corporation, historically one of the long-term players in the industry. Foster Grant had long been known for its quality products and was respected as a major company in the industry. In addition to sunglasses, the firm had been actively involved in the development of plastic materials. Over time, however, the sunglass business had become a larger part of the sales mix, and by 1971, Foster Grant had captured 35 percent of the sunglass market, selling the higher-priced Renauld line in department stores and the lower-priced Foster Grant line in general merchandise and discount stores. Like Pennsylvania Optical, however, it had been acquired several times during the past few years, first by United Brands Corporation, and soon thereafter by Hoechst A.G., a major German chemical manufacturer. Hoechst had hoped to use Foster Grant to establish an important position in the U.S. petrochemical market. Soon after its acquisition by Hoechst, Foster Grant began losing its dominant position in the sunglass industry. Most recently, the firm was sold to Andlinger & Company, a private investment banking group.

The financial structuring of the Foster Grant acquisition by Andlinger involved heavy use of high-yield debt, which later proved untenable, given the firm's level of cash flows.[2] The company had since been placed in receivership and the bankruptcy courts were searching for an acquirer. While not particularly interested in buying Foster Grant, Bonneau decided

---

[2] The acquiring group had hoped that sales would increase to a point that would allow the firm to service the debt. However, the sales growth never materialized.

they should at least take a look at the situation. Shortly thereafter, they decided to make an offer. The key questions now facing management are the offering price and how to finance the acquisition.

Bank Financing of the Acquisition

The Bonneau Company's primary source of financing its previous acquisitions had been a local bank, so Bonneau and Dortch decided to approach the same bank about the Foster Grant deal. The company has had a long-standing relationship with the bank, which had recently been acquired by a large bank holding company. Based on early visits with bank officers, both Dortch and Bonneau believed the bank was interested in financing the purchase. Still, both men were acutely aware of all the recent "dead bodies" of those who used heavy debt financing in acquiring other companies. Dortch notes:

> When we acquired Pennsylvania Optical in 1986, which was not much different from what we are considering with the Foster Grant acquisition, we told the bank what we were doing; it was virtually all verbal. They simply said, "If you think it's good, then it's okay with us." I don't think they saw anything to speak of until just a few days before it was time to transfer the money. But now, they of necessity look very carefully at the transaction and how much debt it brings onto our balance sheet. There are so many more bank examiners and more surveillance regarding leverage transactions or LBOs and things like that.

The Analysis of the Foster Grant Acquisition

Bonneau's management began taking a serious look at Foster Grant in September 1990, and the timing represented a major problem in making the deal. Most decisions by major chain stores regarding the next year's purchases of sunglasses are made in October and November. Thus, time was of the essence. If the deal could not be closed within the next 60 days or so, there was a strong likelihood of losing an entire year of sales and the risk that those lost sales could not be recouped in the following year since vendors could well be slow to return. This fact was weighing heavily on the Bonneau management.

As they studied the proposed acquisition, the Bonneau management was given a package of information that the Foster Grant people believed summarized the current situation and the firm's outlook. Among these documents were (1) the most recent balance sheet (Exhibit 2); (2) a historical statement of operating income, which excludes interest expense and other financing costs (Exhibit 3); and (3) a statement of Foster Grant's strengths as perceived by the company's management (Exhibit 4).

The package of information clearly shows Foster Grant's desperate situation, despite management's note of optimism in identifying the com-

EXHIBIT 2

Foster Grant Corporation

Consolidated Balance Sheet
June 30, 1990
(thousands)

Assets

Cash and investments	$1,051
Accounts receivable	9,625
Inventory	10,036
Prepaid expense	417
Total current assets	$21,129
Property, plant, and equipment	7,320
Other assets	324
Total assets	$28,773

Liabilities and Equity

Short-term debt	10,325
Current portion of long-term debt	801
Accounts payable	2,985
Accrued liabilities	11,926
Accrued taxes	192
Revolver	21,245
Current liabilities	$47,474
Subordinated debt	$17,941
Other liabilities	5,181
Total noncurrent liabilities	$23,122
Total liabilities	$70,596
Common stock	$69
Paid-in surplus	1,714
Treasury stock	(332)
Retained earnings from prior years	(39,048)
Net earnings in current year	(4,226)
Total stockholders' equity	($41,823)
Total liabilities and equity	$28,773

pany's strengths and opportunities. As Ed Bonneau examined the information, several points stood out:

1. Foster Grant essentially has three major operations: the distribution of sunglasses, the manufacturing of sunglasses, and the technical products division. Bonneau has never been involved in the manufacturing and technical sides of the business, and he questions the advisability of making a move into areas where he has very limited experience. Thus, it would be his intent to discon-

––––––––––––––––––––––––––––––––– EXHIBIT 3 –––––––––––––––––––––––––––––––––

Foster Grant

Income Statement History
(millions)

	1984	1985	1986	1987	1988	1989	1990 Plan
Gross sales	$66.6	$60.6	$59.6	$60.1	$54.2	$52.9	$45.2
Returns	6.9	5.4	5.3	7.6	9.3	9.8	5.5
Allowances	0.7	0.8	0.7	0.4	0.8	0.4	0.3
Net sales	59.0	54.4	53.6	52.1	44.1	42.7	39.4
Total cost of goods sold	25.9	25.3	23.5	27.7	26.1	32.3	25.6
Gross profit	33.1	29.1	30.1	24.4	18.0	10.4	13.8
Direct marketing	8.0	7.6	8.0	7.2	5.6	7.8	3.6
Field sales	7.5	7.5	8.1	7.8	5.2	5.6	5.0
Distribution	5.1	4.4	5.2	5.1	4.0	3.7	2.8
Marketing & administration	1.9	2.1	0.8	0.8	1.4	1.1	0.8
Corporate administrative	5.1	5.1	4.2	3.8	3.5	3.4	2.4
Other expenses	1.4	3.3	0.6	1.2	0.8	8.4	0.3
Total expenses	29.0	30.0	26.9	25.9	20.5	30.0	14.9
Earnings before interest and taxes	4.1	(0.9)	3.2	(1.5)	(2.5)	(19.6)	(1.1)

tinue the manufacturing and technical products divisions if they do not prove profitable.

2. After reviewing the detailed schedule of the Foster Grant receivables and the information provided by his own people about the inventories, Bonneau considers the receivables to be worth about $3 million and the inventory subsequent to an acquisition to be worth about the same amount. By the time any acquisition could be consummated, the cash balance for Foster Grant is expected to be depleted.

3. The property, plant, and equipment accounts include equipment with a book value of about $1 million, but which Bonneau believes could be liquidated for only $500,000.

4. Without doubt, the Foster Grant name is of value, and Bonneau fully intends to continue Foster Grant as a separate entity if he decides to acquire the company; to do otherwise would be to lose one of the primary advantages of the acquisition. However, he is confident of only retaining about half of the most recent year's sales in sunglass distribution. Thus, he does not believe there will be more than $20 million in sales in the first year after the acquisition—that is, 1991. Still, he thinks that with a concerted effort, some of the loss

----------------------------------- **EXHIBIT 4** -----------------------------------

Foster Grant Company Strengths and Opportunities

(Prepared by Foster Grant management as part of its business plan)

Strengths

1. *Brand Name.* Not only does Foster Grant have high awareness (96 percent), but the brand still has a great deal of salience.
2. *Technology.* The Technical Products Division in Leominster stands alone in the world in lens-making, mold-making, and overall know-how in sunglass manufacturing. This provides not only the foundation for gaining the position of innovator in the industry but also the basis for a large technical products business as well.
3. *Manufacturing.* As the potential low-cost producer of sunglasses and reading glasses, Foster Grant is in a unique position in the industry. Its captive production facility ensures better quality control, quicker turnaround time to meet market demand, and better margins to enable the funding of aggressive consumer marketing programs.
4. *Patents/Licenses/Know-How.* Foster Grant's assets here are considerable. The most important are: (a) Space Tech—the NASA coating that is five times more scratch-resistant than any other plastic; (b) Polarized Sheets—the only patent in the industry outside of Polaroid's; (c) Contact Mates—a technology partnership for sunglasses suitable for contact lens wearers.
5. *Sales and Service.* Recent months have seen some real progress with key trade accounts—Wal-Mart, Payless, Eckard, and Drug Emporium ("Vendor of the Year"). Given proper resources, the programs implemented in 1989 and 1990 can be expanded to provide a base for profitable growth in the future.
6. *People.* Foster Grant continues to have some excellent people. The talent, experience, and commitment of these people needs only to be motivated by new investment and stability.

Opportunities

There are four major business oportunities that can be pursued immediately:

1. *Sunglasses.* The sunglass turnaround plan will include continued participation in the contract and premium segments, with increased sales velocity and improved margins; and in the standard catalog business.
2. *Reading Glasses.* Market dominance will be the Foster Grant objective.
3. *Technical Products.* Stunning underexploited lens technology will be built into a sizable, profitable business.
4. *International.* This important segment will provide an opportunity for significant growth and eliminate seasonality.

---

could be recovered in 1992 and that sales would increase by 20 percent in that year. Any sales increases beyond 1992 would probably be around 5 percent through 1995, and 3 percent at best thereafter.

5. Bonneau is not willing to assume any of Foster Grant's indebtedness. The acquisition would relate to the assets only, with no assumption of any debt being part of the transaction.

Although the Bonneau personnel believe they know how to value accounts receivable and inventories in the sunglass business, they are less sure of what the technical products division and the manufacturing facilities are worth. However, after visiting the various Foster Grant sites, Dortch estimates that the plant and equipment related to manufacturing could be sold for about $1.5 million. Valuing the technical products division is more problematic. Although there is no ready answer as to its value, Dortch and Bonneau believe that $1 million is a conservative estimate of its potential sales price. Moreover, any of the building leases related to these operations could be terminated or renegotiated, since Bonneau would not be liable for any contracts or agreements made by the old Foster Grant Corporation.

A key question that the Bonneau management has considered at great length is the obvious lack of profitability of the Foster Grant operations. Everyone recognizes the danger that the Bonneau management will not be able to operate the newly acquired firm at an acceptable profit. An even worse prospect—albeit an unlikely one, they believe—is that they will not be able to eliminate the losses, and that these could threaten the Bonneau Company itself.

After some agonizing, the Bonneau management has come to the conclusion that they can turn around the situation at Foster Grant with respect to the distribution of sunglasses. They have decided, however, to sell the technical products division. They have also determined to sell the manufacturing plant and equipment and focus on what they know best—selling sunglasses.

With respect to Foster Grant's sunglass sales business, the Bonneau management has carefully analyzed the potential cost reductions that could be realized, especially in terms of duplicate functions that could be eliminated and by renegotiating terms relative to the leasing of existing facilities. Also, there would always be the possibility that some of the warehousing facilities could be eliminated and use could be made of the excess capacity in the existing Bonneau facilities.

Everything considered, Dortch believes that the operating profit margin on sales could approach 6 percent in 1991, increasing to 8 percent in 1992, and 10 percent thereafter. Also, based on experience, Dortch has made the following assumptions regarding the investment requirements related to the Foster Grant acquisition:

1. None of the cash held by Foster Grant will be received by Bonneau. Thus, some cash will need to be made available for transactions balances. Experience suggests that needed cash should be around one percent of sales.

2. Investments in accounts receivables and inventories will approximate 30 percent and 20 percent of sales, respectively, for the indefinite future. However, some of this investment in working capital would be offset by spontaneous sources of financing, such as credit allowed for purchasing inventories, and should amount to about 15 percent of sales each year.

3. Beyond equipment replacements, there should be no additional investment in plant and equipment in 1991. There is ample excess space and capacity

within the Bonneau Company to meet any needs for the first year. After 1991, plant and equipment would probably amount to 5 percent of any increases in sales.

4. Investments in other assets should be about 1 percent of sales.

Decision Time

Ed Bonneau has called a meeting of his vice presidents and other key managers to be held in three days. They plan to convene at the local airport hotel for the convenience of those coming from out of town. The purpose of the meeting is to close the door and focus on the opportunity before them. A decision must be made quickly, and he wants the input of all his key personnel. He has asked you to prepare a recommendation, both regarding the offering price that should be made for Foster Grant and the feasibility of the use of bank financing to fund the entire purchase. You believe that a cost of capital of 15 percent is appropriate for evaluating the acquisition, and you estimate that the relevant tax rate of the analysis is 30 percent. What recommendation will you make?

CASE 38

Fort Meyers Lincoln-Mercury Dealership, Inc.

Valuation of a Privately Held,
Small Business

In late 1990, Dr. Mark Johnson, a finance professor at City University, was asked to determine the value of the stock in a small privately held car dealership located in Fort Meyers, Florida. George Stone, the owner, wished to give a portion of his stock in the company to his children, George Jr. and Wanda. In order for the accountant, John Morris, to determine the appropriate tax treatment of the gifts, he needed to know the fair market value of the shares of stock. Morris sent Johnson copies of the company's financial statements for the past nine years and pro forma statements for the current year. Thus, 10 years of income statements, balance sheets, and tax returns were included in the package sent to Johnson. Morris also encouraged Johnson to visit the dealership in order to make judgments regarding the company's performance. Since Morris needed to know the value of the company before completing the 1990 tax return, Johnson had to begin his analysis rather quickly.

After reviewing all the data, he generated the financial statements found in Exhibits 1 and 2 and went to see George Stone to discuss his business. Stone told Johnson that he had purchased the dealership in 1977 and that it was "in the red" at the time. Subsequent to the acquisition, the dealership had been expanded three times—with added space for parts, service, and autobody repair. To keep up with the growing needs of his

EXHIBIT 1

Fort Meyers Lincoln-Mercury, Inc.

Statement of Income for Year Ended December 31

	1981	1982	1983	1984	1985	1986	1987	1988	1989	1990
Gross sales	$3,746,834	$4,835,263	$5,800,303	$7,525,966	$9,695,709	$11,444,244	$12,481,501	$11,682,350	$15,183,710	$15,999,530
Dividends	14,186	20,824	9,870	4,558	5	257	3,429	217	0	0
Interest income	17,723	25,934	24,895	15,513	11,040	6,455	8,395	3,318	2,934	3,060
Gross rents	28,019	6,794	5,884	0	2,293	0	3,403	800	0	0
Other income	35,722	36,191	34,622	34,974	72,350	150,710	109,760	194,341	207,990	159,837
Total income	3,842,484	4,925,006	5,875,574	7,581,011	9,781,397	11,601,666	12,606,488	11,881,026	15,394,634	16,162,427
Cost of goods sold	3,139,031	4,075,972	5,201,925	6,723,419	8,701,031	10,229,103	11,081,912	10,471,835	13,864,162	14,680,708
Officer compensation	131,775	154,877	179,143	201,243	217,500	293,698	322,750	316,400	325,000	340,100
Depreciation	58,321	39,778	37,712	48,324	49,727	44,717	42,126	49,567	50,629	64,951
Other operating expenses	308,584	412,248	435,072	428,110	550,220	747,004	917,930	764,238	767,099	827,265
Total operating expenses	3,637,711	4,682,875	5,853,852	7,401,096	9,518,478	11,314,522	12,364,718	11,602,040	15,006,890	15,913,094
Earnings before interest and taxes	204,773	242,131	21,722	179,915	262,919	287,144	241,770	278,986	387,744	249,333
Interest expense	76,738	73,291	73,142	53,275	78,871	58,721	51,038	40,462	69,878	70,743
Ordinary gains	1,875	1,439	307	2,128	(120)	0	(75)	0	(1,039)	
Capital gains	3,716	15,314	42,575	18,929	0	0	0	0	0	
Profit before taxes	133,626	185,593	(8,538)	147,697	183,928	228,423	190,657	238,524	316,827	178,590
Taxes	2,873	14,628	0	0	5,043	86,367	57,197	69,172	101,385	57,149
Profit after taxes	$130,753	$170,965	($8,538)	$147,697	$178,885	$147,056	$133,460	$169,352	$215,442	$121,441
						0.37	0.30	0.29	0.32	0.32
Dividends	($39,000)	($40,000)	($40,000)	($60,000)	($60,000)	($60,000)	($60,000)	($60,000)	($75,000)	($75,000)
Retained earnings	$91,753	$130,965	($48,538)	$87,697	$118,885	$87,057	$73,460	$109,352	$140,443	$46,442

EXHIBIT 2

Fort Meyers Lincoln-Mercury, Inc.

Balance Sheets as of December 31

Assets

	1981	1982	1983	1984	1985	1986	1987	1988	1989	1990
Cash	$145,127	$230,002	$278,047	$265,110	$168,721	$264,043	$371,052	$364,841	$448,821	$487,989
Accounts receivable	123,304	122,749	95,032	94,737	143,516	97,343	207,769	181,786	246,609	168,170
Inventory	744,461	919,363	941,289	1,441,645	1,593,910	1,577,057	1,504,902	1,718,935	1,976,222	1,998,845
Other current assets	20,011	20,417	16,781	10,230	9,800	4,690	3,220	0	2,374	7,308
Total current assets	1,032,903	1,292,531	1,331,149	1,811,722	1,915,947	1,943,133	2,086,943	2,263,565	2,674,026	2,662,812
Land	60,438	60,438	60,438	60,438	60,438	60,438	60,438	60,438	60,438	60,438
Buildings	465,265	461,867	471,913	605,940	604,513	622,207	627,776	805,773	743,975	785,202
Accumulated depreciation	(131,145)	(159,263)	(191,785)	(240,109)	(274,065)	(318,183)	(360,309)	(409,876)	(379,376)	(418,518)
Net buildings	394,558	363,042	340,566	426,269	390,886	364,462	327,905	456,337	427,037	427,122
Other assets	31,166	32,378	66,789	75,613	43,396	41,604	45,377	58,268	142,020	148,615
Other investments	231,539	167,189	114,442	134,893	107,428	81,907	3,640	7,260	7,260	8,914
Total assets	$1,690,166	$1,853,140	$1,852,946	$2,448,497	$2,457,657	$2,431,106	$2,463,865	$2,787,430	$3,250,343	$3,247,463

Accounts payable	$74,453	$64,242	$82,261	$75,954	$42,000	$90,892	$139,460	$158,535	$164,368	$136,225
Notes payable	992,705	1,021,032	1,082,380	1,593,385	1,578,051	1,464,192	1,499,778	1,684,775	2,006,906	1,994,623
Other current liabilities	36,462	58,429	39,231	45,953	41,271	46,150	37,695	5,928	3,199	400
Total current liabilities	1,103,620	1,143,703	1,203,872	1,715,292	1,661,322	1,601,234	1,676,933	1,849,238	2,174,473	2,131,248
Long-term debt	297,098	290,024	276,199	272,633	216,878	163,359	46,959	88,867	86,102	120,562
Total liabilities	1,400,718	1,433,727	1,480,071	1,987,925	1,878,200	1,764,593	1,723,892	1,938,105	2,260,575	2,251,810
Capital stock	112,200	113,200	113,200	113,200	113,200	113,200	113,200	113,200	113,200	94,144
Paid-in surplus	21,502	21,502	21,502	21,502	21,502	21,502	21,502	21,502	21,502	0
Retained earnings	155,746	286,711	238,173	325,870	444,755	531,812	605,272	714,624	855,067	901,509
Total equity	289,448	421,413	372,875	460,572	579,457	666,514	739,974	849,926	989,769	995,653
Total liabilities and equity	$1,690,166	$1,855,140	$1,852,946	$2,448,497	$2,457,657	$2,431,107	$2,463,866	$2,787,431	$3,250,344	$3,247,463

customers, Stone believes significant expansion will be necessary in the next several years.

Stone's experience with auto dealerships dates from the mid-1940s, when he acquired his first dealership in Virginia. Although both of his first two acquisitions were losing money when he purchased them, he was able to turn them around within four years.

Stone's two children, George Jr. (age 44) and Wanda (age 38), were active in the daily operation of the business, George serving as vice president and general manager and Wanda as sales manager and used car appraiser. Successor management-ownership is assured and facilitated, since Ford Motor Company has already accepted the children as the next owners of the dealership.

Besides family members, 36 other employees, many with several years' experience in car dealerships, work for the company. Stone believes that low employee turnover (relative to the industry) and the resulting high level of customer service give the dealership a strong competitive advantage.

Stone also told Johnson that the dealership has 10 to 11 percent of the local new-auto market—significantly higher than the national average of 6.7 percent. The Fort Meyers dealership is ranked third in market penetration among Lincoln-Mercury dealerships, a ranking Stone attributed to four interrelated factors:

1. Very strong customer service.
2. Low employee turnover.
3. Less reliance on advertising than most dealerships, which allows funding of a special account for "policy adjustments" to reimburse repairs/service contracts. Because of this policy, the dealership enjoys a positive customer perception.
4. Highly experienced management in sales and service.

At the same time, Stone noted several risk factors that might make it difficult to maintain market share and/or sales growth:

1. The industry had entered a downward trend in its business cycle. Following several very steady sales years, it was historically customary for auto sales to slump for several years. Even rebates and severe price reductions by the car manufacturers could not reverse these trends.
2. There was significant growth in the number of auto dealerships in the Fort Meyers area. Although the residents of the area were primarily older, and thus preferred large, comfortable touring cars, price competition had become quite aggressive, with new Nissan and Toyota dealerships exerting increasing competitive pressure.
3. The dealership does not have a strong position in the truck market—a growth segment for most auto dealers in the late 1980s.

As Johnson reviewed his notes from his meeting with Stone, as well as the industry literature Stone had given him, he noted that the data regarding general economic conditions were beginning to point toward a recession—supporting Stone's prediction of a downward trend in revenue for the car and truck industry. The latest monthly report of the government's index of 11 leading economic indicators showed a decline for the third consecutive month; this month's index was down 1 percent from the previous month, bringing the three-month decline to 3.2 percent. There was no longer any doubt that the economy was in a recession, and most business and economic analysts were now wondering how deep it would be and how long it would last.

The *Value Line Investment Survey* was currently forecasting U.S. auto sales of 9.9 million units in 1991 and 9.7 units in 1992. This forecast was supported by the 4.55 percent sales drop in the most recent month. Auto manufacturers were already reducing production of the new model cars currently being unveiled and longer-term forecasts were for industry sales to remain flat for several years. Revenue was expected to grow by only 2 percent annually through the year 2000 because of slow growth of the U.S. economy during that period, changing U.S. demographics, and reduced replacement demand for automobiles resulting from the strong growth from 1984 to 1988.

Johnson also noted that the rate of return on U.S. long-term government bonds was approximately 9.0 percent and declining. In fact, the Federal Reserve was expected to lower the discount rate soon. The price-earnings ratios for the Standard and Poor's 500 index had varied recently between 14.5 and 15.0. Similar price-earnings ratios for companies in the car dealership industry were difficult to locate since most car dealerships were privately owned, but seemingly comparable companies were priced at approximately 10 to 11 times annual earnings. The *Value Line Investment Survey* estimated that the return on the Standard and Poor's 500 index was expected to be 18 to 22 percent in the forecast future. The estimated return for the auto industry was lower than this.

Johnson determined that the valuation should use the data from the most recent five years of financial reports since earlier data were too old to be predictive of future revenue and expenses. The 1990 data had been estimated by Morris, Stone's accountant, and Johnson felt comfortable that these data would accurately reflect actual year-end results. With this basic information, he began the valuation process.

First he created the common-size income statements and balance sheets for both the company and the industry for the past five years. Exhibits 3 and 4 detail these calculations. Exhibit 5 shows the financial ratios for the company and the industry that Johnson would analyze. Industry data were gathered from *Robert Morris and Associates' Annual Statement Stud-*

EXHIBIT 3

Fort Meyers Lincoln-Mercury, Inc.

Percentage Income Statements for Company and Industry, 1986–1990

	Company					Industry (SIC 5511)				
	1986	1987	1988	1989	1990	1986	1987	1988	1989	1990
Gross sales	98.6%	99.0%	98.3%	98.6%	99.0%					
Dividends	0.0%	0.0%	0.0%	0.0%	0.0%					
Interest income	0.1%	0.1%	0.0%	0.0%	0.0%					
Gross rents	0.0%	0.0%	0.0%	0.0%	0.0%					
Other income	1.3%	0.9%	1.6%	1.4%	1.0%					
Total income	100.0%	100.0%	100.0%	100.0%	100.0%	100.0%	100.0%	100.0%	100.0%	100.0%
Cost of goods sold	88.2%	87.9%	88.1%	90.1%	90.8%	85.5%	85.5%	85.9%	85.5%	85.9%
Officer compensation	2.5%	2.6%	2.7%	2.1%	2.1%					
Depreciation	0.4%	0.3%	0.4%	0.3%	0.4%					
Other operating expenses	6.4%	7.3%	6.4%	5.0%	5.1%	12.4%	12.7%	12.6%	13.6%	13.3%
Total operating expenses	97.5%	98.1%	97.7%	97.5%	98.5%	97.9%	98.2%	98.5%	99.1%	99.2%
Earnings before interest and taxes	2.5%	1.9%	2.3%	2.5%	1.5%	2.1%	1.8%	1.5%	0.9%	0.8%
Interest expense	0.5%	0.4%	0.3%	0.5%	0.4%					
Ordinary gains	0.0%	0.0%	0.0%	0.0%	0.0%					
Capital gains	0.0%	0.0%	0.0%	0.0%	0.0%					
Profit before taxes	2.0%	1.5%	2.0%	2.1%	1.1%	2.1%	1.8%	1.6%	1.2%	1.1%

ies. Johnson deemed the company position to be quite good, its five-year averages of both return on equity and return on assets higher than the industry averages. The company seemed to have achieved these returns by better-than-average profitability, higher-than-average investment efficiency (total assets turnover, inventory turnover, and accounts receivable turnover), and lower-than-average risk stemming from debt financing. The company's cash flow, as detailed in Exhibit 6, was also quite positive for a small privately held business.

Johnson decided that several valuation techniques would be useful in determining the fair market value of the business. First he revalued the assets to determine the liquidation value of the business. This primarily necessitated estimating the value of the land and the building owned by the dealership as well the value of the franchise. For this, Johnson used the estimates provided by Stone after verifying them in the current county tax records. Exhibit 7 details this information. Johnson had little reason to doubt that this value of the equity represented the fair market value of the company if the company were to be dismantled.

Still, he felt that this technique did not capture the added value of the earnings potential of the business. That is, if the business were to be sold as a "going concern" with earning and cash flow capacity, Johnson felt that it would sell for a different price. He attempted to value this cash flow capacity by using a price-earnings multiple applied to "average" earnings, as well as a discounted cash flow technique.

Before applying either of these techniques, Johnson adjusted the earnings and cash flows of the company for the past five years to reflect higher-than-industry-average officer compensation, changes in tax laws, and the tax shelter of interest expenses. Exhibit 8 provides the details of these calculations. For each year, the historic profit before taxes was increased to reflect the excessive officer compensation paid to the owner. Thus, this adjusted profit before taxes should be comparable to public companies.

Taxes were recomputed to register the 1986 tax law changes so that future earnings and cash flows would reflect current tax laws. Adjusted net profit was revised for depreciation expenses, other operating cash flows from the statement of cash flows, and the tax shelter provided by historic interest expense. The result was five estimates of adjusted net profit and five estimates of operating cash flow or cash flow to asset investment.

Exhibit 9 details how Johnson used these net incomes to estimate average or "normalized" earnings. Equity value was determined by multiplying the "normalized" earnings by the industry average price-earnings ratios of 10.5.

Johnson first estimated a "normalized" cash flow for the company and then used estimates of growth to forecast future cash flows (Exhibit 10). Three stages of growth were forecasted: strong growth for five years,

EXHIBIT 4

Fort Meyers Lincoln-Mercury, Inc.

Percentage Balance Sheets for Company and Industry, 1986–1990

	Company					Industry (SIC 5511)				
	1986	1987	1988	1989	1990	1986	1987	1988	1989	1990
	Assets									
Cash	10.9%	15.1%	13.1%	13.8%	15.0%	6.1%	6.4%	7.3%	3.7%	5.4%
Accounts receivable	4.0%	8.4%	6.5%	7.6%	5.2%	9.6%	9.5%	9.7%	8.6%	8.8%
Inventories	64.9%	61.1%	61.7%	60.8%	61.6%	63.3%	63.3%	61.9%	66.0%	65.7%
Other current assets	0.2%	0.1%	0.0%	0.1%	0.2%	3.5%	3.3%	2.8%	2.8%	2.9%
Total current assets	79.9%	84.7%	81.3%	82.3%	82.0%	82.5%	82.5%	81.7%	83.1%	82.8%
Land	2.5%	2.5%	2.2%	1.9%	1.9%					
Buildings	25.6%	25.5%	28.9%	23.0%	24.2%					
Accumulated depreciation	−13.1%	−14.6%	−14.7%	−11.7%	−12.9%					
Net buildings	15.0%	13.3%	16.4%	13.1%	13.2%	10.0%	9.7%	10.5%	9.8%	10.1%
Other assets	1.7%	1.8%	2.1%	4.4%	4.6%	7.2%	7.5%	7.5%	6.5%	6.6%
Other investments	3.4%	0.1%	0.3%	0.2%	0.3%					
Total assets	100.0%	100.0%	100.0%	100.0%	100.0%	99.7%	99.7%	99.7%	99.4%	99.5%

Liabilities and Owners' Equity

Accounts payable	3.7%	5.7%	5.7%	5.1%	4.2%	5.3%	5.2%	5.3%	5.5%	5.9%
Notes payable	60.2%	60.9%	60.4%	61.7%	61.4%	47.1%	49.7%	49.5%	53.3%	53.5%
Other current liabilities	1.9%	1.5%	0.2%	0.1%	0.0%	9.7%	8.5%	9.1%	7.6%	6.9%
Total current liabilities	65.9%	68.1%	66.3%	66.9%	65.6%	62.1%	63.4%	63.9%	66.4%	66.3%
Long-term debt	6.7%	1.9%	3.2%	2.6%	3.7%	9.5%	9.4%	9.9%	9.7%	10.0%
Total liabilities	72.6%	70.0%	69.5%	69.5%	69.3%	71.6%	72.8%	73.8%	76.1%	76.3%
Capital stock	4.7%	4.6%	4.1%	3.5%	2.9%					
Paid-in surplus	0.9%	0.9%	0.8%	0.7%	0.0%					
Retained earnings	21.9%	24.6%	25.6%	26.3%	27.8%	28.4%	27.2%	26.2%	23.9%	23.7%
	27.4%	30.0%	30.5%	30.5%	30.7%	28.4%	27.2%	26.2%	23.9%	23.7%
Total liabilities and equity	100.0%	100.0%	100.0%	100.0%	100.0%	100.0%	100.0%	100.0%	100.0%	100.0%

EXHIBIT 5

Fort Meyers Lincoln-Mercury, Inc.

Ratio Analysis

	Company						Industry (SIC 5511)					
	1986	1987	1988	1989	1990	Avg.	1986	1987	1988	1989	1990	Avg.
Liquidity												
Current ratio	1.21	1.24	1.23	1.23	1.25	1.23	1.3	1.3	1.3	1.2	1.2	1.26
Quick ratio	0.23	0.35	0.30	0.32	0.31	0.30	0.2	0.2	0.2	0.2	0.2	0.20
Productivity ratios												
Sales/total assets	4.8	5.1	4.3	4.7	5.0	4.8	4.9	4.7	4.8	4.2	4.3	4.6
Sales/net fixed assets	31.8	38.4	26.0	36.0	37.8	34.0	76.9	73.3	70.3	68.0	64.7	71.0
Sales/current assets	6.0	6.0	5.2	5.8	6.1	5.8						
Sales/accounts receivable	119.2	60.7	65.4	62.4	95.9	80.7	60.2	62.1	61.3	61.2	59.1	60.8
Average collection period	3.0	5.9	5.5	5.8	3.8	4.8						
Sales/inventory	7.4	8.4	6.9	7.8	8.1	7.7	6.7	6.3	6.6	5.5	5.6	6.1
Leverage												
Debt/total assets	72.6%	70.0%	69.5%	69.5%	69.3%	70.2%	71.6%	72.8%	73.8%	76.1%	76.3%	71.1%
Fixed assets/net worth	63.7%	52.5%	60.8%	49.3%	49.0%	55.1%	30.0%	30.0%	30.0%	30.0%	40.0%	32.0%
EBIT/interest	5.3	4.7	6.9	5.5	3.5	5.2	3.2	3.0	2.8	2.1	2.0	2.6
Profitability												
Pretax net profit margin	2.0%	1.5%	2.0%	2.1%	1.1%	1.7%	2.1%	1.8%	1.6%	1.2%	1.1%	1.6%
Operating profit margin	2.5%	1.9%	2.3%	2.5%	1.5%	2.2%	2.1%	1.8%	1.5%	0.9%	0.8%	1.1%
Gross profit margin	11.8%	12.1%	11.9%	9.9%	9.2%	11.0%	14.5%	14.5%	14.1%	14.5%	14.1%	14.3%
Pretax return on assets	9.6%	7.7%	8.6%	9.7%	5.5%	8.2%	8.2%	6.6%	5.7%	4.0%	3.8%	5.7%
Pretax return on equity	35.0%	25.8%	28.1%	32.0%	17.9%	27.8%	33.4%	28.8%	25.5%	18.7%	19.0%	25.1%

EXHIBIT 6

Fort Meyers Lincoln-Mercury, Inc.

Statement of Cash Flow

	1986	1987	1988	1989	1990
Beginning cash balance	$168,721	$264,043	$371,052	$364,844	$448,821
Funds from operations					
Profit after taxes	147,056	133,460	169,352	215,442	121,441
Depreciation	44,717	42,126	49,567	50,629	64,931
Accounts receivable	46,173	(110,426)	25,983	(64,823)	78,139
Inventories	16,853	72,155	(214,033)	(257,287)	(22,623)
Other current assets	5,110	1,470	3,220	(2,374)	(5,134)
Accounts payable	48,892	48,568	19,075	5,833	(28,143)
Notes payable	(113,859)	35,586	184,997	322,131	(12,283)
Other current liabilities	4,879	(8,455)	(31,767)	(2,729)	(2,799)
Total funds from operations	$199,821	$214,484	$206,394	$266,823	$193,529
Funds from investing					
Land	0	0	0	0	0
Buildings	(18,293)	(5,569)	(177,999)	(21,329)	(65,016)
Other assets	1,792	(3,773)	(12,891)	(83,752)	(6,595)
Other investments	25,521	78,267	(3,620)	0	(1,654)
Total funds from investing	$9,020	$68,925	($194,510)	($105,081)	($73,265)
Funds from financing					
Long-term debt	(53,519)	(116,400)	41,908	(2,765)	34,460
Dividends	(60,000)	(60,000)	(60,000)	(75,000)	(75,000)
Capital stock	0	0	0	0	(40,558)
Total funds from financing	($113,519)	($176,400)	($18,092)	($77,765)	($81,098)
Cash flow	$95,322	$107,009	($6,208)	$83,977	$39,166
Ending cash balance	$264,043	$371,052	$364,844	$448,821	$487,987

---

slower growth for five years, and constant, steady growth of 3.5 percent forever. The discount rate of 15.75 percent was used to estimate both the terminal value and the discounted cash flow. Johnson derived this rate by using the 9.0 percent rate for government securities and adding to it a 4.50 percent premium for business risk and a 2.25 percent premium for financial risk; the 6.75 premium for risk seemed consistent with current market conditions. The value of the company's assets was determined by discounting the forecasted cash flow. Value of the equity was calculated by subtracting the long-term liabilities from the value of the assets.

At last Johnson was ready to summarize his report of the car dealership's value to John Morris, but he wondered how he could justify pre-

---
EXHIBIT 7

Fort Meyers Lincoln-Mercury, Inc.

Adjusted Market Estimate of Book Value

	Book Value	Adjustment	Adjusted Book Value
	Assets		
Cash	$487,989	100%	$487,989
Accounts receivable	168,470	100%	168,470
Inventory	1,998,845	100%	1,998,845
Other current assets	7,508	100%	7,508
Other investments	8,914	100%	8,914
Land	60,438	500%	302,190
Buildings	366,684	200%	733,368
Other assets	148,615	100%	148,615
Franchise	0	NA	500,000
Total Assets	$3,247,463		$4,355,899
	Liabilities		
Accounts payable	$136,225	100%	136,225
Notes payable	1,994,623	100%	1,994,623
Other current liabilities	400	100%	400
Long-term debt	120,562	100%	120,562
	$2,251,810		$2,251,810
Value of equity	$995,653		$2,104,089

senting three separate estimates. Which one was correct? In frustration, he had merely weighted each of the three estimates. He knew that he had not discounted the value of the company for any lack of marketability or minority interest. Once the gifts of stock had been completed, Stone would still own more than 51 percent of the shares. With Stone retaining effective control of the company, the minority shares would be worth less than his own shares. Also, neither George Jr. nor Wanda would be able to sell their shares of stock easily. The IRS would allow a discount for the lack of marketability of the gifted shares. Johnson estimated that a 20 percent discount might be appropriate, but wondered how he might verify this number. Exhibit 11 provides his resulting calculations of fair market value.

EXHIBIT 8

Fort Meyers Lincoln-Mercury, Inc.

Adjusted Earnings and Cash Flow

	1986	1987	1988	1989	1990
Profit before taxes	$233,423	$190,657	$238,524	$316,827	$178,590
Adjustments for Officer compensation*	144,923	160,490	164,529	127,612	132,106
Adjusted profit before taxes	378,346	351,147	403,054	444,439	310,696
Adjusted taxes†	129,960	119,815	139,176	154,613	104,727
Adjusted net profit	$248,385	$231,332	$263,877	$289,826	$205,969
Plus: depreciation	43,132	40,504	48,446	48,874	62,389
Plus: adjustment for operating cash flow from cash flow statement	8,048	38,898	(12,525)	751	7,157
Plus: adjustment for interest expense tax shelter‡	20,038	19,037	15,092	26,064	26,387
Adjusted operating cash flow	$319,603	$329,771	$314,891	$365,515	$301,902

*Officer compensation was reduced to 1.3 percent of revenue.

†Taxes were computed by $16,813 plus 37.3 percent times the income over $75,000. This includes both federal and state taxes. The 37.3 rate was found by .34 + .05 * (1 − .34) (federal plus state).

‡Interest was multiplied by the new, marginal tax rate for the appropriate year (e.g., 37.3 percent).

EXHIBIT 9

Fort Meyers Lincoln-Mercury, Inc.

Estimated Value Using Normalized Earnings and Price-Earnings Multiple

Year	Adjusted Net Income (2)	Weight (3)	Product (2) × (3)
1986	$248,385	0.2	$49,677
1987	231,332	0.2	46,266
1988	263,877	0.2	52,775
1989	289,826	0.2	57,965
1990	205,969	0.2	41,194
		1.00	$247,878
Normalized earnings			$247,878
Value of equity			$2,602,717

EXHIBIT 10

Fort Meyers Lincoln-Mercury, Inc.

Estimated Value Using Discounted Cash Flow Techniques and Forecasted Normalized Cash Flow

Year	Adjusted Cash Flow (2)	Weight (3)	Product (2) × (3)
1986	$319,603	0.2	$63,921
1987	329,771	0.2	65,954
1988	314,891	0.2	62,978
1989	365,515	0.2	73,103
1990	301,902	0.2	60,380
		1.00	$326,336
	Normalized cash flow		$326,336

Estimated Value

Year	Growth Rate (2)	Forecasted Cash Flow (3)	15.75% Discount Rate (4)	Product (3) × (4)
1991	7.0%	$349,180	0.7464	$260,620
1992	7.0%	373,623	0.6448	240,918
1993	7.0%	399,776	0.5571	222,707
1994	7.0%	427,761	0.4813	205,871
1995	7.0%	457,704	0.4158	190,309
1996	5.0%	480,589	0.3592	172,634
1997	5.0%	504,618	0.3103	156,601
1998	5.0%	529,849	0.2681	142,057
1999	5.0%	556,342	0.2316	128,864
2000	5.0%	584,159	0.2001	116,896
Terminal Value*		4,935,546	0.2001	987,653
Value of assets				$2,825,130
Less long-term debt				$120,562
Value of equity				$2,704,568

*Assumes a 3.5 percent constant growth rate and a 15.75 percent discount rate. Cash flow in 2000 was increased by 3.5 percent and the result capitalized by 12.25 percent (15.75 percent minus 3.5 percent).

—————————————— **EXHIBIT 11** ——————————————
Fort Meyers Lincoln-Mercury, Inc.

Summary of Value

Technique of Valuation	Value	Weight	Product
Adjusted book value	$2,104,089	0.2	$420,818
Normalized earnings	2,602,717	0.4	1,041,087
Discounted cash flow	2,704,568	0.4	1,081,827
		1.0	$2,543,732

Value of equity		$2,543,732
Number of shares outstanding		14,414
Value per share		$176.47
Discount for lack of marketability and minority interest	20%	($35.29)
Value per share		$141.18

QUESTIONS*

1. Analyze the dealership's financial statements. Use the company calculations and industry data provided in Exhibits 1 through 6.

2. Comment on the usefulness of the adjusted book value technique of valuation. Use the data provided in Exhibit 7 as an example. What are the advantages and disadvantages of this technique? Where does "goodwill" enter into this analysis?

3. Comment on the usefulness of the adjusted earnings and cash flow calculations. Be prepared to explain how you determined these calculations.

4. Comment on the usefulness of the price-earnings multiple technique. What are the advantages and disadvantages of this technique? How are the data determined?

5. Comment on the usefulness of the discounted cash flow technique. What are the advantages and disadvantages of this technique? How are the data determined?

6. How would you reconcile the three different numbers to George Stone?

7. How might you determine an appropriate discount for "lack of marketability and minority interest"?

*The computer spreadsheet is named "MEYERS.wk1."

CASE 39

Wyoming Energy Development, Inc.

Cost of Capital

In May 1991, Linda Bellich, a recent M.B.A. graduate and newly appointed assistant to the comptroller of Wyoming Energy Development, Inc. (WED), was given a list of six new investment projects proposed for the following year. It was her job to analyze these projects and be prepared to present her findings before the board of directors at its annual meeting to be held in 10 days.

Wyoming Energy Development was founded in Laramie, Wyoming, in 1963 by Scott Heywood. WED gained recognition as a leading producer of high-quality coal, with the majority of its sales being made to Japan. During the rapid economic expansion of Japan in the 1960s, demand for coal and other energy products boomed, and WED's sales grew rapidly. As a result of this rapid growth and recognition of new opportunities in the energy market, WED began to diversify its product line. While retaining its emphasis on coal production, it expanded operations to include uranium mining and the production of electrical generators, and finally, it went into all phases of energy production. By 1990, WED's sales had reached the $140 million level, with net profit after taxes attaining a record $6.7 million.

As WED expanded its product line in the early 1980s, it also formalized its capital budgeting procedure. Until 1982, capital investment projects were selected primarily on the basis of the average return on investment calculations, with individual departments submitting these calculations for projects falling within their division. In 1986, this procedure was replaced by one using present value as the decision-making criterion. This change was made to incorporate cash flows rather than accounting profits into the decision-making analysis, in addition to adjusting these flows for the time value of money. At that time, the cost of capital for WED was determined to be 4.36 percent, which has been used as the discount rate for the past five years. This rate was determined by taking a weighted average of the costs WED had incurred in raising funds from the capital markets over the previous 10 years.

It had originally been Bellich's assignment to update this rate over the most recent 10-year period and determine the net present value of all the proposed investment opportunities using this newly calculated figure. However, she objected to this procedure, stating that while this calculation gave a good estimate of "the past cost" of capital, changing interest rates and stock prices made this calculation of little value in the present. Bellich suggested that current costs of raising funds in the capital markets be weighted by their percentage makeup of the capital structure. This proposal was reviewed enthusiastically by the comptroller of WED, and Bellich was given the assignment of recalculating WED's cost of capital and providing a written report for the financial board of directors explaining and justifying this calculation.

To determine a weighted average cost of capital for WED, it was necessary for Linda Bellich to examine the costs associated with each source of funding used. In the past, the largest sources of funding had been the issuance of new common stock and internally generated funds. Through conversations with the comptroller and other members of the board of directors, Bellich learned that the firm, in fact, wished to maintain its current financial structure since it is in accordance with the book value weights shown in Exhibit 1. She further determined that the strong growth patterns that WED had exhibited over the past 10 years were expected to continue indefinitely because of the dwindling supply of U.S. and Japanese domestic oil and the growing importance of, and U.S. and Japanese dependence on, coal and other alternative energy resources. Through further investigation, Bellich learned that WED could issue additional shares of common stock, which had a par value of $25 per share and were selling at a current market price of $45. The expected dividend for the next period would be $2 per share, with expected growth at a rate of 6 percent per year for the foreseeable future. The underwriting commission paid to WED's investment banker would amount to $2 per share and would be for insuring the issue against the risk of adverse market fluctuations in the stock's selling price during the distribution process, in addition to performing the function of actually selling the security and providing advice as to the timing and pricing of the issue.

———————— **EXHIBIT 1** ————————
Wyoming Energy Development, Inc.

Balance Sheet
for Year Ending April 30, 1991

Assets

	1991
Cash	$ 9,000,000
Accounts receivable	31,000,000
Inventories	12,000,000
Total current assets	$ 52,000,000
Net fixed assets	193,000,000
Goodwill	7,000,000
Total assets	$252,000,000

Liabilities and Equity

Accounts payable	$ 850,000
Current debt	10,000,000
Accrued taxes	1,150,000
Total current liabilities	$ 12,000,000
Long-term debt	72,000,000
Preferred stock	43,000,000
Common stock	114,000,000
Retained earnings	11,000,000
Total liabilities and equity	$252,000,000

Preferred stock at 6 percent also could be issued with the help of an investment banker at $97 per share with a par value of $100 per share. Of this $97, 3.1 percent would go to the investment banker for his help in marketing the issue, with the remainder of the funds going to WED.

Finally, Bellich learned that it would be possible for WED to raise an additional $1 million through a one-year loan from WED's Chicago bank at 9 percent. Any amount raised over $1 million would cost WED 14 percent. Short-term debt has always been used by Wyoming to finance capital expenditures, and as WED grows, it is expected to maintain its proportion in the capital structure to support capital expansion. Also, $6 million could be raised through a bond issue with 30 years' maturity with a 10 percent coupon at 98 percent of face value. On this issue, 2 percent of the face value would be charged as an underwriting commission. If it became necessary to raise more funds via long-term debt, $3 million more could be accumulated through the issuance of additional 30-year bonds sold at 95 percent of face value, with the coupon rate being raised to 11 percent and 2 percent of the face value being charged as an underwriting commission. While any additional funds raised via long-term debt would necessarily have a 30-year maturity with a 14 percent coupon yield and be sold at 95 percent of face value, 2 percent of this face value would be charged as an underwriting fee. Here again, this fee would go to the investment banker for his help in marketing the issue.

In the past, WED has calculated a weighted average of these sources of funds to determine its cost of capital. In discussions with the current comptroller, the point was raised that while this served as an appropriate calculation for externally generated funds, it did not take into account the fact that much of the funds used for capital expenditures by WED were internally generated. For example, WED is expected to produce $5 million in depreciation-generated funds in addition to retaining $4 million of its earnings during the coming period. The comptroller agreed that there should be some cost associated with retained earnings financing incorporated into the calculations, but depreciation charges should not be included since they, as opposed to all other financing methods, do not appear on the liability side of the balance sheet. Although Bellich was not completely convinced by the comptroller's logic, she continued with her work.

QUESTIONS

1. Should Linda Bellich assign a cost to any depreciation-generated funds? If so, what should be the cost assigned? Should this cost be used in the calculations of the average cost of capital? If not, what is its significance?

2. Should Bellich assign a cost to funds from retained earnings? Why or why not? If so, what cost should be assigned? (Assume no personal taxes or brokerage fees.) Would this cost change if the stockholder pays an income tax on dividends in addition to incurring brokerage costs when reinvesting dividend receipts?

3. Assume that WED wishes to continue with the existing capital structure. What is the average cost of capital associated with the next $25 million increase in gross assets? (Use a 50 percent corporate tax rate for WED.)

4. Graph WED's marginal cost of capital associated with the first $40 million generated; again assume that WED desires to maintain its current capital structure. Observing this supply curve of capital, do you now feel it is possible to determine the cost of capital independently of the amount of funds to be raised?

5. At the board of directors meeting, the projected costs and internal rates of return for the six capital investment projects are given as follows:

Project	Cost (millions)	IRR
1	$7	8.73%
2	7	8.40
3	8	9.60
4	5	9.14
5	5	8.20
6	8	8.18

Graph the internal rates of return on investment projects against the marginal cost of capital. Which projects should be selected?

6. If dividends are expected to be as given here, and the net proceeds to the company from the sale of a share of stock are $43.25, what is the cost of equity capital?

$$D_1 = 1.00$$
$$D_2 = 2.00$$
$$D_3 = 3.00$$
$$D_4 = 4.00$$
$$D_5 \text{ through } D_\infty = 6.00$$

7. If the projects being selected by WED have a higher degree of risk than current projects do, what will happen to the cost of capital over time? If projects being selected have less risk than current projects do, what will happen to the cost of capital over time?

8. How might a change in the long-term interest rate (a change upward or a change downward) affect the marginal cost of equity capital and the overall marginal cost of capital?

CASE 40

Texon Production, Inc.

Cost of Capital

In 1923, Imir Swenson, a young Swedish immigrant, migrated to the south plains of Texas to begin cotton farming. His farming operation continued to expand, with the only downturn coming during the Depression of the 1930s. After the Depression, his operation resumed a growth posture; however, in 1960, he made a decision to retire. At this time, his two sons, only nearing their 20s, assumed control of the farming interests and proved to be excellent farmers and equally capable businessmen. The business scope remained virtually unchanged over the years until Joseph Swenson convinced his brother Herman that the processing of raw cotton would represent a profitable expansion of business interests. With the financial support of their father, the necessary plant and equipment were acquired. This additional capability became operational in October 1977.

During the ensuing years, the mixture of the firm's revenues gradually shifted from farm production to cotton processing. As this change in business purpose became more extensive, the existing partnership came under pressure for additional capital. When the Swensons approached prospective investors, some hesitancy was encountered as a result of the current form of business—that is, the partnership. The private parties being contacted were simply not interested in subjecting themselves to the unlimited liability associated with a partnership. For this reason, the business was incorporated in 1983, with the new corporate entity being designated Texon Productions, Inc.

At the time of incorporation, Joseph Swenson became president of the business, with the complete emphasis of the firm being placed upon the processing of cotton. During his presidency, the company has continued to prosper, with both sales and earnings growing at a relatively stable rate. (The company's financial condition for the past five years is reflected in Exhibit 1.) Earnings before interest and taxes have been running at approximately 25 percent of net sales, with an increase to about 30 percent by 1996 expected. (The projected sales levels for the next five years are shown in Exhibit 2.) The reason for the projected improvement in the profitability margins comes largely from improved processing equipment.

Since the inception of the corporation, capital assets have expanded at a rate approximating 10 percent per year. Exhibit 3 provides an indication of the growth pattern in capital expenditures within the past five years. Capital needs for 1994 are expected to be significantly larger than experienced in prior years, with an estimate having been set at $275,000. These funds are to be used in renovating the plant and to purchase new processing and distribution equipment. Joseph Swenson is particularly interested in a new process that would allow for more efficient cleaning of the cotton fiber. Although the 1994 projection for capital needs is substantially higher than in previous periods, the management policy of appropriating a portion of retained earnings for investments has not been altered to account for the forthcoming investment level.

As to the corporation's financial policies, management has maintained a relatively constant capital structure and dividend payout ratio. The firm's capital structure is considered by Joseph Swenson to be optimal and at a level that should be maintained for the foreseeable future. He maintains this conviction in spite of the fact that the percentage of debt financ-

---

EXHIBIT 1

Texon Production, Inc.

Comparative Balance Sheets, 1989–1993

	1989	1990	1991	1992	1993
		Assets			
Cash	$ 16,811	$ 18,430	$ 21,203	$ 19,821	$ 20,611
Marketable securities	125,874	136,216	148,821	153,260	176,215
Receivables	45,617	42,210	62,533	78,330	89,800
Inventory	178,343	184,355	211,216	203,820	224,074
Property, plant and equipment, net	616,634	653,212	717,240	784,215	816,107
Total assets	$983,279	$1,034,423	$1,161,013	$1,239,446	$1,326,807

Liabilities and Stockholders' Equity

Trade payables	$ 16,593	$ 18,219	$ 23,416	$ 21,210	$ 22,311
Short-term notes (6%, due 12/31/94)	17,359	16,230	21,870	23,210	25,637
Notes payable (8%, 15 years, due 1/1/04)	30,882	30,882	30,882	30,882	30,882
Bonds payable (8%, 20 years, due 1/1/04)	252,000	252,000	252,000	252,000	252,000
Preferred stock ($9 cumulative $100 par, 2,000 shares authorized, 1,000 shares issued)	100,000	100,000	100,000	100,000	100,000
Common stock ($10 par, 50,000 shares authorized)	254,310	254,830	255,100	253,870	254,900
Paid-in capital in excess of par:					
Preferred	2,000	2,000	2,000	2,000	2,000
Common	34,198	50,103	128,557	169,182	209,175
Retained earnings:					
Appropriated	55,325	63,280	68,412	77,526	176,215
Free	220,612	246,879	278,776	309,566	253,687
Total liabilities and stockholder's equity	$983,279	$1,034,423	$1,161,013	$1,239,446	$1,326,807
Net sales	$449,206	$447,683	$508,133	$539,571	$576,424
Cost of goods sold	255,980	243,012	289,642	307,558	332,341
Operating expenses	80,913	86,003	91,472	97,125	100,998
Earnings before interest and taxes	$112,313	$118,668	$127,019	$134,888	$143,085
Interest	23,672	23,604	23,942	24,023	24,168
Taxable earnings	$ 88,641	$ 95,064	$103,077	$110,865	$118,917
Income taxes	35,307	38,026	41,362	44,359	47,567
Earnings after taxes	$ 53,334	$ 57,038	$ 61,715	$ 66,506	$ 71,350
Preferred dividend	9,000	9,000	9,000	9,000	9,000
Net income	$ 44,334	$ 48,038	$ 52,715	$ 57,506	$ 62,350
Earnings per share	$1.74	$1.89	$2.07	$2.27	$2.45
Dividends per share	0.52	0.55	0.62	0.70	0.77

ing for the industry, currently 15 percent, is considerably lower than the same figure for Texon Production. In contrast, Herman Swenson is somewhat concerned regarding the capital mix decision. The basis for his anxiety rests upon several factors, including the firm's poor liquidity position. He contends that if the current financial policy is not changed, any future notes payable, regardless of maturity structure, would have a cost of 11 percent. Furthermore, the existing bonds, which consist of 252 securities

─────── **EXHIBIT 2** ───────

Texon Production, Inc.

Projected Sales, 1994–1998

Year	Projected Sales
1994	$600,000
1995	625,000
1996	668,000
1997	705,000
1998	783,000

─────── **EXHIBIT 3** ───────

Texon Production, Inc.

Capital Outlay, 1989–1993

Year	Outlay
1989	$56,774
1990	62,933
1991	93,089
1992	76,452
1993	83,178

having a $1,000 par value each, are currently depressed at a market value of $855. Finally, the preferred stock has encountered a decrease in market price to $88. For these reasons, he has asked brother Joseph to reconsider his position regarding the concern's financial mix. As to the dividend policy, the company paid out 31 percent of its earnings in 1993. This relationship has been maintained relatively closely in the past and is expected to continue into the indefinite future.

As a new financial policy, Herman Swenson has decided to calculate the firm's cost of capital. He knows very little about the actual computations and associated assumptions, and has approached Texon's treasurer, Bernard Erickson, for assistance. In response, Erickson has begun a search for additional information that would be needed in making the cost-of-capital determination. In this effort, he has come to the conclusion that an issuance of any additional common stock or preferred stock would have a flotation cost of some 10 percent. The expected price per share before any flotation costs is based upon the average 1993 price as computed in Exhibit 4. Any future bond issues would face an 8 percent issuance cost. Furthermore, the current risk-free rate, as reflected by short-term government securities, is 5 percent. Finally, a "beta factor" for Texon Production, Inc.,

———————— EXHIBIT 4 ————————

Texon Production, Inc.

Market Price of Common Stock for 1993

Date	Price
Jan. 31	$14.00
Feb. 28	14.50
March 31	15.25
April 30	14.95
May 31	15.85
June 30	16.60
July 31	17.50
Aug. 31	18.25
Sept. 30	17.90
Oct. 31	18.75
Nov. 30	19.10
Dec. 31	19.50
Average market price for 1993	$16.85

——— EXHIBIT 5 ———

Texon Production, Inc.

Average Annual Return for the Market, 1984–1993

Year	Average Annual Return
1993	.23
1992	.17
1991	(.08)
1990	.02
1989	.13
1988	.09
1987	(.01)
1986	.16
1985	.21
1984	.07

using the last 10 years of annual data, has been ascertained to be 1.32. In this regard, the average annual returns of the market have been computed, with the results indicated in Exhibit 5.

QUESTIONS

1. When management computes its firm's cost of capital, what application(s) might be made of the measurement?

2. What assumptions are attached to the calculations?

3. Using the existing capital structure, expressed in terms of market value as opposed to book value, determine the firm's weighted cost of capital as of January 1, 1994, at the projected 1994 investment level. Assume that (a) the existing capital committed to marketable securities is a viable source of internal funds, (b) the book values for credit and all notes closely reflect the current market value of such forms of indebtedness, (c) no implicit costs exist for trade credit and all trade discounts are taken, and (d) the company tax rate is 40 percent.

4. How well do you consider the assumptions cited in question 2 to have been met?

5. Drawing upon the capital asset pricing model to determine the company's cost of equity, recompute the weighted cost of capital for Texon Production, Inc.

CASE 41

Woods General Producers

Break-even Analysis, Operating Leverage, Financial Leverage

Woods General Producers (WGP) is a medium-sized public corporation that until recently consisted of two divisions. The Retail Furniture Group (RFG) has eight locations in the northeastern Ohio area, mostly concentrated around Cleveland. These retail outlets generate sales of contemporary, traditional, and Early American furniture. Additionally, casual and leisure furniture lines are carried by the stores. The other (old) division of WGP is its Concrete Group (CG). The CG operates three plants in the North Tonawanda area of western New York. These plants produce precast concrete wall panels and concrete stave farm silos. The company headquarters of WGP is located in Erie, Pennsylvania. This community touches Lake Erie in northwestern Pennsylvania and is about 140 miles north of Pittsburgh. Since Erie is almost equidistant between Cleveland and North Tonawanda and is a connecting hub for several interstate highways, it makes a sensible spot for the firm's home offices.

WGP was started 10 years ago as Woods Producers by its current president and board chairman, Kevin Woods. During the firm's existence, it has enjoyed periods of both moderate and strong growth in sales, assets, and earnings. Key managerial decisions have always been dominated by Woods, who openly boasts of the fact that his company has never suffered a year of negative earnings despite the often cyclical nature of both the retail furniture (RFG) and concrete (CG) divisions.

Recently, Woods decided to acquire a third division for his firm. The division manufactures special machinery for the seafood processing industry and is appropriately called the Seafood Industry Group (SIG). The financial settlement for the acquisition took place yesterday. Currently, the SIG consists of one manufacturing plant in Erie. A single product is to be manufactured, assembled, and shipped from the facility. That product, however, represents a design breakthrough and carries with it a projected contribution margin ratio of .37. This is greater than that enjoyed by either of WGP's other two divisions.

WGP's manufacturing operation in Erie will produce a new machine called "The Picker." The Picker was invented and successfully tested by Eric Klang, the major stockholder and manager of a small seafood processing firm in Floresville, Virginia. Klang plans and supervises all operations at Eastern Shore Processors, which specializes in freezing and pasteurizing crab meat. Freezing and pasteurizing procedures have been a boon to the seafood industry, for they permit the processor to retain his product without spoilage in hopes of higher prices at a later date. In comparing his industry with that of agriculture, Klang aptly states, "The freezer is our grain elevator."

The seafood processing industry is characterized by a notable lack of capital equipment and a corresponding heavy use of human labor. Klang will tell you that at Eastern Shore Processors a skilled crab meat picker will produce about 30 pounds of meat per day. No matter how skilled the human picker, however, he or she will leave about 10 pounds of meat per day in the top pieces of the crab shells. This past year, after five years of trying, Klang perfected a machine that would recover about 30 percent of this otherwise lost meat. In exchange for cash, Eastern Shore Processors sold all rights to The Picker to WGP. Thus, Woods established the SIG and immediately made plans to manufacture The Picker.

--- **EXHIBIT 1** ---

Woods General Producers Retail Furniture Group

Income Statement, December 31, Last Year

	Amount
Sales	$40,000,000
Less: Total variable costs	27,685,000
Revenue before fixed costs	$12,315,000
Less: Total fixed costs	8,612,500
EBIT	$3,702,500
Less: Interest expense	447,500
Earnings before taxes	$3,255,000
Less: Taxes @ 50%	1,627,500
Net profit	$1,627,500

EXHIBIT 2

Woods General Producers Concrete Group

Income Statement, December 31, Last Year

	Amount
Sales	$27,500,000
Less: Total variable costs	22,262,500
Revenue before fixed costs	$5,237,500
Less: Total fixed costs	2,680,000
EBIT	$2,557,500
Less: Interest expense	180,000
Earnings before taxes	$2,377,500
Less: Taxes @ 50%	1,188,750
Net profit	$1,188,750

Recent income statements for the older divisions of WGP are contained in Exhibits 1 and 2. Woods has now decided to assess more fully the probable impact of the decision to establish the SIG upon the financial condition of WGP. He knows that such figures should have been generated prior to the decision to enter this special machinery field, but his seasoned judgment led him to the quick choice. He has requested several pieces of information (see the following questions) from his chief financial officer.

QUESTIONS

1. Using last year's results, determine the break-even point in dollars for WGP (i.e., before investing in the new SIG). The break-even point is defined here in the traditional manner where EBIT = $0. (*Hint:* Use an aggregate contribution margin ratio in your analysis.)

2. Using last year's results, determine what volume of sales must be reached to cover *all* before-tax costs.

3. Next year's sales for the SIG are projected to be $15,000,000. Total fixed costs will be $2,497,500. This division will have no outstanding debt on its balance sheet. WGP uses a 50 percent tax rate in all of its financial projections. Using the format of Exhibits 1 and 2, construct a pro forma income statement for the SIG.

4. After the SIG begins operations, what will be WGP's break-even point in dollars (a) as traditionally defined and (b) reflecting the coverage of *all* before-tax costs? Base the new sales mix on last year's sales performance for the older divisions plus that anticipated next year for the SIG. Using your answer to part (b) of this question, construct an analytical income statement demonstrating that earnings before taxes = $0.

5. Using next year's anticipated sales volume for WGP (including the SIG), compute (a) the degree of operating leverage, (b) the degree of financial leverage, and (c) the degree of combined leverage. Comment on the

meaning of each of these statistics. Refer to questions 3 and 4 for next year's sales.

6. Using projected figures, determine whether acquisition of the SIG will increase or decrease the vulnerability of WGP's earnings before interest and taxes (EBIT) to cyclical swings in sales. Show your work.

7. Review the key assumptions of cost-volume-profit analysis.

CASE 42

Foster Brewing Company

Financial Structure: Overview

The Foster Brewing Company was founded in 1937 by Adolph Foster, who had immigrated to the United States in 1922 at the age of 20. His family owned and operated a brewery in Germany, and by 1937, Foster had attained his goal of establishing a brewery in the United States to carry on the family tradition. During its initial years of operation, the brewery was small and known only locally. However, Foster's insistence on quality caused the reputation of the beer to spread. He had also managed the company well, so even though he insisted on high-quality standards, he had managed to keep operating costs low. It was not unusual to see Adolph Foster roaming through the brewery looking to spot areas that could be run more efficiently. By holding the line on costs, he had kept profits high enough to finance the firm's expansion through internally generated funds.

The Fosters had three sons, Adolph Jr., George, and Frank. Adolph Jr. and Frank had never been interested in the brewing industry and had entered other professions—Adolph Jr. was a practicing attorney in St. Louis, and Frank was a physician who had set up a medical practice in a nearby town. The middle son, George, had agreed to help out with the family business. Although George was the heir apparent to the presidency of the company, Adolph Sr. had refused to relinquish control of operations. When he died suddenly in April 1989, George took over the management of the brewery.

The ownership of Foster Brewing Company was divided into four equal parts: one-quarter to Adolph's widow, Anna, and one-quarter to each of the three sons. Current ownership information is given in Exhibit 1.

After Adolph Sr.'s death, profits began to slide. In 1990, the company had been forced to reduce its generous dividend payment, and in 1991, dividends were suspended until such time as the company began to show a profit again. Exhibits 2 and 3 contain the income statements and balance sheets for the past four years.

It is now February 1992, and the company is in a state of crisis. The Alscan National Bank, with which the company has been doing business for years, has turned down Foster's request for an increase in the amount

---

EXHIBIT 1

Foster Brewing Company

Ownership of Foster Brewing Company

	Anna	Adolph Jr.	George	Frank
Stock in Foster Brewing Co. (book value)	$66,000	$66,000	$66,000	$66,000
Loans to Foster Brewing Co.	6,250	11,250	26,250	11,250
Total	$72,250	$77,250	$92,250	$77,250

EXHIBIT 2

Foster Brewing Company

Income Statements, 1988–1991

	1988	1989	1990	1991
Sales	$900,000	$1,020,000	$1,090,000	$1,050,000
Cost of goods sold	635,000	755,000	850,000	871,000
Excise taxes	54,000	61,000	65,000	63,000
Marketing, administrative, and general expenses	115,000	133,000	142,000	140,000
Operating income	$96,000	$71,000	$33,000	$(24,000)
Interest expense	3,000	6,000	17,000	20,000
Earnings before taxes	$93,000	$65,000	$16,000	$(44,000)
Tax expense (refund)	37,000	26,000	6,000	(18,000)
Net income	$56,000	$39,000	$10,000	$(26,000)
Dividends	$30,000	$30,000	$10,000	—
Earnings available for reinvestment in the firm	26,000	$9,000	—	$(26,000)

EXHIBIT 3

Foster Brewing Company

Balance Sheets, 1988–1991

	1988	1989	1990	1991
Assets				
Cash	$54,000	$61,000	$65,000	$65,000
Accounts receivable	74,000	91,000	93,000	87,000
Inventory	40,000	47,000	71,000	84,000
Current assets	$168,000	$199,000	$229,000	$236,000
Cash value life insurance*	25,000	30,000	35,000	40,000
Plant and equipment	201,000	229,000	276,000	283,000
Total assets	$394,000	$458,000	$540,000	$559,000
Liabilities and Net Worth				
Accounts payable	$36,000	$41,000	$44,000	$42,000
Notes payable, bank	25,000	61,000	133,000	146,000
Notes payable, insurance co.	—	—	—	20,000
Notes payable, loans from family members	25,000	35,000	40,000	55,000
Deferred tax and other accruals	27,000	31,000	33,000	32,000
Current liabilities	$113,000	$168,000	$250,000	$295,000
Common stock, $10 par	100,000	100,000	100,000	100,000
Retained earnings	181,000	190,000	190,000	164,000
Total liabilities and net worth	$394,000	$458,000	$540,000	$559,000

*The company owns life insurance policies on key managers, with itself as beneficiary.

of its note with the bank. Furthermore, the bank is refusing to renew the current note in the amount of $146,000. To receive a short-term line of credit, the company will have to increase its current ratio above 1.5 and reduce its total debt to total assets ratio to the industry average of 40 percent. The bank cited the recent losses and increase in short-term financing as reasons for including a current ratio and total debt covenant in any new short-term financing arrangement. In addition to these problems with the bank, Adolph's widow, Anna Foster, is upset because she is not receiving dividends, which she had counted on to support herself. She has reminded George of the promise that he made in 1990 to restore total dividends to a level of $30,000 as soon as the company showed a profit of more than that amount. In short, the company's recent losses have produced a severe cash shortage that has endangered its relationships with the bank and one of its stockholders.

Since George had already loaned all his available cash to the company, he asked his brothers if they would be willing to increase their loans to the company. The two brothers, however, were reluctant to invest further in what they viewed as a failing family business.

Because of his limited expertise in financial affairs, George hired a consultant, Robert Smith of Financial Consulting Services, to advise the company on how to obtain the necessary financing to continue operations.

Smith immediately recognized that the solution to the company's problems will require some changes in operations to improve profitability. In addition, the company has asked for specific recommendations on how to restructure its liabilities in order to meet the loan covenants its bank is requiring to secure a short-term line of credit. Finally, the company undoubtedly requires additional sources of financing to pay down the current bank note.

To begin his analysis, Smith prepared a table of average ratios for firms of comparable size in the brewing industry (Exhibit 4), planning to use these industry average ratios to spot operating difficulties of the firm and to prepare pro forma income and balance sheets. To fill in the other items on the pro forma statements, Smith looked for typical historical relationships that existed in the past statements. He decided to use the current interest rate level of 11 percent to estimate interest expense. He determined that at the current level of plant and equipment, Foster had sufficient capacity to supply annual sales of approximately $1,230,000. If sales were to exceed this amount, however, the industry average ratios suggest that plant and equipment would have to be increased at a rate of approximately $230 for each additional $1,000 of sales.

--------------------- **EXHIBIT 4** ---------------------

Foster Brewing Company

Average Industry Ratios

Ratio	Average
Current ratio	1.5
Average collection period*	30 days
Inventory turnover†	21.8X
Cost of goods sold as a percentage of sales	71
Marketing, administrative, and general expenses as a percentage of sales	13
Plant and equipment as a percentage of sales	23
Total debt to total assets ratio	40
Dividend payout ratio	42

*Uses a 365-day year.

†Inventory turnover = sales/inventory.

QUESTIONS

1. What areas of operations would you recommend be changed to improve the profitability and financial position of the firm?

2. Prepare a pro forma income and balance sheet for Foster Brewing Company for the next three years. In these pro forma statements, make reasonable assumptions on future sales and working capital requirements. Along with these statements give details of any new sources of financing that you have included in the pro forma balance sheet. Be sure to incorporate a convincing argument as to why the company should be able to obtain these additional sources of capital.

3. What other sources of financing could the firm rely on for reserve borrowing capacity?

CASE 43

J. B. Fuller, Inc.

Financial Leverage Analysis

J. B. Fuller, Inc. (JBFI), is located in Toledo, Ohio. The firm was founded in 1919 by J. B. Fuller, who served as its president and chairman of the board until his death in early 1955. Both positions are now filled by J. J. Fuller, J. B.'s grandson, who is carrying on his grandfather's dogmatic tradition of "high-quality products for a quality industry"—a trademarked phrase that appears in all JBFI's advertisements. Dan Cullinane, vice president of finance, has often argued, formally and informally, against the total emphasis contained in the last four words of that phrase, feeling that by concentrating on supplying component parts solely to the auto industry, the enterprise has assumed an undue exposure to basic business risk.

JBFI manufactures a very wide range of component parts, subassemblies, and final assemblies for sale to the major automobile producers that are largely concentrated 61 miles north in Detroit. Standard items in the product line include hubs, rims, brakes, antiskid units, and mirrors. J. B. Fuller had taken immense pride in all facets of JBFI's activities, ranging from the early decision to locate in Toledo to the firm's solid reputation within key offices in Detroit's Fisher Building. In retrospect, the location decision was a fine one. The expressway that connects Toledo with Detroit makes truck transportation extremely swift. Further, Toledo is located on the west end of Lake Erie and has a good port facility that enables the firm to receive raw materials via marine transportation and to ship finished goods to other key automotive centers, such as Cleveland, across the lake.

The Fuller family interests own 51 percent of the common stock of JBFI. Over the years, outside financing has been almost completely shunned by the organization. The JBFI annual reports for the past four years contain this statement: "We will continue to finance corporate growth primarily through the internal generation of funds." Recent auto industry trends, however, have necessitated a shift by JBFI management away from strict adherence to that policy. A national recession saw last year's motor vehicle factory sales of passenger cars drop 24 percent from the previous annual period. This, in turn, adversely affected the profitability and funds-generating capacity of JBFI. In addition, the officials of JBFI have decided upon a major product mix shift. The firm underestimated the demand for disc brakes, which have been installed on about 84 to 86 percent of passenger cars in recent years (see Exhibit 1). JBFI's capacity to produce in this area will be increased during the coming year. The volume achieved on the sale of antiskid units has proved to be a disappointment. Accordingly, some factory space and equipment devoted to this product line will be used for other, more profitable activities.

Noting the public's acceptance of rear window defoggers, the firm has developed the technology necessary to be competitive in this product. To effect this expertise, however, substantial equipment purchases will be required within the next six months. The end result is that JBFI must raise $10 million in the capital markets through either the sale of new common stock or the issuance of bonds. The new common shares could be sold to net the firm $50 per share. The common stock price of JBFI shares in the marketplace is now $56. Henrie Schmidt, a partner in the investment banking house long used by JBFI, has assured Dan Cullinane that the new bond issue could be placed with a 10 percent interest rate. Schmidt's counsel has

---

EXHIBIT 1

J. B. Fuller, Inc.

Factory Installations of Selected Equipment
(percentage of total units installed upon)

Automobile Equipment	Most Recent Year	One Year Earlier
Power brakes, 4-wheel drum	2.4	1.0
Power brakes, 2- or 4-wheel disc	64.8	74.5
Disc brakes manual	19.2	11.2
Skid control device	0.9	1.9
Rear window defogger	21.5	16.4

Source: 1975 Automobile Facts & Figures, Motor Vehicle Manufacturers Association, p. 21.

always been highly valued by both Cullinane and other members of the JBFI top management team.

A preliminary meeting took place one week ago with Cullinane, Schmidt, and Fuller in attendance. The only topic discussed was the $10 million financing choice facing JBFI. Exhibits 2, 3, and 4 were analyzed at length. Cullinane felt that the firm's owners would benefit if the asset expansion were financed with debt capital. Also, Fuller liked having total control over the firm's operations. With 51 percent of the common shares family owned, Fuller knew that he could personally choose a course of action when a tough situation faced JBFI. The corporate charter of JBFI does not provide for the election of directors via a cumulative voting procedure.

Cullinane pointed out to Fuller that apart from the family, no "public" investor controlled as much as 5 percent of the outstanding common shares. Thus, he noted that effective control of the firm's operations would remain with the Fuller family should the debt alternative be elected. Cullinane did not think it would be prudent to elect the debt alternative *only* because it would ensure Fuller family control over JBFI in the strictest sense.

Both Cullinane and Fuller were concerned about the effect of additional financial leverage on the firm's price-earnings ratio. To deal with this question, Schmidt had his staff prepare Exhibit 4. Schmidt suggested to Fuller that his firm prepare for the "worst that could happen." He stated

---
EXHIBIT 2
J. B. Fuller, Inc.

Abbreviated Balance Sheet, December 31, Last Year

	Amount
Assets	
Current assets	$17,360,000
Net plant and equipment	22,650,000
Other	1,750,000
Total assets	$41,760,000
Liabilities and Equity	
Current liabilities	$ 4,879,000
Long-term debt:	
First mortgage bonds, 20 years	
to maturity, at 9%	3,000,000
Common stock, $5 par	7,500,000
Capital surplus	12,000,000
Retained earnings	14,381,000
Total liabilities and equity	$41,760,000

---------------------------------- EXHIBIT 3 ----------------------------------

J. B. Fuller, Inc.

Income Statement, December 31, Last Year

	Amount
Sales	$125,000,000
Variable costs	91,250,000
Fixed costs (excluding interest)	13,239,000
Interest expense	270,000
Earnings before taxes	$ 20,241,000
Taxes @ 40%	8,096,400
Net profit	$ 12,144,600

---------------------------------- EXHIBIT 4 ----------------------------------

J. B. Fuller, Inc.

Main Competitors' Selected Financial Relationships

Firm	Debt Ratio*	TIER†	P/E Ratio‡
Atlas Auto Components	32.7%	7	4.2
Autonite	20.1	38	6.2
Kalsey-Ways Ltd.	24.2	14	5.7
L-G Parts	26.8	14	5.7
Morgan-Wells, Inc.	19.0	29	7.7
Simple average	24.6%	20.4	5.9

*Total debt divided by total assets.
†Times interest earned ratio.
‡Price-earnings ratio.

that JBFI's price-earnings ratio might remain unchanged from its present level of 6.03 times if the debt alternative were chosen. He did not, however, believe such an occurrence to be highly likely. Schmidt's best guess was that JBFI's price-earnings ratio would fall to 5.91 times if bonds were sold and would rise to 6.13 times if the common stock alternative were selected.

Prior to taking the question before the entire board of directors, Fuller wanted to review a more substantial body of analysis with Cullinane and Schmidt. He gave Cullinane a week to prepare the information requested in the following questions.

QUESTIONS

1. Dan Cullinane has projected that the firm's variable cost to sales ratio will be .70 after the $10 million expansion is effected. In addition, fixed costs apart from interest will rise to an annual level of $15.0 million. These

assumptions hold for the remaining questions. Calculate the level of sales that will equate earnings per share regardless of whether the subject $10 million is financed with bonds or common stock.

2. Set up income statements for bond financing and common stock financing by using the sales volume given and demonstrate that earnings per share will indeed be the same under the assumed conditions.

3. Use last year's results as the base period. Compute earnings per share under each financing alternative for sales levels equal to (a) 60 percent, (b) 80 percent, (c) 100 percent, (d) 110 percent, and (e) 120 percent of the base period results.

4. Using the price-earnings ratios suggested by Henrie Schmidt, project the common stock prices for each financing choice at the sales levels just analyzed.

5. Again taking Schmidt's "best guess" price-earnings ratios, determine the sales level that will equate market price per share regardless of the financing source chosen.

6. After reviewing recent marketing department forecasts of sales levels, J. J. Fuller concluded, "Rarely will JBFI experience revenues below the $90.2 million mark." If Fuller is correct, which financing alternative do you recommend?

CASE 44

DeSmedt-Baker, Inc.

Leverage Analysis

In 1969, after graduating from college with a degree in chemistry, Bob DeSmedt took a job as a sales representative for a large chemical supply firm. While this job was relatively well-paying, particularly given DeSmedt's sales skills, it just wasn't satisfying. As a result, he looked closely for an opportunity to start his own business.

In his interaction with various clients, DeSmedt noticed there was a shortage of propylene gycol, a gelatin used in stick deodorants. Moreover, he felt the price charged for propylene gycol was excessive, given its chemical makeup. Feeling that this was the chance of a lifetime, in 1970 he summoned one of his college chums, Rhody Baker, who had a background in chemical engineering, and together they started Phi Alpha Chemicals.

The two men borrowed and mortgaged all they could to raise the funds to build a plant to produce propylene gycol. Initially, this was Phi Alpha's only product, and the company's main customers were deodorant makers. Propylene gycol is the primary gelatin to which sodium stearate and perfumes are added to produce antiperspirants like Right-Guard, Speed Stick, and Power Stick. Over time, Phi Alpha became the primary supplier of propylene gycol in the United States. In addition, it branched out to produce other chemical compounds, primarily for use in the health-care industry.

During the 1980s, the company continued to grow at a steady pace, and finally, in 1987, Phi Alpha was sold to a large conglomerate. DeSmedt and Baker continued to do research in the area, however, and in early 1992, they were ready to form a new company, DeSmedt-Baker Inc., to market one of their new developments. This new product, which DeSmedt developed, is an antiperspirant compound that goes on dry without leaving the chalky white residue that characterizes aluminum zirconium tetra-chlorohydrexgyl, the most commonly used antiperspirant compound. Moreover, the compound he developed, which he named OWU, was significantly less expensive than aluminum zirconium. Another major reason DeSmedt felt that OWU would be able to displace aluminum zirconium as the active ingredient of choice in antiperspirants concerned the possible health hazards associated with the use of aluminum. Specifically, similarities between Alzheimer's disease and aluminum toxicity have led to some speculation that there is a causal relationship between them.

While no one is quite sure what causes Alzheimer's disease, a number of potential suspects, including genetic makeup, viruses, the effect of aging on the body's immune system, and environmental toxins—specifically, aluminum—have come under investigation. The debate over the relationship between aluminum and Alzheimer's disease is fierce and undecided, although most evidence seems to suggest a lack of causality. Those who feel there is no connection cite the fact that Alzheimer's disease is characterized by brain atrophy, which in the later stages can be recognized by the naked eye. With aluminum toxicity (encephalopathy), on the other hand, the brain appears to be macroscopically normal and the senile plaques that are characteristic of Alzheimer's disease are absent. Moreover, although neurofibrillary tangles are present in both Alzheimer's disease and aluminum toxicity, they differ significantly: those in patients with aluminum toxicity are made up of normal neurofibril fibers, whereas those in people with Alzheimer's disease are distinctly abnormal. On the other side of the debate are those who point to aluminum as a cofactor in the development of Alzheimer's disease. While this may not support a linkage between the two, it surely suggests at least the possibility of a relationship.

Suspicion that there is a relationship between aluminum and Alzheimer's disease originated in the early 1970s, when Dr. Ronald McLachlan, a neurologist at the University of Toronto, found high levels of aluminum in the brain tissue of patients with Alzheimer's disease. More recent studies in France and England have shown a prevalence of Alzheimer's disease in areas with high amounts of aluminum in the drinking water. Other support for a linkage between the two comes from studies in which aluminum injected into the brains of rabbits caused pathological changes and the finding that patients on dialysis have developed dementia or memory loss and other impairments of brain functions when the aluminum concentration in the water used to prepare the dialysis solution was too high. Finally, a clinical experiment recently conducted by McLachlan suggests that removing aluminum from the brains of people with Alzheimer's disease can slow the rate of mental deterioration by 50 percent.

In summary, while some well-respected experts strongly believe there is absolutely no causal relationship between Alzheimer's disease and aluminum, other equally well-respected experts believe a causal relationship does exist. While the jury is still out on this question, enough concern has been raised to convince DeSmedt that there would be considerable consumer interest in a product that avoids these potential health concerns. As he says, "Why should you be exposed to something that you think might be harmful when it is not necessary? It's this health concern that should let us displace aluminum as the active ingredient of choice in antiperspirants."

Test marketing of OWU, which was based on very limited production, has shown a strong customer preference for an aluminum-free antiperspirant, particularly when customers are informed about the possible dangers associated with aluminum. Unfortunately, producing OWU at an economically feasible level requires a significant investment in plant and equipment. Moreover, while a number of health-care firms have expressed considerable interest in this new product, DeSmedt-Baker has received no firm orders for it. Thus, this is a somewhat risky venture since it is impossible to forecast with certainty what future demand will be, although DeSmedt and Baker have been able to determine sales estimates for 1993 (Exhibit 1).

In order to produce OWU efficiently at the expected future sales level, it would be necessary to build a new plant and purchase specially designed equipment. The expected cash outlay associated with this, including additions to working capital, is $20 million, irrespective of the choice of method of production. The choices DeSmedt and Baker face in funding this outlay are either to sell common stock or to sell some combination of common stock and bonds.

If they decide to go ahead with the project, DeSmedt and Baker next face questions regarding the production method. Because of the complex nature of OWU, the production process is made up of 27 distinct production steps. DeSmedt and Baker have identified two feasible production

----

EXHIBIT 1

Sales Estimates for OWU in Pounds

Probability	Sales in Pounds
5%	20,000
20%	60,000
50%	75,000
20%	90,000
5%	130,000

plans. *Plan 1* involves a fully automated production facility and a minimum number of employees. Fixed costs would be $10 million per year, primarily for the leasing of specially designed robotics equipment. The variable costs would be $90 per pound of OWU, while the selling price would be $300 per pound. *Plan 2* calls for considerably less automation. Fixed costs would run to $3 million per year and variable costs of OWU would be $210 per pound. Under either of these production plans, the expected sales price would remain constant at $300 per pound. Given the amount of OWU that would be used in each stick of antiperspirant, this would make OWU slightly less expensive than aluminum zirconium.

In addition to settling on a method of production, DeSmedt and Baker must decide exactly how this expansion is to be financed. On September 11, 1992, a board meeting was called to discuss the two options. At that meeting, those present, in addition to DeSmedt and Baker, were John Gladfelter of the financial consulting firm of Swabby Associates, Edgar Boles of the law firm of Boles and Associates, and Tom Hatch, founder of the Pink Pork Barbecue Pit franchise.

As the discussion began, Gladfelter clearly became the advocate for financing the expansion through the issuance of additional debt, on the grounds that long-term debt is generally less expensive than other forms of financing because (1) investors view debt as a relatively safe investment alternative, and therefore demand a lower rate of return; and (2) interest expenses are tax deductible. In addition, he noted that since payments to bondholders are limited to interest, they would not participate in any extraordinary profits that might result from this project. Finally, he observed that since bondholders do not have voting rights, there would not be any potential challenge to the management resulting from the issuance of debt. Gladfelter then went on to state that as the economy continued its recovery, inflation and interest rates would rise, making this an ideal time to issue debt at what might be historically low rates. Moreover, he felt that the LBO boom of the 1980s had brought about a fundamental change in what investors viewed as an appropriate debt level; investors were now much more willing to accept higher debt levels and, in fact, were demanding them. For all these reasons, he argued that financing the new company largely with debt was totally warranted.

Boles disagreed sharply with Gladfelter, stating that to go primarily with debt financing at this point would be less than prudent. First, he disputed Gladfelter's contention that investors preferred companies with more debt. In fact, he stated, firms with higher debt ratios tend to have lower price-earnings ratios. To prove his point, he provided a schedule containing the estimated relationship between long-term debt and total capitalization (Exhibit 2). After a bit of discussion, Gladfelter agreed with Boles that this relationship did in fact hold.

—————————— **EXHIBIT 2** ——————————

Relationship Between the Long-Term Debt to Total Capitalization Ratio and the Firm's P/E Ratio

LT Debt/Total Capitalization	P/E Ratio
0.0% to 50.0%	16.00 times
50.1% to 65.0%	14.00 times
65.1% to 80.0%	9.75 times
80.1% to 95.0%	8.00 times

From that point on, much of Boles's argument in favor of issuing stock centered around his fear of too much leverage and the associated risks. For example, if sales did not reach expectations, Boles stated, the firm would still be obligated to make its interest payments. However, if common stock was issued, there would be no legal obligation to pay common stock dividends. Boles further argued that because common stock has no maturity date, the firm does not have a cash outflow associated with its redemption. However, if desired, the firm can repurchase its stock in the open market. Thus, Boles stressed, common stock would give them a level of flexibility that could not be achieved if the project was financed with debt. Finally, Boles commented on the effect financing with common stock would have on the future financing flexibility of the firm. He stated that by financing with common stock, the financial base of the firm would be expanded, thereby increasing its borrowing capacity. On the other hand, a debt offering at this time, he felt, would preclude any future debt offerings until the existing equity base was expanded. Boles's closing comments dealt with the direction of future interest rates. Here again, his opinion conflicted with Gladfelter's: he felt interest rates were still on their way down.

As the meeting closed, there was no clear consensus as to what should be done. Tom Hatch thought that more information was needed before a decision could be made. Specifically, the riskiness of the alternative plans and the effect of financing with debt versus stock needed to be analyzed. Your assignment is to provide DeSmedt and Baker with the information they need to choose between the two plans of production and to decide on the best method of financing.

QUESTIONS

1. Should DeSmedt and Baker produce OWU using the highly automated production plan or the less highly automated production plan involving lower fixed costs? To answer this question, examine the degree of operating leverage for each production method. In addition, determine the

expected level of earnings before interest and taxes and the break-even point for each production plan.

2. How might the proposed financing method interact with the decision on which production plan is most appropriate? To answer this question, calculate the degree of operating leverage and degree of combined leverage for each production plan, assuming first that the new project is financed with a mix of 90 percent debt carrying a 15 percent interest rate and 10 percent common stock, and then that it is financed totally with stock. Discuss how the relationship between the choice of a method of production and the method of financing affects the degree of combined leverage.

3. The question now becomes how to finance the new project. First, let us assume that the product cannot be produced at a high enough quality to be attractive to the health-care industry if it is not produced using the more automated method. Therefore, Baker and DeSmedt have decided to go ahead with the more automated plan, which involves fixed costs of $10 million per year. Before OWU can be produced, a new plant must be built, which involves an initial outlay of $20 million. These funds can be raised by issuing either common stock or a combination of common stock and bonds. Given the current market price of DeSmedt-Baker's stock, it is estimated that a new issue will net $35 per share—regardless of how much stock is issued.

    If debt is issued, it is not clear exactly what the interest rate associated with the debt offering would be. In talking to investment bankers, DeSmedt and Baker have discovered that the interest rate on the new debt would vary according to how much debt they decide to issue. Specifically, they found the following relationship between the interest rate on new debt and the total level of new borrowing:

Total Level of New Borrowing	Before-Tax Interest Rate on Total Amount of Funds Borrowed
$0.00–$ 9.0 million	10.00%
$9.01–$12.0 million	11.00%
$12.01–$15.0 million	14.00%
$15.01–$18.0 million	19.00%

In determining how best to finance the new project, assume that a minimum of $9 million of debt must be issued and that a maximum of $18 million in debt can be raised, and that the debt can only be raised in $3 million increments. To help in deciding how best to finance this project, determine the stock price, assuming first that no new debt is issued, then that $9 million of debt is issued, $12 million, $15 million, and finally, $18 million. In doing this, first determine the number of shares that will be outstanding (this will be used to determine the EPS); then determine the firm's price-earnings ratio (this is determined by the long-term debt to total capitalization ratio); finally, determine the firm's EPS, which is equal to: (expected EBIT − interest payments) (1 − tax rate) / (number of shares outstanding). You can assume that the federal and state tax rate is 40 percent.

4. DeSmedt and Baker intend to invest all their savings in this new company. How might this fact influence the financing decisions discussed in question 3?

5. If DeSmedt and Baker diversify their savings in other securities and investments in addition to investing in the new company, how would this fact influence the decisions discussed in question 3?

6. In making these kinds of decisions, how would the type or method of compensation received by the decision makers affect the outcome of their decisions? For example, consider the effect of all management compensation being in the form of stock options, with the exercise price set above the current market price of the stock.

CASE 45

Colorado Business Instruments

Long-Term Financing Choices

Eric Knutson was hired by Colorado Business Instruments (CBI) 10 months ago as an assistant to comptroller Doug Fisher. Since that time, his main task has been to analyze the profitability of CBI's various products. At the completion of this project, Knutson asked to be given a more challenging assignment, and as a result, on December 1, 1991, he was given the task of analyzing the various proposals that have been suggested for raising $28 million in additional funds in the capital market needed for the production and promotion of some new products.

CBI was founded in Ann Arbor, Michigan, in 1894 by Mike Bellich to produce manual typewriters. Through the 1920s, CBI grew at a rapid pace, expanding its product line to include manual calculators and improving and expanding its typewriter line. With the business slowdown of the 1930s, CBI's growth stopped and did not begin again until the early 1950s. At that time, CBI went through a major change in both its management personnel and its product line, resulting in five years of strong company growth. Electric typewriters and calculators replaced their manual counterparts as CBI's major products, and extensive research was done into computer applications in these fields. After 10 years of moderate stagnation in sales, this research paid off in the late 1960s, resulting in a strong growth pattern once again. This growth pattern, which continued through the 1980s, was largely a result of CBI's increased emphasis on the calculator and computer markets.

Although the new growth was encouraging, it has not been very stable, especially during the 1990–1991 recession, when CBI's earnings dropped sharply. As a result of this profit instability, CBI had in recent years a low price-earnings ratio relative to other growth stocks in the market, in spite of the fact that CBI had shown above-average growth for seven years (see Exhibits 1 and 2). However, from discussions with several Wall Street analysts, Fisher has come to believe that if CBI could show a strong comeback from the 1990–1991 slowdown, indicating that it has returned to its earning ways of the past several years, the stock would be looked upon favorably by investors. This could perhaps result in a doubling of the firm's price-earnings ratio. As the current need for funds is directly related to

EXHIBIT 1

Colorado Business Instruments

Comparative Industry Price-Earning Ratios, 1984–1991

Year	CBI's Average P/E Ratio	Industry Average P/E Ratio	Industry Average P/E Ratio for Companies Exhibiting a 20% Compound Growth Rate in EPS over the Past 7 Years
1991	16.76	9.53	31.46
1990	11.64	6.91	25.24
1989	19.81	17.46	37.42
1988	20.16	19.22	39.25
1987	19.74	18.72	38.91
1986	17.60	17.64	38.71
1985	15.63	17.26	36.12
1984	14.91	17.80	35.56

EXHIBIT 2

Colorado Business Instruments

CBI's Stock Performance, 1984–1991

Year	Average Common Stock Price	Earnings per Share	Dividend per Share
1991	$60.00	$3.58	$1.00
1990	30.61	2.63	.90
1989	64.97	3.28	.88
1988	53.42	2.65	.74
1987	41.85	2.12	.60
1986	29.39	1.67	.47
1985	20.32	1.30	.37
1984	15.21	1.02	.29

CBI's movement into the mini- and desk computer field, it is felt that these products will generate the strong earnings necessary to boost CBI's share price substantially. For this reason, Fisher is somewhat hesitant about issuing additional common stock at a price that is, in his opinion, temporarily depressed. He feels that if the issuance of common stock can be postponed for two years, the stock price may well be doubled, allowing CBI to raise the necessary capital by issuing only half the number of shares currently required. Fisher is quite confident of this, since the 1992 expected level of EBIT is $16 million, whereas the 1994 expected level of EBIT is $22 million, and there is only a minor chance (10 percent) of nonacceptance of the new mini- and desk computer. Even if the mini- and desk computer do meet resistance, it is estimated that the 1994 EBIT cannot fall below $14 million. Moreover, Fisher has stated that to reach an acceptable price-earnings level, the company has adopted a firm policy of not lowering dividends per share regardless of the profit level in that year; this policy is an attempt to make the stock more appealing to institutional investors.

Complicating the financing question is the fact that CBI currently has proportionally more debt in its capital structure than do other companies in the same industry (see Exhibit 3). Through conversations with Fisher, Eric Knutson learned that even though interest rates appear to be at an attractive level, falling substantially from their 1990 peaks, and while it would be possible to raise current funds through the issuance of long-term debt, Fisher feels that this would prohibit the issuance of any additional debt prior to a substantial increase in equity capital and would therefore reduce CBI's future financing flexibility (see Exhibits 4 and 5). This is due to the potentially unfavorable effect of excess long-term debt on CBI's bond rating and its common stock price. CBI's long-term debt problem is magnified by the fact that the company, in effect, considers preferred stock to be a form of subordinated debt, refusing ever to pass a preferred stock dividend.

The decision as to how to finance the $28 million in new funds is further complicated by the fact that in three years CBI will again have to

---
EXHIBIT 3

Colorado Business Instruments

Comparative Capital Structures, December 1, 1991

Capital Structure	CBI Distribution	Industry Average, Business Instruments Companies Distribution
Debt	52%	45%
Preferred stock	14	15
Common stock and earned surplus	34	40

---------------------------- **EXHIBIT 4** ----------------------------

Colorado Business Instruments

Balance Sheet as of December 1, 1991
(thousands)

	1991
Assets	
Cash	$ 10,000
Accounts receivable	14,000
Inventory	29,000
Total current assets	$ 53,000
Fixed assets, net	56,000
Deferred charges	1,000
Total assets	$110,000
Liabilities and Net Worth	
Accounts payable	$ 1,300
Accruals	1,200
Taxes payable	1,500
Total current liabilities	4,000
Long-term debt outstanding	$ 55,000
(sold at par due 1999, 6.0%, no sinking fund requirements)	
Preferred stock	15,000
($6.00 cumulative, $100 par)	
Common stock (985,000 shares outstanding)	985
Paid-in capital	15,015
Retained earnings	20,000
Total liabilities and net worth	$110,000

---

tap the financial markets for an additional $28 million. Although the need for current funds is related to CBI's movement into the mini- and desk computer market, the additional funds needed in three years will be primarily related to the company's introduction and promotion of product line improvements.

Currently, CBI has several improved automatic copy-typewriters nearing the final development stage. Production of these products is not scheduled to begin until early 1995, but $28 million in outside funding will be needed in three years to purchase the specialized production equipment. Production could be postponed somewhat and the equipment introduced at a slower speed, but that would quite possibly allow the competition to develop substitutes, thus drastically reducing the potential profitability of the product.

CBI plans to engage the services of an investment banker in offering

———————————— **EXHIBIT 5** ————————————

Colorado Business Instruments

Statement of Income
Fiscal Year Ended December 1, 1991
(thousands)

	1991
Net sales	$77,462
Cost of goods sold	53,524
Selling, general, and administrative expense	11,782
EBIT	$12,156
Interest	3,300
Income before taxes	$ 8,856
Taxes	4,428
Earnings after taxes	$ 4,428
Preferred stock dividends	900
Earnings available to common stockholders	$ 3,528
Shares outstanding (985,000)	985
Earnings per common share (in dollars)	$3.58

its proposed issue to the public, but management has decided to solicit the investment banking services on a competitive bid rather than on a negotiated bid basis. Thus, it will be necessary for CBI to assemble the new offering prior to inviting bids from investment bankers. After CBI has assembled the security package, it will sell it to an investment banker, who will, in turn, sell the securities to the public. With this in mind, Fisher has already solicited the opinion of several of his staff members as to the appropriate design of the new issue and has compiled a list of four possible alternatives. It is Knutson's job to review and evaluate these alternatives critically and to provide Fisher with a recommended strategy for raising the necessary funds in the capital market.

The four alternatives to be evaluated by Eric Knutson are as follows:

1. Rather than offer common stock directly to the public, CBI could offer the new common stock to the current shareholders on a privileged subscription basis. This action is not required by CBI's corporate charter, but it has been argued by several of Fisher's assistants that as the common stock is currently selling for what is considered to be a depressed price, this alternative would allow existing shareholders to maintain their proportionate ownership or benefit from the sale of the rights, thus keeping the shareholders happy. Under this proposal, CBI would issue additional stock through a rights offering with a price of $48 per share. The expected flotation costs would amount to approximately $1 per share for each share successfully subscribed to.

2. Alternatively, CBI could offer common stock directly to the public. Under this plan, new shares would be sold to the public at a price of $57 per share with underwriting costs amounting to $2 per share.

3. A third possibility for raising new funds is through the issue of 10-year 5½ percent nonconvertible debentures. These could be issued at par with 2 percent of the par value going to the investment banker in return for performing the tasks of distribution and underwriting the issue. This issue would include a sinking fund requirement of $4,000,000 per year due every year, with the first payment due three years after the issue is floated.

4. Finally, CBI could raise the needed funds through the issuance of 10-year 5 percent convertible subordinated debentures callable at 107, which could be sold at par with 2 percent of the par value going to the investment banker in return for services. These bonds would be convertible at $75 a share after one year. This conversion price would hold for two years and then rise to $90 per share, and subsequently increase $10 per share every three years until maturity. If the bonds were not converted after three years, a sinking fund requirement of $4,000,000 per year would become effective.

Knutson was given two days in which to prepare his recommended strategy as to the proper method CBI should undertake to raise the necessary funds in the capital market. He was instructed by Fisher to consider the obvious risk-return trade-offs in addition to the effect of the current decision on future financing.

QUESTIONS

1. What factors should be considered in making the financing decision faced by CBI? Discuss each briefly.

2. To raise the needed $28 million, how many shares of stock must be sold under the rights offering proposal, assuming all shares are subscribed?

3. Compute the number of rights required to buy a share of stock.

4. Compute the value of a right when the stock is selling at $60 per share rights-on.

5. Compute the value of the stock when it goes ex-rights.

6. Is it likely they will all be exercised?

7. Under alternative 2, how many new shares of common stock must be issued to raise the needed $28 million?

8. What is the initial conversion ratio of the convertibles proposed in alternative 4?

9. What is the initial conversion value of each debenture? What is the meaning of this value?

10. How many shares must be issued if all debentures are converted at the initial conversion price?

11. What is the purpose of the stepped-up conversion prices?

12. For the EBIT level of $16 million, calculate the earnings per share for

each of the alternative methods of financing: assume a 50 percent tax rate and that conversion of the convertibles (a) has not taken place and (b) has taken place at the $75 conversion price.

13. Examine the interest coverage ratio for 1992 and 1994, assuming an expected EBIT level in 1992 of $16,000,000 and in 1994 an expected EBIT level of $22,000,000, with the minimum possible level of $14,000,000. Are there any modifications in this ratio that might be interesting? If additional information were available, what other ratios might be interesting?

14. Which financing alternative identified in the case would serve the best interests of CBI? Might any other methods be considered?

CASE 46

Richardo Oil and Gas Corporation

Lease versus Purchase Analysis

Since its formation in 1983, the Richardo Oil and Gas Corporation (ROGC) has experienced rapid growth in both the scope of its operations and its earnings. The company was started by Malcom and John Richards after both spent several years working in oil and gas exploration. The firm enjoyed almost immediate success with discoveries made in the Marston Field and The Delaware Basin (both located in West Texas).

ROGC faces bright prospects for future development, with over 1 million acres of undeveloped oil leases under contract. Exhibit 1 contains a brief historical description of the firm's investment in undeveloped oil leases. In addition, ROGC plans to spend more than $80 million on exploration and development over the next four years.

The firm has a 65 percent working interest in a 2,000-acre block in Brazos County. The field is relatively unexplored, with only one test well underway at the present time. However, geologists' reports indicate the existence of a promising layer of oil sand at about 4,000 feet. Thus, ROGC plans to drill relatively shallow wells in the field. Most of the firm's previous operations have involved wells of 12,000 to 18,000 feet in depth. To drill to these depths requires the use of much larger and more expensive drilling rigs than are required for shallower wells. In fact, recent developments in the technology of the drilling industry have produced a portable rig (called Porta-Drill) that is capable of drilling to depths of 8,000 feet. The

---------------- EXHIBIT 1 ----------------

Richardo Oil and Gas Corporation

Undeveloped Oil Leases, 1983–1988

Year	Undeveloped Acres	Investment
1983	201,119	$ 3,755,000
1984	202,140	3,911,000
1985	486,101	7,446,000
1986	628,429	9,821,000
1987	940,020	13,633,000
1988	1,201,000	18,000,000

---------------- EXHIBIT 2 ----------------

Richardo Oil and Gas Corporation

Porta-Drill Cost of Operating Information

Base price (drilling rig only)	$2,250,000
Shipping	4,000
Options:	
Mud tanks	30,000
Heavy-duty diesel engine	6,000
Four-ton tractor	18,000
Total	$2,308,000

principal advantages of such a rig are (1) its lower initial cost, (2) the speed with which it can be put into place and dismantled after the well has been drilled, and (3) the smaller crew required to operate the rig while it is running. In addition, it can be easily transported from one field to another. The major disadvantages associated with the rig relate to the limitation on the depth to which it can drill and the speed with which it can drill through rock formations.

ROGC is currently considering the acquisition of a Porta-Drill. Cost information is found in Exhibit 2. The firm feels that the $2,308,000 figure is very close to the actual cost of acquiring the portable rig and getting it into operation. However, there is some question as to whether the Porta-Drill represents an economically feasible investment. ROGC's cost analysts estimate that the smaller rig will last for 10 years and produce cash flow savings of $506,236 per year over the use of the firm's larger drilling rigs. In addition, the Porta-Drill is estimated to be worth $15,000 as scrap at the end of its 10-year life. The estimated cost savings are based on savings over current operating costs for the firm's larger drilling rigs and the assumption that the firm will have a need for the shallow-drilling Porta-Drill throughout the next 10 years.

ROGC utilizes an 18 percent required return on investments in its drilling operations. In addition, it uses a target financing mix consisting of 30 percent debt and 70 percent owner-supplied capital. At present, the firm is borrowing its funds at an annual rate of 12 percent and faces a tax rate on income of 30 percent.

ROGC is also considering the possibility of leasing the Porta-Drill. The First Bank and Trust of Mariwell, Texas, has offered, through its lease company subsidiary (Leasequip, Inc.), to lease the drilling rig to ROGC for $375,000 per year. The lease arrangement would cover the full 10-year expected life of the drilling rig and includes insurance premiums and maintenance valued at $4,800 per year.

QUESTIONS

1. Calculate the net present value of acquiring the Porta-Drill unit. Should the asset's services be acquired via the purchase arrangement?

2. Calculate the net advantage in leasing the Porta-Drill. Is the lease favored over the purchase option? Discuss. (You may assume the use of straight-line depreciation.)

CASE 47

Hamlin Duplicating Company

Lease versus Purchase Decision

Hamlin Duplicating Company, Inc. (HDC), is a leading copying company in Fort Myers, Florida. It was founded 22 years ago by Skip and Marvin Hamlin. The brothers had both had difficulty in college duplicating class materials, so after they graduated, they had the idea to found a business based on duplicating materials for college courses. This service was particularly useful for professors who wished to use their own materials in classrooms or who required large quantities of duplicated materials. Colleges and universities encouraged their professors to use Hamlin's services since students paid the duplication expenses by purchasing materials directly from Hamlin.

Hamlin also catered to local businesses by providing duplication of all kinds of promotional materials. However, the commercial side of the business represented only 27 percent of revenue and 38 percent of income before interest and taxes. Hamlin grew and by 19x0 had franchises in 97 locations.

In 19x0, Skip Hamlin was considering the purchase of new duplicating machine that would triple the duplicating speed of the company. The new machine was also capable of duplicating in multicolors, collating, stapling, and binding. Skip estimated that it would increase the firm's revenue through higher job productivity. The first year's added revenue was estimated to be $75,000; thereafter, revenues would increase by the rate of inflation, 5 percent.

Since the machine could be programmed by the operator and then left to complete a job, only one fully trained operator would be required to maintain the entire print facility. Thus, purchase of the machine would save $79,000 in salaries and benefits. The capital budgeting analysis indicated that the purchase of the machine had an internal rate of return of 16.2 percent over four years. Since the company used a 12.7 percent after-tax cost of capital for projects of such low risk, the project clearly was worth undertaking.

The machine had an invoice price of $1,250,000, including delivery, installation, and training. The asset would be depreciated over three years using MACRS (thus, annual depreciation rates of 33, 45, 14, and 7 percent, respectively, were required). The net financing required for the system, if Hamlin borrows the money, would be the purchase price borrowed from South Florida National Bank on a four-year amortized note. The loan would carry an interest rate of 11.5 percent with annual principal and interest payments. If Hamlin purchases the equipment, the manufacturer will provide maintenance service for a fee of $75,000 per year.

The machine is expected to have a useful life of six years at the rate at which Hamlin will use it, and Marvin Hamlin is concerned that the purchase will lock the company into using equipment that will be obsolete in four years or less. Lease Plan, Inc., the manufacturer, has a plan that allows a client to lease the duplicator for four years. This lease requires an annual payment of $425,000, payable at the beginning of the year, and also provides for maintenance.

In four years, Lease Plan should be able to sell the machine to a smaller company that does not require leading-edge equipment. The selling price at that time is estimated to be $65,000. Lease Plan views leasing as an alternative to lending the funds at 11.5 percent. Lease Plan has a marginal tax rate of 38 percent. Hamlin, however, is a much smaller company, so its marginal tax rate is only 20 percent.

If you were Skip and Marvin Hamlin, would you purchase or lease the equipment?

QUESTIONS*

1. Calculate the net present value of leasing and purchasing the equipment from the Hamlin brothers' point of view. Compute the net advantage to leasing. Do you recommend that Hamlin purchase or lease the equipment?

*The spreadsheet model is named "HAMLIN.wk1."

2.   To the nearest $10, what lease payment would make Hamlin indifferent between leasing and purchasing?

3.   Skip Hamlin recognizes that the analysis is influenced by the selection of the uncertain residual value of the duplicator in year 4. The equipment could be worth the values below. Perform a scenario analysis using these data. How does this information affect your recommendation?

Residual Value	Probability
$10,000	.20
$65,000	.40
$100,000	.20

4.   Suppose you learned that Hamlin's tax rate was about to increase substantially. What effect would this have on your analysis? (*Hint:* Use a data table to evaluate the effect of differing tax rates.)

5.   Interest rates have been very volatile lately. Skip Hamlin thinks that rates could increase to 12.5 percent or decrease to 10.5 percent within the next few weeks. He also expects the lease payment to change if the interest rates change. The table below illustrates his expectations. Analyze the effects of potential interest rate changes. (Maintain the tax rate and residual value at their expected levels.)

Interest Rate	Lease Payment
10.5%	$400,000
11.5	425,000
12.5	450,000

6.   Evaluate the lease from Lease Plan's point of view. What are the net present value and internal rate of return?

7.   Perform a scenario analysis on the lease using various residual values and tax rates for Lease Plan.

8.   To the nearest $10, at what payment does Lease Plan earn exactly 11.5 percent? Use the original residual value and tax rate.

9.   What is the range of negotiation on the lease payment?

CASE 48

Barringer Fabricators, Inc.

Refunding a Bond Issue

Seven years ago, Barringer Fabricators, Inc., entered the tire recapping business by acquiring an old line recapping firm. Since that time, Barringer has expanded its recapping operations, making major inroads into the "off-the-road" vehicle field. In March, Barringer reported earnings of $1.15 per share for the fiscal year just ended, with over 85 percent of its sales attributable to the firm's recapping operations.

Prospects for future growth look particularly good for Barringer in light of the fact that the firm holds exclusive rights to a newly patented "hot capping" process (Bondtread), which, according to informed industry sources, will revolutionize the off-the-road tire recapping business. Bondtread boasts lower cost and roughly the same performance characteristics as the conventional "cold process." The new process achieves its cost savings through the use of a less expensive rubber compound and reduced handling. The tire is coated, bonded, and patterned in a single revolution through the machine.

Barringer's recapping business has led to a marked improvement in the financial posture of the firm over the past five years. In conjunction with the company's improved financial stature, the general easing of credit conditions has resulted in a drastic lowering in the cost of borrowed funds to the firm. In May 1970, for example, Barringer issued $10 million of first mortgage bonds. These bonds carried a 9¼ percent rate of interest and were not callable for a period of five years after issuance.[1] In the five years since the bond issue, Barringer's bond rating has improved from Baa to A (Moody's Investor Service). Combined, these factors have resulted in a lowering of the cost of new debt to an estimated 8 percent.

The lower cost of new debt funds was brought to the attention of Barringer's management by the investment banking house that handled the 1970 bond issue. The rather substantial (125-basis-point) reduction in borrowing cost along with the expiration of the five-year delayed call on the outstanding issue, according to the investment banker, make the refunding of the issue worth considering by Barringer. Since Barringer has never refunded a public offering, the firm's management has a number of serious questions and misgivings concerning both how the refunding should be analyzed and whether it should be undertaken even if it is found to be profitable.

--------------------------------- EXHIBIT 1 ---------------------------------

Barringer Fabricators, Inc.

Bond Indenture Characteristics

The outstanding issue had the following characteristics:

Coupon rate	9¼ percent
Par value	$1,000
Issue size	$10 million
Due date	May 15, 2000
Call premium	One year's interest in the first year in which the bonds are callable and declining by ½ percent per year until the eighteenth year and zero thereafter
Unamortized discount	$500,000
Unamortized issue expense	$100,000

The corresponding characteristics of the refunding issue are as follows:

Coupon rate	8 percent
Par value (also the price at which the bonds are expected to be sold)	$1,000
Due date	May 15, 2000
Underwriter's spread	1½ percent of the face value of the issue plus a $400,000 fee
Overlap period (during which time both the old and new issues will be outstanding)	2 months
Return on Treasury bill investment during the overlap period	6 percent

---

[1]Pertinent information regarding the outstanding issue and the refunding issue is found in Exhibit 1.

J. J. Bows, Barringer's financial vice president, felt that the refunding probably would be profitable, but was concerned over the path of interest rates in the months to come. His chief concern was that the firm would give up the opportunity to refund at a more desirable time in the future if delayed-call bonds were sold at the present time. The firm had had to live for five years with the 9¼ percent bonds because of the delayed-call provision, and Bows wanted to be very sure that the firm was making the right move before any action was taken.

Bow's assistant, Jerry Wilson, was not convinced that the current refunding was in the best interests of the firm. This belief was founded on the fact that Barringer had just approved a record $20 million capital budget for fiscal year 1975. Wilson felt that the proposed refunding of a $10 million bond issue, along with the need to enter the capital market for an added $15 million to help finance the planned capital expenditures, would be viewed as excessive by the market and could result in a higher cost of funds to the firm. A second assistant to the financial vice president, Jim Koss, indicated that the refunding should not affect the other capital-raising plans of the firm since the total financing of the company would not be altered. In fact, if anything, the refunding should improve the ability of the firm to raise the needed funds since the new issue would be less expensive.

Bows suggested that the profitability of refunding be analyzed using the net present value technique employed by the firm in making capital investment decisions. However, he was not sure whether Barringer's after-tax cost of capital (approximately 10 percent) or some other rate, such as the after-tax, risk-free rate (the before-tax yield on 90-day U.S. Treasury bills is 6 percent), should be used in discounting the cash flows. Even if refunding now were found to be profitable, Bows wondered if the refunding should be delayed until the path of future interest rates could be determined.

Based on their discussion of the proposed refunding, the two assistants to the financial vice president were asked to prepare a recommendation as to whether the refunding should be undertaken. The analysts specifically were asked to address their report to the appropriate rate of discount for the refunding cash flows and the timing problem.

QUESTIONS

1. What rate of discount is appropriate to refunding cash flows? Explain.
2. Compute the net present value of refunding at the present time. You may assume a 50 percent marginal income tax rate.
3. How can the problem of selecting the optimal time for the refunding be solved? Discuss the feasibility of successfully timing the issuance of new bonds to obtain the maximum interest savings from the refunding.

CASE 49

Salem Rack Company, Inc.

Bond Refunding

Salem Rack Company, Inc. (SRC), manufactures display shelving for use by retailers such as department stores, grocery stores, and tire companies. Eight years ago, SRC embarked on a strategy of growth by acquiring small competitors. Four separate firms were acquired, giving SRC a national exposure. In the last fiscal year, SRC reported earnings of $2.34 million on revenue of $43.33 million.

The total cost of the four firms, $10 million, had been financed by an issue of long-term unsecured bonds. The bonds were issued in July 19x0, when interest rates were near an all-time high. The coupon rate was 17.25 percent, paid semiannually with a 20-year maturity. The bonds sold at a discount relative to par, and the current unamortized discount was $500,000. Since rates were at a historical high in 19x0, SRC's chief financial officer, Jeff Madsen, had insisted that the bonds contain a call provision. Management, in concert with the investment banking firm, had settled on a deferred-call provision, which protected the investors against the bonds being called for five years. Beginning in the fifth year, the bonds could be called, though a call premium of one year's interest would be required.

Now, in early June 19x5, interest rates have fallen to an eight-year low. SRC's investment bankers estimate that the manufacturer could float a new 15-year bond issue with an 11.0 percent coupon. Investors are more receptive to long-term issues in 19x5 than they were in 19x0; hence, flotation costs on the issue would be 2 percent, or $200,000. If it is decided to call the original bonds, there would be a two-month overlap between the issuance of the new bonds and the calling of the old ones. Proceeds from the new issue would be temporarily invested in short-term Treasury securities, which are currently yielding 6.9 percent before taxes.

Madsen brought the matter of the bond refinancing before the board of directors at the last quarterly meeting. Rick Gish, president of a local insurance company and a long-term member of the board, argued that calling the bonds for refund would not be well received by the institutional investors that are the primary holders of the issue. He stated that insurance companies such as his, as well as pension funds, had purchased the bonds expecting to hold them until they matured. They had also written contracts based on the expectation of receiving the 17.25 percent coupon return. These investors would be very disturbed if the bonds were called because they would have to reinvest the proceeds at a return of only 13 percent or so, which would seriously affect their funds' rates of return. Since Salem anticipates financing its planned growth by floating new bonds, Gish warned that it would be most unfortunate if institutional investors developed an ill-feeling toward the company.

Another member of the board, Barbara Browning, chief economist for a major regional bank, disagreed with Gish's arguments. She stated that institutional investors are sophisticated enough to know that high-coupon callable bonds will be called if interest rates decline, and that coupon rates reflect the call provision. Still, Browning expressed some opposition to a call at this time because she thought that interest rates would decline even further. She is heavily involved with interest rate forecasts—her bank receives several forecasts from econometric forecasting firms and she does her own forecasting as well—and the consensus view is that while short-term rates are likely to remain constant for the next 12 months, long-term rates will probably be the same or lower next year. In fact, Browning estimated the probability distribution of coupon rates for SRC one-year hence as given in Exhibit 1. SRC has a marginal tax rate of 38 percent. Exhibit 2 summarizes the details of the two bond issues.

EXHIBIT 1

Salem Rack Company, Inc.

Distribution of Forecasted Interest Rates in One Year

Probability	Coupon Rate
7%	17.25%
10	16.25
37	15.00
29	14.50
12	13.50
4	12.25
1	11.00

—————————— EXHIBIT 2 ——————————

Salem Rack Company, Inc.

Summary of Bond Issue Characteristics

Characteristic	Outstanding Issue	New Issue
Coupon rate	17.25%	11%
Par value	$1,000	$1,000
Issue size	$10 million	$10 million
Time to maturity	15 years	15 years
Call premium	1 year's interest	None
Float	2% of face	2% of face
Unamortized discount	$500,000	None
Unamortized issue exp.	$300,000	NA

General Information:
2-month overlap period during which both the old and new issues will be outstanding.
7.02% return on Treasury security investment during the overlap period.

Madsen began to prepare the final report for the board. He intended to use the net present value technique to analyze the financial impact of the decision, but he was not sure whether to use the company's cost of capital (12.9 percent), as he normally would in a capital budgeting decisions, or some other rate, such as the after-tax cost of debt or even the after-tax risk-free rate.

QUESTIONS*

1. Determine the net present value of refunding now. What discount rate is appropriate to refunding cash flows? Discuss the merits of using the after-tax cost of capital, after-tax cost of old debt, after-tax cost of new debt, and after-tax cost of Treasury securities.

2. Determine the current net present value of refunding the bond issue one year from now. Assume that a 14-year bond issue would be used at that time. (*Hint:* Use a data table to determine the various NPVs.) Remember to discount back to the current year.

3. Should the refunding be undertaken at this time or should Salem wait one year? Discuss the probability of maximizing net present value in bond refunding decisions—that is, refunding when interest rates are at their lowest point.

*The spreadsheet model is named "SALEM.wk1."

CASE 50

Commute Air

Bond Refunding Decision*

James T. Ward is the founder and sole stockholder of Commute Air, a commuter airline based in Orlando, Florida, that had its first flight in 1981. Commute Air operates small overwing propeller aircraft that seat 20 to 30 passengers. It developed a niche in the business travel market by providing low-cost transportation over short distances. In addition, it offers flights to the small regional airports that major airlines have ignored.

In the early 1980s, Commute Air's revenue was expanding rapidly and not much attention was being paid to cost control activities. However, in the late 1980s, businesses cut back on their travel expenses and substituted automobile transportation for air travel for short-distance business trips. Thus, Commute Air's revenues have leveled off since 1988, and Ward is very concerned (see Exhibit 1). To increase profits, he and his financial manager have instituted several cost-saving ideas over the last year.

Ward has also asked his financial manager to find a way to reduce the interest expense of Commute Air. Since he wants to remain the sole stockholder, an issue of stock to replace the outstanding bonds is not an option. The financial manager has suggested a bond refunding, though he is not sure that it will be beneficial. Current interest rates are slightly lower than the interest rate on the outstanding bonds, and the financial manager be-

*This case was authored by Kevin L. Woods of the University of Central Florida.

EXHIBIT 1

Commute Air

Income Statements, 1987–1990

	1990	1989	1988	1987
Net sales	$50,175,647	$49,981,342	$50,247,168	$54,543,281
Cost of sales	28,822,953	28,686,939	28,873,018	31,880,297
Gross profits	21,352,694	21,294,403	21,374,150	22,662,984
Operating expenses	3,357,326	3,895,529	3,457,589	3,077,910
Operating income	17,995,368	17,398,874	17,916,561	19,585,074
Interest expense	10,000,000	10,000,000	10,000,000	10,000,000
Income before taxes	7,995,368	7,398,874	7,916,561	9,585,074
Income taxes	2,718,425	2,515,617	2,691,631	3,258,925
Net income	$5,276,943	$4,883,257	$5,224,930	$6,326,149

---

lieves a bond refunding may reduce the overall debt costs. Ward has asked his financial manager to investigate the possibility of refunding the outstanding debenture issue.

Commute Air is in the 34 percent tax bracket and has a $100 million, 10 percent debenture issue outstanding, with 20 years remaining to maturity. The unamortized flotation costs and discount on the old bonds total $4 million. These bonds contain a call provision and can be called at $105 (i.e., $105 for each $100 of par). The financial manager has been told that the bonds could be replaced with a $100 million issue of 9 percent 20-year bonds, providing the firm with $97 million after flotation costs. Thus, the discount on the new bonds is $3 million. An additional $600,000 in issuing expenses would be incurred with the new debenture issue. The overlap period during which both issues will be outstanding is expected to be one month.

James Ward has given his financial manager two days to analyze the bond refunding decision.

QUESTIONS

1. What is the appropriate discount rate to use in the bond refunding decision analysis?
2. How should the financial manager analyze the bond refunding decision?
3. Assume you are the financial manager. Analyze the bond refunding decision and make a recommendation.
4. How would the analysis be handled if the maturity on the old bonds was shorter than the maturity on the new bonds?

CASE 51

Rollins Manufacturing Co., Inc.

Convertible Securities

The Rollins Manufacturing Company, Inc., a producer of consumer hardware and industrial cleansing solvents and applicators, was founded in 1964 by Jonathan Rollins. For several years, the business was only marginally profitable. Finally, in 1969, profits improved significantly as the result of a long-term government contract to supply the military with specially formulated cleansing solvents to be used with electronic gear systems. After several profitable years, Rollins decided to retire from business in 1980. Thus, when James Reed and Robert Hall approached him regarding the possible sale of his firm, he was quite interested. By the end of the year, the terms were finalized, and the operation changed leadership on January 1, 1981. In financing the enterprise, Reed and Hall provided approximately 69 percent of the equity, with an additional 25,000 shares being purchased by other investors. (The total equity capital at that time was 80,500 shares of $1 par common stock.) Then, in 1983, to acquire long-term financing for the purpose of funding growth, an additional 19,500 shares were placed with interested parties. Throughout the financial decision-making process, Reed and Hall agreed that maintaining in excess of 50 percent control was of key importance to them.

In the year subsequent to the acquisition, Reed, as president of the firm, and Hall, as executive vice president, undertook a study to determine the direction Rollins Manufacturing should take in the future. The result was a 10-year plan for further expansion into recently developed cleansing solvents and accessories. Thus, additional plant facilities became a pressing issue. The company purchased a building adaptable to its needs from John Bradshaw, the sole owner of a wholesale operation who had recently become ill. After his illness, he began to liquidate the assets of the business and agreed to accept 5,000 shares of 4 percent preferred stock from the Rollins organization in payment for the building.

By 1982, the firm, under its new management, was experiencing excellent growth, and in five years, it had outgrown the facilities acquired from Bradshaw. Hence, in 1989, as the second phase in the 10-year expansion plan, the management issued $1,750,000 of 6 percent senior debt having a maturity of 20 years. These funds were invested in additional plant and equipment for the express purpose of increasing production capacity in the following year.

Growth has continued to be excellent, and the need for additional capital equipment is again becoming a reality. The management of Rollins indicates that $750,000 is needed to meet the corporate financial requirements for the immediate future. These funds will be applied to the con-

---

EXHIBIT 1

Rollins Manufacturing Co., Inc.

Income Statements, 1988–1992

	1992	1991	1990	1989	1988
Sales	$9,000,000	$8,460,000	$8,100,000	$4,057,500	$3,367,000
Cost of goods sold	4,050,000	3,785,850	3,240,000	1,704,150	1,438,800
Gross profit	$4,950,000	$4,674,150	$4,860,000	$2,353,350	$1,928,200
Operating expenses*	3,939,620	3,715,690	3,962,422	1,804,963	1,604,200
Earnings before interest and taxes	1,010,380	958,460	897,578	548,387	324,000
Interest	129,220	129,290	138,530	150,710	35,000
Taxable income	$ 881,160	$ 829,170	$ 759,048	$ 397,677	$ 289,000
Taxes†	416,457	391,502	357,843	184,385	180,220
Income after taxes	464,703	437,668	401,205	213,292	108,780
Preferred dividends	20,000	20,000	20,000	20,000	20,000
Earnings available to common	$ 444,703	$ 417,668	$ 381,205	$ 193,292	$ 88,780
Earnings per share	$4.45	$4.18	$3.81	$1.93	$0.89

*Include $225,000 of depreciation charges for 1992.

†Tax rate is 22 percent for $0 to $25,000; 48 percent for over $25,000.

struction of facilities essential in meeting the obligations of a new government contract. To meet the terms of the contract, the plant must be started within three months. With this new addition, plant and equipment should be adequate for operations until 2001.

The financial statements for Rollins are provided in Exhibits 1 and 2, covering the period 1988–1992. Based upon these data, sales in 1993 are expected to be 105 percent of 1992 sales, excluding revenues contributed by the new government contract. Cost of goods sold and operating expenses are expected to maintain the same percentages as experienced in 1992.

Reed contacted an investment banking firm for advice regarding the raising of the needed funds. After a study of the company, the banker developed three alternatives.

1. Sell stock at $60 per share (current market value) less an approximate 10 percent for flotation costs. The current price-earnings ratio is considered by both management and the investment banker to be somewhat low in view of

---

EXHIBIT 2

Rollins Manufacturing Co., Inc.

Balance Sheets, 1988–1992

	1992	1991	1990	1989	1988
Cash	$ 550	$ 500	$ 450	$ 400	$ 300
Accounts receivable	850	700	600	450	500
Marketable securities	200	150	150	150	50
Inventories	1,000	800	700	650	500
Net plant and equipment	2,400	2,550	2,600	2,700	1,250
Total assets	$5,000	$4,700	$4,500	$4,350	$2,600

Liabilities and Equity

	1992	1991	1990	1989	1988
Trade payables	$ 250	$ 250	$ 200	$ 200	$ 400
Short-term notes (7%)	96	97	229	403	500
Long-term bonds (7%)	1,750	1,750	1,750	1,750	0
Preferred stock (4%)	500	500	500	500	500
Common stock par ($1 par)	100	100	100	100	100
Capital surplus	900	900	900	900	900
Retained earnings	1,404	1,103	821	497	200
Total liabilities and equity	$5,000	$4,700	$4,500	$4,350	$2,600

Selected 1981 industry norms:

Current ratio	4.00X
Return on assets (before interest and taxes)	17.5%
Total debt to total assets	35%
Preferred to total assets	5%
Return on common	15%

historical figures for both Rollins and the industry. Both groups feel that a return to a more normal price-earnings ratio of 14.75 (based upon fully diluted earnings per share) will occur within the next six months. The 14.75 ratio is independent of future financing. Furthermore, the stock price should then continue to grow for several years at a 10 percent annual rate, after which a 6 percent rate could be expected.

2. Sell subordinated convertible debentures at a $1,000 market price with an 8 percent coupon rate and a 20-year life. Costs of underwriting and managing the issue would be 2.597 percent of the market price of the security. The conversion ratio would "step down" as time elapses, with the ratios being as follows:

Years 1– 3	14.25
Years 4–10	13.25
Years 11–20	12.00

3. Sell subordinated convertible debentures at a $1,000 market price with a 7 percent coupon rate, maturing in 20 years and having a conversion price of $65. Flotation costs would be the same as for the 8 percent debentures. The call price for the convertibles in either alternative 2 or 3 will be as follows:

Years	Call Price
1–5	105
6–12	104
13–16	102
17–20	100

Rollins's outstanding senior debt is currently selling to yield 8 percent, while subordinated debentures having a risk class similar to the debentures under consideration, but without the conversion privilege, are selling at 10 percent. Also, the financial consultant recommended not executing the call feature until the conversion value exceeds the call price by 20 percent. Both Reed and Hall concur with such a policy.

QUESTIONS

1. From the perspective of Reed and Hall, which financing alternative should be undertaken?

2. What is the impact of each of the convertible issues upon the firm's earnings per share (both with and without the potential dilution effect being recognized)? In making your calculations, assume that the same percentage return on investment (before interest and taxes) can be achieved with the new funds as occurred in 1992 with existing assets. Also assume that the interest in 1993 will be equivalent to interest charges in 1992 if no financing occurs.

3. For alternative 2 (8 percent convertibles), determine as of the time of issue:
   a. The conversion value.
   b. "The bond value floor"—that is, the market price of the convertible

issue when the conversion privilege is of no value owing to a depressed common stock price.

   c. The premium-over-conversion value and the premium-over-bond value.

4.
   a. Why is a "step-down" conversion ratio employed?

   b. In view of the firm's call policy and the expected price movement, when would the issue be called? Answer in terms of both market price of the issue and approximate time.

   c. What would you expect the premium-over-conversion value and bond value to be at the time the issue is called?

   d. Experience shows that as the conversion value falls to approximately 50 percent of the "bond value floor," the market value of a convertible debenture essentially becomes equivalent to the floor. In this context, compute both premiums if the anticipated increase in the stock price did not materialize but rather decreased to a low of $24.

5. With the results from the previous questions, develop a graph at the expected time of the call that reflects the *approximate* relationships between (a) the bond value floor, the conversion value, and the market value of the 8 percent convertible debentures; and (b) the price of the common stock. (Let the vertical axis comprise the market, bond, and conversion value of the convertible security, while the horizontal axis depicts the price of the common stock.)

6. Based upon the prior computations, explain the reasons for the premium-over-conversion value and the premium-over-bond value. Also explain the relationship of the two premiums.

CASE 52

Computer Synectics

Agency Theory and Capital Structure

For 10 years, Annette Evans worked in the research department of a major computer company. Most of her time was spent developing sophisticated graphics hardware and software to be used in engineering applications. Recently, she designed a computer monitor and software system called "Ultragraph" that could significantly expand the graphics capabilities of existing spreadsheet, data-base, and word processing packages. Nevertheless, the computer company she worked for showed little interest in investing funds in the further development of Ultragraph. Consequently, Evans studied the possibility of buying the rights to Ultragraph and pursuing its development and ultimate production and marketing herself.

The computer company agreed to sell Evans the rights to Ultragraph in 1991 for $20,000. She figured that further research and development of Ultragraph, necessary to demonstrate its compatibility with several other commercially available software packages, would require an additional investment of $80,000 in 1991. Thus, for Evans to begin this venture on her own, she had to come up with $100,000 in 1991. Evans decided to form a corporation called Computer Synectics, of which she would be president and holder of a minority interest, and to raise all of the initial $100,000 cost for acquiring the rights to Ultragraph and for further research and development by issuing shares of common stock.

It took Computer Synectics one year to complete the necessary research and development on Ultragraph. It is now 1992 and Evans hopes to be able to make a commitment this year to begin building the production facilities and marketing networks necessary for the ultimate selling of the Ultragraph system to the public. She estimates that to begin production and marketing of Ultragraph will require an investment of $640,000 in 1992.

Evans is convinced that Ultragraph is a more powerful and convenient add-on graphics package than anything currently available in the market. The problem she faces is to convince the capital market of the strengths of her product. The investment banker Computer Synectics has hired to advise it concerning alternative methods of raising the needed $640,000 in capital has told Evans that the capital market is skeptical of the claims made for the power and convenience of Ultragraph in an article in the newsletter *Graphline*, which is published by Computer Synectics. He has estimated that the market, based on its own inferences from the *Graphline* article, is currently making the forecasts outlined in Exhibit 1 for the total value of the Ultragraph project in 1994, two years after the $640,000 investment for starting the project is made.

The investment banker has also proposed the following two alternative plans for financing the $640,000 investment required to begin production and marketing of Ultragraph in the current year 1992:

Plan A

1. Raise all the $640,000 by issuing new, additional shares of common stock.
2. The stockholders' required rate of return will be 25 percent, given forecasts based on the *Graphline* article.

EXHIBIT 1

Computer Synectics

*1992 Market Forecasts of Value
in 1994, Based on the* Graphline *Article*

State of Economy	Probability	*1994 Value of All Discounted Future Net Cash Flows*
Boom	.2	$1,500,000
Normal	.6	1,000,000
Recession	.2	500,000

Required rates of return for Exhibit 1 data:

Plan A: Stockholders' required rate of return = 25%.

Plan B: Stockholders' required rate of return = 40%.
Bondholders' required rate of return = 16.72258%.

Plan B
1. Issue 600 discount bonds that promise to pay $1,000 per bond when they mature in 1994.
2. Finance the rest of the $640,000 by issuing new shares of common stock.
3. The bondholders' required rate of return will be 16.72258 percent and the stockholders' required rate of return will be 40 percent if plan B is adopted, given forecasts based on the *Graphline* article.

The market projections for the project's value in 1994 provided by the investment banker in Exhibit 1 were extremely disappointing to Annette Evans. She feels that the Ultragraph system is worth more than the capital market is currently forecasting, and she is convinced that the capital market will place a much higher valuation on the Ultragraph system once *Compu-Tech Magazine* completes its own research and publishes its findings concerning the power and convenience of Ultragraph. In fact, Evans estimates that when the *Compu-Tech* research is made public, the market will revise its estimates of the project's 1994 value to those given in Exhibit 2.

Unfortunately, the *Compu-Tech* article will not be available to the public until after the new financing must be obtained. It may be assumed, however, that once the report is released, the market will revise its forecasts to those given in Exhibit 2. At the same time, investors will also change their required rates of return on the Ultragraph project. After the *Compu-Tech* article is released, investors' new required rates of return will be as follows:

Plan A
1. Stockholders' revised required rate of return: 20 percent.

EXHIBIT 2

Computer Synectics

*Revised 1992 Market Forecasts of Value
in 1994, After Release of the* Compu-Tech *Article*

State of Economy	Probability	Revised 1994 Value of All Discounted Future Net Cash Flows, After Compu-Tech Article
Boom	.1	$2,600,000
Normal	.8	1,800,000
Recession	.1	1,000,000

Required rates of return for Exhibit 2 data:

Plan A: Stockholders' required rate of return = 20%.

Plan B: Stockholders' required rate of return = 28%.
Bondholders' required rate of return = 7.66825%.

Plan B
1. Stockholders' revised required rate of return: 28 percent.
2. Bondholders' revised required rate of return: 7.66825.

QUESTIONS

1. Assume that financing plan A is adopted. (*Note:* Question 1 deals with *stockholder value* under plan A.)
   a. Given that the market is currently using the forecasts set forth in Exhibit 1, what is the current (1992) total market value of the stock?
   b. What is the current (1992) total market value of the stock from the point of view of an investor such as Annette Evans, who can anticipate the revised forecasts given in Exhibit 2 before they are actually released?
   c. From the point of view of an investor like Evans, how much will the stockholders gain in total when the *Compu-Tech* article is released?

2. Answer parts (a), (b), and (c) of question 1 under the assumption that financing plan B is adopted. (*Note:* Question 2 deals with *stockholder value* under plan B.)

3. (*Note:* Question 3 deals with *bondholder value* under plan B.)
   a. What is the 1992 total value of the bonds using Exhibit 1 to forecast the cash flows to the bondholders?
   b. What is the 1992 total value of the bonds when the forecasts are revised, because of the release of the *Compu-Tech* article, to those given in Exhibit 2?
   c. How much do bondholders gain from the release of the *Compu-Tech* article?

4. Which financing plan will be preferred by Evans and other stockholders? What causes the two plans to have different net present values to the stockholders?

5. How would your answer to question 4 be affected by the following:
   a. The bonds in plan B were callable at any time at some fixed call price.
   b. Plan B was changed to use a level of debt that was small enough to prevent the possibility of any future default even under the circumstances forecasted in Exhibit 1.

As it turned out, by an incredible stroke of luck, *Compu-Tech* was able to publish its article more quickly than envisioned, so the market immediately adjusted its forecast to that given in Exhibit 2. Also, Computer Synectics decided to raise the necessary $640,000 in capital *by using plan B*.

It is now 1993. It is important to note that the forecasts given in Exhibit 2 were made under the assumption that Computer Synectics would contract with Micro Systems, Inc., the world's largest marketer of computer systems, to do the actual marketing of the Ultragraph system because Ev-

---
EXHIBIT 3

Computer Synectics

*Forecasts Given That Ultragraph
Is Marketed by Computer Synectics*

State of Economy	Probability	1994 Value of All Discounted Future Net Cash Flows
Boom	.3	$3,500,000
Normal	.4	1,800,000
Recession	.3	100,000

Required rates of return for Exhibit 3 data:

Plan A: Stockholders' required rate of return = 25%.

Plan B: Stockholders' required rate of return = 40%.
Bondholders' required rate of return = 16.72258%.

---

ans thought that she could substantially reduce the risk of uncertain market acceptance of Ultragraph by having it marketed through the trusted and well-known Micro Systems. However, an alternative option available to Computer Synectics is to market the Ultragraph system independently. Although Evans estimates that the cost of both alternative marketing plans would be the same, she feels that the market would view the plan in which Computer Synectics does its own marketing as the riskier of the two. In fact, she feels that if Computer Synectics does its own marketing, the market would revise its forecasts for the value of the Ultragraph project to those indicated in Exhibit 3.

If Computer Synectics markets Ultragraph itself, the investors will return to using the original required rates of return specified for plan B (i.e., 40 percent for stockholders and 16.72258 percent for bondholders). If Micro Systems markets Ultragraph for Computer Synectics, then investors will use the revised required rates of return specified for plan B (i.e., 28 percent for stockholders and 7.66825 percent for bondholders).

QUESTIONS (cont.)

6.   a. What will be the 1993 total value of the stock and the bonds if the market thinks that Micro Systems will do the marketing for Ultragraph? (*Remember that* the *Compu-Tech* article has now been released, so the data in Exhibit 2 apply and Computer Synectics is using financing Plan B.)

   b. What will be the 1993 total value of the stock and the bonds if the market thinks that Computer Synectics will do its own marketing of Ultragraph? (See data in Exhibit 3.)

   c. Which marketing option will be preferred by the stockholders of Computer Synectics? Why?

7. Assume that Evans has announced to the market that she would use Micro Systems to market Ultragraph and that the prospective bondholders believed this. What would happen to the wealth of the stockholders of Computer Synectics if, after the investment capital was raised, Evans switched her decision and announced that Computer Synectics would do its own marketing of Ultragraph? What would happen to the stockholders' wealth under the same circumstances if, at the time the capital was raised, the bondholders had assumed that Computer Synectics would market Ultragraph (i.e., the bondholders anticipated the switch)?

CASE 53

Bronson Electronics Company

Convertible Bonds:
Options Pricing Model

Bronson Electronics Company is a small electronics firm located in Livermore, California. The company was founded in 1968 by Jack Bronson. Since that time, it has achieved an average annual growth rate of 25 percent of sales, mainly from the development of technological advances by its founder, Bronson, and other charter owners of the firm. The research and development group has recently been experimenting with a new form of electronic chip for use in one of its current product lines. Since further development and marketing of this chip requires a $750,000 capital outlay, Bronson has asked his chief financial officer, Max Clemens, to devise a strategy to raise the needed funds.

In the past, expansion of the firm has been accomplished through a combination of internally generated funds and the sale of new shares of common stock. The company was therefore in the rare position of having no debt in its capital structure. Unfortunately, all internally generated funds for the current year have already been earmarked for other capital projects. Clemens therefore consulted an investment banker about the feasibility of issuing new common stock. The investment banker advised him that this was not a good time for a new issue of common stock since the market, in general, was depressed. In addition, the earnings for Bronson Electronics were down for the past year, and he felt that a new stock issue would require a 5 to 10 percent discount from the current market price of 14 ⅝ per share.

Clemens agreed with the investment banker that a common stock issue would only be used as a last resort. He was reluctant to issue bonds, however, because of the past variability of profits for Bronson Electronics. He explained to the investment banker that they needed to raise the money to develop a new electronic chip and that the payoff from this investment would not begin for another four or five years. At that time, however, he expected profits to grow so fast that there would be tremendous investor interest in the company.

The investment banker suggested that Clemens consider zero coupon convertible bonds to finance the new project. To conserve cash, no coupons would be paid but the investor would have the option of converting the bond to a stated number of shares of stock on or before maturity. He suggested the following terms for the security:

Face value	$1,000
Conversion ratio	40 shares
Time to maturity	5 years
Number of bonds issued	1,000
Proceeds from the bond issue	$750,000

When Clemens reported back on the zero coupon convertible bond option, Bronson thought that this was the answer to his problem. Still, he was concerned about how much investors would be willing to pay for such a security. He remembered hearing at a recent financial seminar that convertible bonds could be priced using the options pricing model. The reasoning was as follows: A convertible bond is simply the combination of a regular, nonconvertible bond and an option to purchase a portion of the firm's stock at an exercise price equal to the face value of the bond. A check of his file from the seminar produced Exhibit 1, which contains more details on how to value convertible securities.

Bronson also obtained the following information on the firm for use in the convertible bond formula:

Number of shares of common stock outstanding	360,000
Market price of common stock	14 ⅝
Variance rate of the firm's assets	.04
Dividends (the firm does not anticipate paying any dividends during the next five years)	
Interest rate on a 5-year Treasury bond	8%

―――――――――――――――――― **EXHIBIT 1** ――――――――――――――――――

Bronson Electronics Company

Valuation of a Zero Coupon Convertible Bond

Consider a firm that has only one issue of nonconvertible debt and equity in its capital structure. By definition, the value of the nonconvertible debt, D, is equal to the value of the firm, V, minus the value of the common stock, E, or

$$D = V - E \tag{1}$$

The stock of the firm can, however, be viewed as an option to purchase the assets of the firm, V, from the bondholders at the maturity date of the bond for an exercise price equal to the face value of the bond.

Using the options pricing model, the value of the stock as an option on the assets on the firm is

$$E = VN(b_1) - Be^{-rt}N(b_2) \tag{2}$$

where

V = total value of the firm
B = total face value of the debt
r = risk-free rate of interest
t = time to maturity of the bond
$b_1 = [\ln(V/B) + (r + s^2/2)t]/s\sqrt{t}$
$b_2 = b_1 - s\sqrt{t}$
s^2 = variance rate of the firm's assets
$N(.)$ = cumulative normal probability density function
e = exponential function ≈ 2.718

The value of the conversion feature can also be obtained using the options pricing model. In addition to the regular bond, the convertible bondholders have an option to purchase a proportion of the firm's assets, k, at an exercise price equal to the face value of the bond. The proportion of the assets that the bondholders receive is equal to

$$k = n/(n+N)$$

where

N = number of shares of stock before conversion
n = total number of shares for which the bond issue can be exchanged

Since the bondholders will own k percent of the firm after conversion, the symbol k can be viewed as the dilution factor. Using the options pricing model, the value of the conversion privilege, CP, is equal to

$$CP = kVN(c_1) - Be^{-rt}N(c_2) \tag{3}$$

where

$c_1 = [\ln(kV/B) + (r + s^2/2)t]/s\sqrt{t}$
$c_2 = c_1 - s\sqrt{t}$

The value of convertible debt, D_c, is equal to the value of a regular nonconvertible bond plus the conversion privilege, or

$$D_c = D + CP \tag{4}$$

Putting equations (1), (2), (3), and (4) together, the value of the convertible bond issue is equal to

$$D_c = [V - VN(b_1) + Be^{-rt}N(b_2)] + [kVN(c_1) - Be^{-rt}N(c_2)]$$

The first term on the right-hand side of the equation represents the value of a similar nonconvertible debt issue, D; the second term represents the total value of the conversion privilege, CP.

QUESTIONS

1. What proportion of the firm will the bondholders own after conversion?

2. Bronson wants to know how the price of the convertible bond will vary with the value of the firm. Fill in the following table for the various values of the firm.

Value of the Firm	Total Value of the Nonconvertible Bonds	Total Value of the Conversion Privilege	Total Value of the Convertible Bonds	Total Value of the Stock
V	D	CP	$D_c = D + CP$	$S = V - D_c$
$ 100,000				
400,000				
700,000				
1,000,000				
2,000,000				
3,000,000				
4,000,000				
5,000,000				
6,000,000				
7,000,000				
8,000,000				
10,000,000				
12,000,000				

3. Using the table in question 2, prepare a graph with the value of the firm on the horizontal axis and the total value of the convertible bonds on the vertical axis.

4. Place a line on your graph that represents the total conversion value of the bonds for various values of the firm. (*Hint:* Remember that the bondholders will own k percent of the firm after conversion.)

5. In your own words, explain why the convertible bond issue would be priced as shown in your table and graph. (*Hint:* Break your explanation into approximately three segments of the firm value—$0–$1,000,000, $1,000,000–$4,000,000, and $4,000,000–$10,000,000.)

6. Why does the convertible bond sell for a premium over its conversion value?

7. Holding everything else constant, what would happen to the value of the convertible security (increase, decrease, or stay the same) under each of the following conditions?
   a. Increase in the value of the firm.
   b. Increase in the face value of the bond.
   c. Increase in the risk-free rate of interest.
   d. Increase in the dilution factor, k.

8. If the bonds originally sold for $750 each and if the bond is never converted and the investor receives the full $1,000 face value at maturity, what would be the effective annual interest rate that the company pays on the bond?

9. It has been shown that bondholders should never convert before maturity except possibly just before the stock pays a dividend or just before the conversion terms are changed. In both cases, the bondholder suffers a loss of wealth and must determine whether the value of his or her investment would be greater by converting or by continuing to hold the convertible bond. Suppose that four and one-half years have passed and that the total value of the Bronson Electronics Company has risen to $11,360,000. The company announces that it will be paying a dividend of $1 per share to shareholders of record. The company fully expects to continue to pay a dividend of $1 or more on an annual basis. Should you convert your bond to receive the dividend? (*Hint:* If the bondholders convert before payment of the dividend, they will own $n/(n+N)$ percent of the firm. If they do not convert, they will own, after payment of the dividend, a convertible bond on a firm worth $11,000,000 with one-half year to maturity.)

CASE 54

Traner Furniture Company

Dividend Policy

The Traner Furniture Company (TFC) is a diversified manufacturer of household furnishings located in Rocky Mount, North Carolina. The firm's expansion program, begun in the early 1960s, has been continued to the point where the company is now represented in most major furniture lines that have national appeal. About 55 percent of sales for the company are generated by its lines of wooden furniture; the other 45 percent are attributed to its upholstered products. Throughout all its product lines, TFC has been able to offer very high quality for every dollar spent by consumers. TFC's many competitors praise its quality control and point to it as a major reason for the organization's solid reputation in the industry.

That reputation is buttressed by a pervasive respect among both competing manufacturers and security analysts for the leadership and overall managerial abilities of John Collberg, president of TFC. Collberg has unique sales and styling talents that almost provide him with a mystique in the furniture profession. These attributes allow him to run the affairs of this publicly held corporation quite sternly.

It is Monday, and Collberg has his executive staff preparing for the quarterly meeting of the board of directors, which will take place on Friday. Several economic developments directly affecting the financial picture of TFC are disturbing its chief executive officer. Alan Boyer, the head purchasing agent for the company, today presented Collberg with the information shown in Exhibit 1. Boyer felt certain that, on the average, a 10 percent price rise in the various woods used in quantity by TFC would be experienced during the next fiscal year.

Because of the firm's total commitment to quality merchandise, Collberg would not hear of using some cheaper grades of lumber to dampen the effect of the price increases expected by the purchasing department. "A few cracked frames, and there goes 70 years' worth of reputation," he argued.

After Boyer's information reached Collberg, J. R. Wilson discussed with the company president the prospects for interest rate levels over the coming year. Wilson is the vice president of finance for TFC. During the past month of October, he digested numerous governmental reports, commercial and Federal Reserve bank letters, and brokerage house publications that touched upon interest rate projections for next year. The composite tone of these forecasts was not at all good for the furniture industry. Wilson put together his own projections, influenced by the materials that he had been examining, and offered them to Collberg in the form of Exhibit 2.

Wilson's prognostication did not please Collberg. Interest rate levels are extraordinarily critical to the furniture manufacturing industry.

"Look at this!" Collberg yelled as he pushed a table (Exhibit 3) of figures in front of the vice president. "I just received this from the Regional Furniture Manufacturers' Association."

Collberg's usually calm and composed manner disintegrated as he informed Wilson that the Manufacturers' Association was projecting annual new housing starts at a rate below 1 million units for the first quarter of next year. This would be the lowest rate since late 1966, if the forecast

---
EXHIBIT 1

Traner Furniture Company

Wood Price Increases

Division	Location	Key Products	Wood Inputs	Projected Price Rise
Maplemount	Greenwood, N.C.	Quality recliners	Hackberry, plywood, oak	15%
Hazeldown	Dublin, Ga.	Juvenile furniture	Oak, pine	8
Ballett	Ballett, Va.	Bedroom, dining room	Poplar, oak, tupelo, hackberry	8
Hickory Style	Hickory, N.C.	Upholstered furniture	Mixed hardwoods	9
Victoria	Wellsville, Pa.	Correlated tables	Mahogany, pecan	12

─────────────────────── **EXHIBIT 2** ───────────────────────

Traner Furniture Company

Recent Interest Rate Levels and Forecasts

Time	3-Month Treasury Bills	Prime Bankers' Acceptances	4- to 6-Month Commercial Paper
Current year*	7.04%	8.08%	8.15%
1 year ago	4.07	4.47	4.69
2 years ago	4.35	4.85	5.11
3 years ago	6.46	7.31	7.72
Next July	7.53	11.77	11.80
Next August	8.80	12.07	11.60
Next September	8.82	11.47	11.58

*Includes 11 months of actual data and a forecast for December.

─────────────────────── **EXHIBIT 3** ───────────────────────

Traner Furniture Company

Housing Starts
New Private Housing Units Authorized*
(seasonally adjusted annual rates, in thousands)

January	2,233	May	1,838	September	1,596
February	2,209	June	2,030	October	1,316
March	2,129	July	1,780	November	1,314
April	1,939	August	1,750	December	1,231

*Authorized by issuance of local building permits for the current year; the December figure is preliminary.

proved true, and a startling 60 percent below the rate that culminated the 1970–1973 housing boom.

"I'll need the fiscal year financial statements by tomorrow, along with your projection of sales, net income, and earnings per share for each of the four quarters of next year," Collberg told Wilson. "We need to make a firm recommendation to the board of directors as to our most prudent dividend policy in the light of these developments."

Collberg reminded Wilson of the executive staff's decision to increase its hourly wage schedule at the Virginia and North Carolina production facilities. As labor is somewhat tight in both these states, the top management of TFC decided to offer higher wages than some of the competition to attract a steady supply of help.

Wilson left the president's office and signaled for Barney Abbott to enter. As he did so, he quickly moved his right index finger in a semicircular motion across his throat, giving Abbott advance warning of Collberg's general mood. Abbott is now in his tenth year of service to TFC as its corporate attorney. Collberg gave Abbott a copy of a letter that he had received from a shareholder who was expressing displeasure with TFC's dividend policy (Exhibit 4). Collberg said he was unaware that the retention of earnings could be deemed "improper" by the courts. He instructed Abbott to determine whether TFC should be concerned with the implications of the letter received from Adam Randolph.

By Tuesday noon, Collberg's staff had on his desk considerable information pointed toward the question of the firm's dividend policy. As he poured over these data (Exhibits 5 to 10), Collberg became certain that several problems relating to the formulation of next year's dividend policy would be touched upon at the directors' meeting. Some members of the board would seize upon the letter from Adam Randolph to further their cause for an increase in the annual cash dividend. Others would argue strongly for a cut in the cash dividend payout. Another group could be counted on to favor keeping the current 69 cent dividend intact. Finally,

---
EXHIBIT 4
Traner Furniture Company

Mr. John Collberg, President
Traner Furniture Company
Rocky Mount, North Carolina

Dear Mr. Collberg:

I have been a small investor in TFC common shares for approximately three years. It disturbs me that you and your board of directors continue to follow such a highly conservative dividend payout policy as has been evidenced by the recent past.

In light of (1) your firm's extreme liquidity, (2) low level of long-term debt, and (3) high executive compensation level, I believe that TFC is a prime candidate for the accumulated earnings tax. It seems to me that an increase in the cash dividend would be more beneficial to the firm's owners than having to prove in tax court that TFC has not been improperly accumulating surplus.

Sometimes I think the management of TFC continues to act like it is a family-held enterprise rather than a public company whose shares are actively traded over-the-counter.

Sincerely,

Adam Randolph
Upper Vista, Virginia

CC: Internal Revenue Service
      Southeast Region
      Memphis, Tennessee

Traner Furniture Company

Selected Financial Statistics (Traner and Competitors)
(per-share basis)

Item	4 Years Ago	3 Years Ago	2 Years Ago	1 Year Ago	Current Year
Traner					
Cash dividends	$ 0.59	$ 0.61	$ 0.61	$ 0.65	$ 0.69
Earnings	1.58	2.03	2.12	2.79	2.71
Book value	15.69	17.14	18.62	20.77	22.67
Share price (midpoint of yearly high-low range)	26.46	40.18	43.60	25.48	16.17
Barttonn South					
Cash dividends	$ 0.63	$ 0.86	$ 1.01	$ 0.98	$ 0.98
Earnings	1.36	1.90	1.99	1.93	1.48
Book value	10.18	11.23	12.23	13.17	13.95
Share price	23.03	43.61	47.53	29.89	16.66
Harbor Groupings					
Cash dividends	$ 0.29	$ 0.32	$ 0.33	$ 0.34	$ 0.35
Earnings	0.90	0.72	0.99	1.21	1.64
Book value	5.89	6.29	6.94	7.80	9.08
Share price	14.70	20.09	20.09	12.25	9.80
Sleepy-Boy					
Cash dividends	$ 0.23	$ 0.29	$ 0.29	$ 0.34	$ 0.39
Earnings	0.76	1.14	1.30	1.68	1.54
Book value	4.16	5.02	6.93	8.30	9.47
Share price	43.12	22.05	37.73	26.95	9.31

Traner Furniture Company

Selected Financial Ratios of Traner and Competitors
(latest 12 months)

Item	Traner	Barttonn South	Harbor Groupings	Sleepy-Boy
Net working capital per share	$14.21	$8.24	$5.59	$6.31
Current ratio	8.60X	7.75X	4.01X	3.98X
Long-term debt to total equity	1.4%	3.3%	20.7%	11.6%
Inventory turnover (COS/EI)	4.56X	4.61X	4.23X	3.75X
Return on equity (net income/total equity)	11.8%	10.7%	17.7%	16.4%
Return on assets (net income/total assets)	10.8%	9.6%	12.3%	12.2%

---------------------------------- EXHIBIT 7 ----------------------------------

Traner Furniture Company

Income Statement
End of Current Fiscal Year

Net sales	$119,664,250
Less: Cost of sales	84,701,301
Gross profit	$ 34,962,949
Less: Selling and administrative expenses	21,539,806
Operating income	$ 13,423,143
Other income and expenses	
Income from investments	555,450
Less: Interest expense	59,436
Miscellaneous, net	234,472
Earnings before taxes	$ 14,153,629
Less: Taxes (federal and state)	6,820,800
Net income	$ 7,332,829
Less: Preferred dividends paid	51,195
Earnings available to common	$ 7,281,634

---------------------------------- EXHIBIT 8 ----------------------------------

Traner Furniture Company

Balance Sheet
End of Current Fiscal Year

	Amount
Assets	
Cash	$ 846,312
Marketable securities	8,340,782
Accounts receivable	14,785,326
Inventories	18,572,714
Prepaid expenses	658,927
Total current assets	$ 43,214,061
Net property and equipment	21,693,493
Other assets	2,886,630
Total assets	$ 67,794,184
Liabilities and Stockholders' Equity	
Total current liabilities	$ 5,027,185
Long-term debt	840,245
Stockholders' equity	
Preferred stock	1,023,904
Common stock (2,686,950 shares)	13,193,250
Paid-in surplus	3,736,582
Retained earnings	44,435,084
Treasury stock	-462,066
Total stockholders' equity	$ 61,926,754
Total liabilities and equity	$ 67,794,184

EXHIBIT 9

Traner Furniture Company

Comparative Annual Remuneration for Top Officers

Position	*Traner*	*Average of Three Main Competitors*
President	$133,468	$105,756
Financial vice president	89,389	88,420
Marketing vice president	88,404	64,555

EXHIBIT 10

Traner Furniture Company

Selected Financial Projections, Next Year
(thousands, for sales and net income)

Item	*First Quarter*	*Second Quarter*	*Third Quarter*	*Fourth Quarter*
Sales	$22,965	$21,729	$28,741	$27,614
Net income	784	1,099	2,289	2,312
Earnings per share	$0.29	$0.41	$0.85	$0.86

some board members from all of these camps would argue strongly against the company's policy of paying a regular quarterly dividend of 14 cents; the remainder has been the declaration of an extra dividend at year-end. TFC has followed this procedure the past five years. Those against it feel that the "extra" portion of the dividend should be built into the regular quarterly payment.

QUESTIONS

1. Prepare a table that contains yearly price-earnings ratios, dividend payout ratios, and market value to book value ratios for TFC and its three main competitors.

2. Compute compound annual growth rates in earnings per share for TFC and competitors. Use

$$\frac{\text{EPS current year}}{\text{EPS 4 years ago}}$$

to develop appropriate interest factors; then convert these interest factors to approximate (and appropriate) growth rates in earnings per share.

3. Compute a five-year composite dividend payout ratio for TFC and competitors by evaluating

$$\sum_{t=1}^{5} D_t/E_t$$

where D_t is cash dividend paid during time period t and E_t is earnings per share during time period t.

4. Recall that the growth rate in the Gordon valuation and cost-of-capital model can be represented by $G = br$, where b is the fraction of current earnings retained and r is the productivity of those retentions. Using information derived from the previous two questions, calculate the implied productivity of retentions for the subject firms.

5. Considering all data, make a recommendation as to the proper *payout ratio* for TFC to strive to maintain over longer periods and as to the *size* of the dividend for each of the four quarters of next year.

CASE 55

Hyatt Petroleum Corporation

Mergers and Acquisitions

The Hyatt Petroleum Corporation is a partially integrated oil company that explores for, produces, refines, and markets petroleum and petroleum products. The corporation was organized in 1944 and its stock is currently traded on the over-the-counter market.

The history of the company dates back to Joseph Hyatt, a student from the University of Nebraska who arrived in Ponca City, Louisiana, in 1932. His professional goal at that time was to revolutionize the oil industry through the latest developments in petroleum geology. After conducting extensive technical research, he leased land that he considered to be the most promising in terms of oil reserves. Drawing upon his own limited financial resources, he immediately began a drilling program. At first, his efforts proved to be disappointing; however, as his funds were quickly approaching complete depletion, a large payload was discovered, which proved to be the foundation of the firm's financial welfare. In 1944, the enterprise was incorporated under the name Hyatt Petroleum Corporation. It has grown successfully throughout the years, maturing into one of the more successful smaller petroleum companies.

Historically, the corporate efforts in oil and gas exploration have primarily been concentrated throughout the southwestern states of Texas, Oklahoma, Arkansas, and Louisiana. In exploring for such natural resources, Hyatt has, on several occasions, been responsible for innovations in drilling. For instance, company researchers have experimented with lasers, electric sparks, and shaped charges. Additionally, exploration teams are implementing high-pressure jets, which offer substantial improvement for injecting mud, an essential ingredient in the drilling process, through the drill bit nozzle. Moreover, Hyatt has been engaged in the active search for new oil and gas reserves in the Gulf of Mexico, near Yucatan, Old Mexico. In these latter efforts in the gulf, a significant portion of the research has been directed toward exploration of the ocean waters through the application of computer technology. Techniques have been developed for analyzing, modeling, and mapping geological and geophysical data and for solving complex seismic ray-path problems in three dimensions. Also, Hyatt has made advances in offshore drilling methods centering on the Hyatt fixation of a drill ship over a particular location in the water. The new approach combines (1) satellite navigation, thereby determining the vessel location; (2) an acoustic beacon to find the ship's position relative to the sea floor; and (3) a computer-controlled thruster propulsion system to control ship movement.

In addition to the petroleum field, Hyatt is engaged in several other operations. These divisions, mostly originating within the past 10 years, include:

1. *The production of coal.* In recent years, the research department has made several breakthroughs in the area of coal production. Such innovations have included a new process for making substitute hydrocarbon fuels from coal, an improved method for producing pollution-free blast furnace coke from coal, and a revolutionary process for the production of clean, synthetic fuels derived from coal.

2. *Industrial chemicals.* Another area of Hyatt's involvement is the supplying of industrial chemicals for use in biodegradable detergents and vinyl plastics. The company's major chemical complex, located in Ruskmore, Louisiana, derives hydrocarbon feedstocks from natural gas and petroleum for the purpose of producing ethylene, vinyl chloride monomer, paraffin, and industrial alcohols. These intermediary products are either sold to commodity customers or represent raw materials for use in further processing within the Hyatt system.

3. *Hard mineral production.* Remaining activities of Hyatt's business are in the exploration for and production of hard minerals. In 1978, the company opened a uranium plant in Overton, Texas, and since then has expanded its search for additional deposits in all four states where its oil and gas exploration efforts are concentrated. The company is presently conducting negotiations with New Mexico for obtaining the drilling rights for a potential copper deposit believed to exist north of Santa Fe. Even though Hyatt is relatively new in the mineral production and research area, this is quickly becoming an area of increasing importance to the enterprise.

More recently, however, the management at Hyatt, owing to increasing costs and long-term commitments, has had to restrain investment in the firm's major research projects. This recent inability to conduct the research deemed to be essential to the business has its roots in two areas. First, the company is encountering a deterioration in its working capital position. As can be seen in Exhibit 1, the current ratio in 1992 was .92, and .80 in 1993. The company is having difficulty generating the cash necessary to meet its everyday working capital needs. For a case in point, the cash po-

---

EXHIBIT 1

Hyatt Petroleum Corporation

Consolidated Balance Sheets as of
December 31, 1992 and December 31, 1993
(thousands)

	1992	1993
Assets		
Current assets		
Cash	$ 1,054	$ 218
Accounts receivables, less allowances	5,254	5,683
Inventories, at lower of costs or market	10,521	11,211
Prepaid expenses	312	112
Total current assets	$17,141	$17,224
Property, plant, and equipment		
Land	455	511
Buildings and improvements	16,238	16,084
Machinery and equipment	21,569	22,773
Allowances for depreciation	(8,522)	(8,984)
Net property, plant, and equipment	$29,740	$30,384
Other assets	723	844
Total assets	$47,604	$48,452
Liabilities and Stockholders' Equity		
Current liabilities		
Accounts payable	$12,543	$13,866
Accrued liabilities	4,595	5,854
Federal income taxes	1,583	1,721
Total current liabilities	$18,721	$21,441
Stockholder's equity		
Common stock, $1.00 par value		
Authorized 25,000,000 shares; issued and		
outstanding 10,000,000 shares since		
1981	10,000	10,000
Additional paid-in capital	4,325	4,325
Retained earnings	14,558	12,686
Total liabilities and stockholders' equity	$47,604	$48,452

sition (Exhibit 1) declined from $1,054,000 in 1992 to $218,000 in 1993. As a result of the working capital shortage, Hyatt has felt compelled to decrease the allocation of funds directed to research and development as well as for plant and equipment expenditures.

The second problem being encountered is the volatility in corporate revenues. As can be seen in Exhibit 2, during the past five years, sales have ranged from a high of $48,293,000 in 1990 to a low of $26,674,000 in 1991. The fluctuations are mostly the result of volatile oil prices. Similarly, the earnings available to common stockholders have been subject to large fluctuations. As a consequence of the uncertainty in profits, dividend payments to the common shareholders have been terminated intermittently during the past several years, including the most recent period.

Because of these circumstances, a special meeting of the board of directors was called on June 27, 1993. At the meeting, James Nolan, vice president of research and development, pressed the other board members to realize that unless the current financial trends of Hyatt were reversed, the company would lag behind competitors in the near-term future. After a convincing presentation on the part of Nolan, the board decided to appoint Albert Green, vice president of finance, as chairman of a special committee to analyze various alternative measures for solving the financial difficulties facing Hyatt. He was to report back to the board concerning his findings, with the board, in turn, developing a presentation for the forthcoming annual stockholders' meeting in December.

EXHIBIT 2

Hyatt Petroleum Corporation

Income Statements for the Years Ending
December 31, 1989–1992
(thousands)

	1989	1990	1991	1992	1993
Net sales	$31,365	$48,293	$26,674	$41,817	$33,542
Cost of goods sold	26,660	38,015	22,940	37,094	28,678
Gross profit	$ 4,705	$10,278	$ 3,734	$ 7,723	$ 1,864
Selling and administrative expenses	2,615	4,811	1,780	3,926	3,002
Earnings before interest and taxes	2,095	5,467	1,954	3,797	1,862
Interest expenses	129	217	183	211	194
Taxable income	1,961	5,250	1,771	3,586	1,668
Federal income taxes	935	2,516	844	1,715	794
Earnings available to common stockholders	$ 1,026	$ 2,734	$ 927	$ 1,871	$ 874
Earnings per share	$0.1026	$0.2734	$0.0927	$0.1871	$0.0874
Dividends per share	—	$0.1000	—	$0.0800	—

On October 23, 1993, Green returned to the board with the committee's analysis. The committee believed that an amount between $12 million and $15 million would be required for providing sufficient capital. These funds would be employed to relieve the existing deficiency in research and development, and for solving the shortage in working capital.

The committee presented three possible avenues for raising the necessary financing:

Alternative 1:   Based upon preliminary discussions with Jeff Jarrett of Warren Brothers, an investment banking firm, concerning the issuance of common stock, Jarrett noted that such an offering could feasibly be made in February 1994. This time frame was selected in view of the fact that market analysts were predicting an upturn in the market in early 1994. Such timing should result in Hyatt receiving a higher price for its stock, thus necessitating issuance of a fewer number of shares. Furthermore, Jarrett believes that the underwriting would net the firm, after flotation costs, approximately $2.87 per share. If this alternative is selected, Green, along with his committee, considers an issuance of 4,725,000 as being essential to raise the necessary funds. Thus, this financing plan would raise $13,560,750, thereby falling in the $12 million to $15 million range of the company's estimated financial needs.

Alternative 2:   Hyatt could also issue long-term 8.5 percent debentures for providing the additional funds. In the preliminary negotiations with Warren Brothers concerning the possibility of such an offering, the underwriters recommend a $13,500,000 issue, out of which flotation costs of $250,000 would have to be paid. A covenant providing for a sinking fund is thought to be essential to creating adequate marketability of the bond. In addition, the bonds would be issued with a 10-year maturity date of 2004. Warren Brothers further advises a postponement in the offering until March 1994. Current estimates indicate a softening of long-term interest rates in conjunction with the anticipated rise in the stock market.

Alternative 3:   The management of Hyatt Corporation has been working with Gaines Corporation, a closely held fertilizer enterprise, concerning the feasibility of a merger between the two firms. Gaines is a small, but well-known, manufacturer and distributor of a specialized fertilizer and an all-purpose, water-soluble insecticide. The plant facilities and offices are located in Atlanta, Goergia. Although the firm was incorporated in 1940, all of the common stock is still being held by the Gaines family (Exhibit 3).

With respect to Gaines's products, the company's fertilizer and insecticides are marketed under the name of Gaines-Rite, with sales being pri-

EXHIBIT 3

Hyatt Petroleum Corporation

*Gaines Corporation Stockholder List**

	Number of Shares	Percentage of Total Number of Shares Outstanding
Robert M. Gaines, Sr.	708,772	70.9%
Joan A. Gaines	170,522	17.1
Carolyn Gaines	84,614	8.5
Robert M. Gaines, Jr.	23,036	2.2
Robert Gaines, Jr. for Lou Ann Gaines	13,056	1.3
Total	1,000,000	100.0%

*No new shares have been issued since 1988.

marily lawn and garden related. The revenues are normally distributed throughout the year on a relatively stable basis and have been steadily increasing each year. The company retails its merchandise in the southern states, with a concentration in Mississippi, Alabama, Georgia, and Florida. The retail outlets include feed and seed stores, hardware stores, and agricultural cooperatives. In addition to the small retailers, the firm deals directly with several large farm operations. Also, the corporation has enjoyed phenomenal success in the area of research and development. Plans are being made to market a new multipurpose fertilizer in the spring of 1994.

Robert M. Gaines Sr., the founder and principal shareholder, served as president of the organization from its inception until 1984, at which time he was succeeded by Robert M. Gaines Jr. The Gaines family have been the only management personnel, and the firm has continued to prosper under their leadership. As may be observed in Exhibit 4, the price of Gaines's common stock has steadily increased during the past three years. Although the stock is not listed on an organized exchange, offers to purchase shares have been received by the Gaines family on an infrequent basis.

Initial conferences with the Gaines family have evidenced a genuine interest on their part in a potential acquisition. Both parties agree that the combination should be conducted via an exchange of common stock, with the Gaines family receiving a specified number of Hyatt shares upon the relinquishment of their shares in the Gaines Corporation. However, final settlement of the exchange ratio has not been accomplished. Robert Gaines maintains that the trade should be based upon the firms' relative earnings per share, while Robert Green, representing Hyatt, contends that the market price of the respective securities would be a more equitable basis. As part of his analysis, he has used financial statements for the two corporations (Exhibits 5–8) and industry norms (Exhibit 9).

―――――――――――――――― **EXHIBIT 4** ――――――――――――――――

Hyatt Petroleum Corporation

*Market Price of Common Stock of Hyatt
Corporation and Gaines Corporation, 1991–1993*

	Hyatt Corporation Market Prices (listed on NYSE)			Gaines Corporation Market Prices*		
	High	*Low*	*Year-End*	*High*	*Low*	*Year-End*
1991	$3.50	$2.75	$3.25	$21.50	$17.50	NA
1992	4.25	3.50	3.75	23.00	21.00	NA
1993	3.50	2.50	3.00	25.50	23.50	NA

NA = not available.

*Estimate based upon offers made to members of the Gaines family.

―――――――――――――――― **EXHIBIT 5** ――――――――――――――――

Hyatt Petroleum Corporation

*Pro Forma Funds Flow Statements, Years Ending
December 31, 1994–1996
(thousands)*

	1994			Combined	
	Hyatt	*Gaines*	*Combined*	*1995*	*1996*
Sources of funds					
Sales	$34,218	$18,355	$52,573	$64,945	$68,554
Less: Cost of goods sold	29,085	14,940	44,025	53,952	55,781
Less: Selling and general expenses	3,108	1,435	4,543	6,083	6,361
Less: Interest	208	—	208	211	213
Earnings before taxes	$ 1,817	$ 1,980	$ 3,797	$ 4,699	$ 6,199
Less: Taxes	866	944	1,810	2,249	2,969
Add: Depreciation	433	315	748	765	780
Total sources	$ 1,384	$ 1,351	$ 2,735	$ 3,215	$ 4,010
Use of funds					
Additions to facilities	3,218	315	3,533	326	334
Sinking fund	453	—	453	453	453
Increase in noncurrent assets	118	52	170	111	115
Common dividends	—	—	—	438	438
Total uses	$ 3,789	$ 367	$ 4,156	$ 1,328	$ 1,340
Additions (deductions) to working capital	$ (2,405)	$ 984	$ (1,421)	$ 1,887	$ 2,670

──────────────── EXHIBIT 6 ────────────────

Hyatt Petroleum Corporation

Projected Earnings per Share for the Years 1994–2001

	1994	1995	1996	1997	1998	1999	2000	2001
Hyatt	$0.095	$0.136	$0.210	$0.140	$0.200	$0.330	$0.240	$0.380
Gaines	1.036	1.090	1.130	1.17	1.20	1.18	1.24	1.30

──────────────── EXHIBIT 7 ────────────────

Hyatt Petroleum Corporation

Gaines Corporation Balance Sheet
December 31, 1993
(thousands)

Assets

Current assets	
Cash	$ 1,012
Accounts receivable	1,315
Inventories	1,611
Prepaid expenses	154
Total current assets	$ 4,092

Property, plant, and equipment	
Land	250
Buildings and improvements	5,378
Machinery and equipment	6,452
Allowances for depreciation	(2,318)
Net property, plant, and equipment	9,762
Total assets	$13,854

Liabilities and Stockholders' Equity

Current liabilities	
Accounts payable	$ 653
Accrued liabilities	477
Federal income taxes	329
Total current liabilities	$ 1,459

Stockholders' equity	
Common stock, $10 par value, authorized 1,500,000 shares; issued and outstanding 1,500,000 shares since 1987	5,000
Retained earnings	7,395
Total liabilities and stockholders' equity	$13,854

―――――――――――――― EXHIBIT 8 ――――――――――――――

Hyatt Petroleum Corporation

Gaines Corporation
Income Statement
for Year Ended December 31, 1993
(thousands)

Sales	$16,743
Cost of goods sold	13,709
Gross profit	3,034
Selling and general expenses	1,085
Earnings before interest and taxes	$ 1,949
Interest expense	—
Taxable income	1,949
Federal income taxes	929
Earnings available to common stockholders	$ 1,020
Earnings per share	$1.02
Dividends per share	0.00

―――――――――――――― EXHIBIT 9 ――――――――――――――

Hyatt Petroleum Corporation

Selected Petroleum Industry Ratios for 1993

Current ratio	1.00
Quick ratio	.80
Cash ratio	.25
Receivable turnover	4.00X
Inventory turnover*	2.80X
Total debt to total assets	40%
Return on investment (before interest and taxes)	7.50%
Times interest earned	9.50X

*Based upon cost of goods sold.

QUESTIONS

1. What do you perceive to be Hyatt's major problem areas?

2. If the acquisition plan is selected, what reason(s) might be given for the exchange ratio to be based upon (a) 1993 earnings per share or (b) the average 1993 market prices?

3. Assume the final exchange ratio is negotiated between the two firms with the basis being a function of the market price. With this additional information, analyze Hyatt's three alternatives for raising funds, citing the advantages and disadvantages of each plan.

CASE 56

Northwest Toy Company

Interest Rate Futures Market

Northwest Toy Company is a medium-sized firm that develops and produces a line of children's toys for general distribution to retail stores. In addition to this regular line, the company produces special-order children's toys for various large chain stores that place their own brand names on the toys. Because most toys are purchased during the Christmas season, the company has an extremely seasonal sales pattern.

It is currently November 1991, and the comptroller, Janet Smith, has just been given a cash budget for the next year that indicates the company will have $1,000,000 of excess cash to invest in March. This money consists mainly of advance payments from chain stores that have placed orders for Northwest's special-order toys. This amount can be invested for 90 days, after which time it will be needed to finance the inventory buildup for the Christmas season. As the inventory buildup continues, the company will need more funds, and the cash budget projects that $3,000,000 of funds must be borrowed for three months from September until December, when the retail stores will be reimbursing the company for their purchases.

In the past, Smith has always invested the firm's excess cash in Treasury bills and has borrowed any financing required from a bank at ½ percent above the prime rate. Recent volatility in the money market, however, has made it impossible for her to provide very accurate forecasts of the company's borrowing costs and income from investment in marketable securities. This has upset Northwest Toy's cost accountants, since they use the company's short-term borrowing costs to forecast the cost of producing each type of toy, and this information is, in turn, used in setting the wholesale price at which the specific toy will be sold to the retail outlets. Because of the competitive nature of the toy industry, it is important that costs not be overstated, for the company would then set too high a price and lose sales to its competitors. On the other hand, if costs are understated, the company could lose money on each item it sells.

The projected income from investment in marketable securities is also very important in determining the company's pricing structure on its line of special-order toys. The typical industry procedure on these special orders is to require an advance deposit in March. This is in contrast to procedure in the regular line of toys, where payments are received after the merchandise has been shipped and invoiced. To compensate the chain stores for the advance deposit requirement, the company discounts the price to the chain store by an amount that implicitly represents the opportunity cost of the funds tied up in the deposit. The discount is therefore typically tied to the money market rates that are in effect at the time of the deposit.

As usual, Smith has been asked for estimates of the company's short-term borrowing costs and the interest that will be earned on investments in marketable securities for the relevant periods in 1992. Economic forecasts indicate that interest rates will moderate somewhat, but the decline is expected to be less than one-half percent in 1992. Smith, however, has used these economic forecasts in the past and has been disappointed when future rates differed from those forecasted. The economists always found plenty of explanations for the discrepancy, but, unfortunately, when the company's profits suffered because of inaccurate forecasts, it was Smith, not the economists, who had to answer to the cost accountants. Smith was therefore willing to go to great lengths to make her forecasts accurate for the coming year.

She has decided to use the Treasury bill futures market to hedge against changes in interest rates. Currently, Treasury bill interest rates are $7\frac{3}{4}$ percent and the prime rate is 10 percent. Past data indicate that the prime rate and Treasury bill rates are reasonably correlated, with the average differential being $2\frac{1}{4}$ percent.

Today's quotations for Treasury bill futures are given in Exhibit 1. Smith's broker has informed her that the commission of $60 per $1 million contract, paid at the order's initiation, is a round-trip fee that includes both the opening and closing commissions. The broker also explained that a margin in the amount of $1,500 per contract must be deposited at the time a futures contract is initiated. When the position is closed out, the investor receives the margin deposit plus or minus any profit or loss on the futures contract.

EXHIBIT 1

Northwest Toy Company

Interest Rate Instruments,
November 4, 1991

Treasury bills (IMM)—$1 mil; pts of 100%

| | | | | | | Discount | | Open |
	Open	High	Low	Settle	Chg	Settle	Chg	Interest
Dec.	92.23	92.32	92.23	92.30	+.07	7.70	−.07	37,090
Mr92	92.63	92.73	92.63	92.70	+.07	7.30	−.07	18,201
June	92.72	92.80	92.72	92.79	+.13	7.21	−.13	848
Sept.	92.54	92.63	92.54	92.61	+.13	7.31	−.13	213
Dec.	92.40	92.45	92.40	92.42	+.12	7.58	−.12	138

Est vol 9,573; vol Fri 8,992; open int 56,490, −615.

QUESTIONS

1. Describe the transaction Smith should execute to hedge against changes in interest rates on the purchase of three-month Treasury bills in March.

2. On March 15, interest rates have decreased and Smith closes out her futures position. The Treasury bill IMM Index is at 93.53 and the spot market discount quote on 90-day Treasury bills is 6.50. If Smith holds the Treasury bills until maturity, what is the total dollar amount of interest earned net of any profit/loss and commissions on the futures transaction?

3. What is the total dollar amount of interest earned if interest rates increase, the IMM Index is at 91.19, and the spot market discount quote on 90-day Treasury bills is 8.84?

4. Explain why the net interest earned is the same whether interest rates go up or down.

5. Describe the transaction Smith should execute to hedge against changes in the company's borrowing rate in September. What is the net interest cost of borrowing if the prime rate in September goes up to 11 percent and the Treasury bill IMM Index is at 91.25? What is the net interest cost of borrowing if the prime rate is 8 percent and the Treasury bill IMM Index is at 93.58?

6. What is the reason for the reduced borrowing cost for the declining interest rate example in question 5? What are some of the other reasons why risks cannot be perfectly hedged using futures markets?

7. Of what relevance are current 90-day interest rates in guaranteeing future borrowing and lending rates for the firm? What are some of the underlying reasons for changes in interest rates on U.S. Treasury bills?

8. Suppose that you forecast a level of interest rates different from the market consensus. For example, suppose you forecast that 90-day Treasury

bill rates will be 9 percent in March 1992. Assume that you do, indeed, have superior predictive powers and that the March Treasury bill IMM Index is at 91.00 on January 21. Show how you can profit from your superior predictive ability through the use of five Treasury bill futures contracts.

9. Some people have argued that futures markets encourage dangerous speculation because the small margin requirement produces a highly leveraged investment that has the potential of large gains and losses relative to the investment needed to open a futures position. From the viewpoint of society and the economy, what are some of the desirable and undesirable effects of futures markets?

APPENDIX A

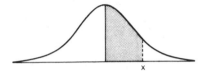

The area indicated in the table is equal to the area between the mean and x standard deviations to the right or left of the mean.

Number of Standard Deviations from the Mean (x)	Area	Number of Standard Deviations from the Mean (x)	Area
.00	.00000	.10	.03983
.01	.00399	.11	.04380
.02	.00798	.12	.04776
.03	.01197	.13	.05172
.04	.01595	.14	.05567
.05	.01994	.15	.05962
.06	.02392	.16	.06356
.07	.02790	.17	.06749
.08	.03188	.18	.07142
.09	.03586	.19	.07535
.20	.07926	.69	.25490
.21	.08317	.70	.25804
.22	.08706	.71	.26115
.23	.09095	.72	.26424
.24	.09483	.73	.26730
.25	.09871	.74	.27035
.26	.10257	.75	.27337
.27	.10642	.76	.27637
.28	.11026	.77	.27935
.29	.11409	.78	.28230
.30	.11791	.79	.28524
.31	.12172	.80	.28814
.32	.12552	.81	.29103
.33	.12930	.82	.29389
.34	.13307	.83	.29673
.35	.13683	.84	.29955
.36	.14058	.85	.30234
.37	.14431	.86	.30511

Number of Standard Deviations from the Mean (x)	Area	Number of Standard Deviations from the Mean (x)	Area
.38	.14803	.87	.30785
.39	.15173	.88	.31057
.40	.15542	.89	.31327
.41	.15910	.90	.31594
.42	.16276	.91	.31859
.43	.16640	.92	.32121
.44	.17003	.93	.32381
.45	.17364	.94	.32639
.46	.17724	.95	.32894
.47	.18082	.96	.33147
.48	.18439	.97	.33398
.49	.18793	.98	.33646
.50	.19146	.99	.33891
.51	.19497	1.00	.34134
.52	.19847	1.01	.34375
.53	.20194	1.02	.34614
.54	.20540	1.03	.34849
.55	.20884	1.04	.35083
.56	.21226	1.05	.35314
.57	.21566	1.06	.35543
.58	.21904	1.07	.35769
.59	.22240	1.08	.35993
.60	.22575	1.09	.36214
.61	.22907	1.10	.36433
.62	.23237	1.11	.36650
.63	.23565	1.12	.36864
.64	.23891	1.13	.37076
.65	.24215	1.14	.37286
.66	.24537	1.15	.37493
.67	.24857	1.16	.37698
.68	.25175	1.17	.37900
1.18	.38100	1.67	.45254
1.19	.38298	1.68	.45352
1.20	.38493	1.69	.45449
1.21	.38686	1.70	.45543
1.22	.38877	1.71	.45637
1.23	.39065	1.72	.45728
1.24	.39251	1.73	.45818
1.25	.39435	1.74	.45907
1.26	.39617	1.75	.45994
1.27	.39796	1.76	.46080
1.28	.39973	1.77	.46164
1.29	.40147	1.78	.46246
1.30	.40320	1.79	.46327
1.31	.40490	1.80	.46407
1.32	.40658	1.81	.46485
1.33	.40824	1.82	.46562
1.34	.40988	1.83	.46638
1.35	.41149	1.84	.46712

Number of Standard Deviations from the Mean (x)	Area	Number of Standard Deviations from the Mean (x)	Area
1.36	.41309	1.85	.46784
1.37	.41466	1.86	.46856
1.38	.41621	1.87	.46926
1.39	.41774	1.88	.46995
1.40	.41924	1.89	.47062
1.41	.42073	1.90	.47128
1.42	.42220	1.91	.47193
1.43	.42364	1.92	.47257
1.44	.42507	1.93	.47320
1.45	.42647	1.94	.47381
1.46	.42785	1.95	.47441
1.47	.42922	1.96	.47500
1.48	.43056	1.97	.47558
1.49	.43189	1.98	.47615
1.50	.43319	1.99	.47670
1.51	.43448	2.00	.47725
1.52	.43574	2.01	.47778
1.53	.43699	2.02	.47831
1.54	.43822	2.03	.47882
1.55	.43943	2.04	.47932
1.56	.44062	2.05	.47982
1.57	.44179	2.06	.48030
1.58	.44295	2.07	.48077
1.59	.44408	2.08	.48124
1.60	.44520	2.09	.48169
1.61	.44630	2.10	.48214
1.62	.44738	2.11	.48257
1.63	.44845	2.12	.48300
1.64	.44950	2.13	.48341
1.65	.45053	2.14	.48382
1.66	.45154	2.15	.48422
2.16	.48461	2.65	.49598
2.17	.48500	2.66	.49609
2.18	.48537	2.67	.49621
2.19	.48574	2.68	.49632
2.20	.48610	2.69	.49643
2.21	.48645	2.70	.49653
2.22	.48679	2.71	.49664
2.23	.48713	2.72	.49674
2.24	.48745	2.73	.49683
2.25	.48778	2.74	.49693
2.26	.48809	2.75	.49702
2.27	.48840	2.76	.49711
2.28	.48870	2.77	.49720
2.29	.48899	2.78	.49728
2.30	.48928	2.79	.49736
2.31	.48956	2.80	.49744
2.32	.48983	2.81	.49752
2.33	.49010	2.82	.49760

Number of Standard Deviations from the Mean (x)	Area	Number of Standard Deviations from the Mean (x)	Area
2.34	.49036	2.83	.49767
2.35	.49061	2.84	.49774
2.36	.49086	2.85	.49781
2.37	.49111	2.86	.49788
2.38	.49134	2.87	.49795
2.39	.49158	2.88	.49801
2.40	.49180	2.89	.49807
2.41	.49202	2.90	.49813
2.42	.49224	2.91	.49819
2.43	.49245	2.92	.49825
2.44	.49266	2.93	.49831
2.45	.49286	2.94	.49836
2.46	.49305	2.95	.49841
2.47	.49324	2.96	.49846
2.48	.49343	2.97	.49851
2.49	.49361	2.98	.49856
2.50	.49379	2.99	.49861
2.51	.49396	3.00	.49865
2.52	.49413	3.01	.49869
2.53	.49430	3.02	.49874
2.54	.49446	3.03	.49878
2.55	.49461	3.04	.49882
2.56	.49477	3.05	.49886
2.57	.49492	3.06	.49889
2.58	.49506	3.07	.49893
2.59	.49520	3.08	.49896
2.60	.49534	3.09	.49900
2.61	.49547	3.10	.49903
2.62	.49560	3.11	.49906
2.63	.49573	3.12	.49910
2.64	.49585	3.13	.49913
3.14	.49916	3.57	.49982
3.15	.49918	3.58	.49983
3.16	.49921	3.59	.49983
3.17	.49924	3.60	.49984
3.18	.49926	3.61	.49985
3.19	.49929	3.62	.49985
3.20	.49931	3.63	.49986
3.21	.49934	3.64	.49986
3.22	.49936	3.65	.49987
3.23	.49938	3.66	.49987
3.24	.49940	3.67	.49988
3.25	.49942	3.68	.49988
3.26	.49944	3.69	.49989
3.27	.49946	3.70	.49989
3.28	.49948	3.71	.49990
3.29	.49950	3.72	.49990
3.30	.49952	3.73	.49990
3.31	.49953	3.74	.49991

Number of Standard Deviations from the Mean (x)	Area	Number of Standard Deviations from the Mean (x)	Area
3.32	.49955	3.75	.49991
3.33	.49957	3.76	.49992
3.34	.49958	3.77	.49992
3.35	.49960	3.78	.49992
3.36	.49961	3.79	.49992
3.37	.49962	3.80	.49993
3.38	.49964	3.81	.49993
3.39	.49965	3.82	.49993
3.40	.49966	3.83	.49994
3.41	.49968	3.84	.49994
3.42	.49969	3.85	.49994
3.43	.49970	3.86	.49994
3.44	.49971	3.87	.49995
3.45	.49972	3.88	.49995
3.46	.49973	3.89	.49995
3.47	.49974	3.90	.49995
3.48	.49975	3.91	.49995
3.49	.49976	3.92	.49996
3.50	.49977	3.93	.49996
3.51	.49978	3.94	.49996
3.52	.49978	3.95	.49996
3.53	.49979	3.96	.49996
3.54	.49980	3.97	.49996
3.55	.49981	3.98	.49997
3.56	.49981	3.99	.49997

Source: This table is condensed and derived from *Tables of Normal Probability Functions*, National Bureau of Standards, Applied Mathematics Series 23 (Washington, D.C.: U.S. Government Printing Office, 1953).

APPENDIX B

TABLE B-1

Compound Sum of $1 for N Years

Interest Rates

N	0.01	0.02	0.03	0.04	0.05	0.06	0.07	0.08	0.09	0.10
1	1.01000	1.02000	1.03000	1.04000	1.05000	1.06000	1.07000	1.08000	1.09000	1.10000
2	1.02010	1.04040	1.06090	1.08160	1.10250	1.12360	1.14490	1.16640	1.18810	1.21000
3	1.03030	1.06121	1.09272	1.12486	1.15762	1.19101	1.22504	1.25971	1.29502	1.33100
4	1.04060	1.08243	1.12551	1.16986	1.21550	1.26247	1.31079	1.36049	1.41158	1.46110
5	1.05100	1.10408	1.15927	1.21665	1.27628	1.33822	1.40255	1.46932	1.53862	1.61050
6	1.06151	1.12616	1.19405	1.26532	1.34009	1.41851	1.50072	1.58687	1.67709	1.77155
7	1.07213	1.14868	1.22987	1.31593	1.40709	1.50362	1.60577	1.71382	1.82803	1.94870
8	1.08285	1.17165	1.26676	1.36856	1.47744	1.59384	1.71817	1.85092	1.99255	2.14357
9	1.09367	1.19508	1.30476	1.42330	1.55131	1.68946	1.83845	1.99899	2.17187	2.35793
10	1.10461	1.21898	1.34391	1.48024	1.62888	1.79083	1.96714	2.15891	2.36734	2.59372
11	1.11565	1.24336	1.38422	1.53944	1.71032	1.89828	2.10483	2.33162	2.58040	2.85309
12	1.12681	1.26823	1.42575	1.60102	1.79583	2.01217	2.25217	2.51815	2.81263	3.13840
13	1.13807	1.29359	1.46852	1.66506	1.88562	2.13290	2.40982	2.71960	3.06576	3.45223
14	1.14945	1.31946	1.51257	1.73166	1.97990	2.26087	2.57850	2.93717	3.34168	3.79745
15	1.16095	1.34585	1.55795	1.80093	2.07890	2.39652	2.75900	3.17214	3.64243	4.17719
16	1.17255	1.37277	1.60468	1.87296	2.18284	2.54031	2.95212	3.42591	3.97024	4.59191
17	1.18428	1.40022	1.65282	1.94788	2.29198	2.69273	3.15877	3.69998	4.32736	5.05140
18	1.19612	1.42822	1.70241	2.02579	2.40658	2.85429	3.37988	3.99598	4.71704	5.55983
19	1.20808	1.45679	1.75348	2.10683	2.52690	3.02555	3.61647	4.31565	5.14156	6.11581
20	1.22016	1.48592	1.80608	2.19110	2.65324	3.20707	3.86962	4.66090	5.60430	6.72738
21	1.23236	1.51564	1.86026	2.27874	2.78590	3.39950	4.14049	5.03377	6.10868	7.40011
22	1.24468	1.54595	1.91607	2.36989	2.92520	3.60346	4.43032	5.43647	6.65846	8.14012
23	1.25712	1.57687	1.97355	2.46468	3.07145	3.81967	4.74044	5.87138	7.25771	8.95112
24	1.26969	1.60841	2.03275	2.56327	3.22502	4.04884	5.07227	6.34109	7.91090	9.84952
25	1.28239	1.64057	2.09373	2.66580	3.38627	4.29177	5.42732	6.84838	8.62287	10.83347
26	1.29521	1.67338	2.15654	2.77243	3.55558	4.54927	5.80723	7.39624	9.39892	11.91790
27	1.30816	1.70685	2.22124	2.88332	3.73335	4.82222	6.21373	7.98794	10.24481	13.10968
28	1.32124	1.74098	2.28787	2.99865	3.92002	5.11155	6.64868	8.62696	11.16683	14.42064
29	1.33445	1.77580	2.35651	3.11860	4.11602	5.41824	7.11409	9.31712	12.17183	15.86309
30	1.34780	1.81132	2.42720	3.24334	4.32181	5.74332	7.61206	10.06248	13.26729	17.44893

TABLE B-1

Compound Sum of $1 for N Years

Interest Rates

N	0.11	0.12	0.13	0.14	0.15	0.16	0.17	0.18	0.19	0.20
1	1.11000	1.12000	1.13000	1.14000	1.15000	1.16000	1.17000	1.18000	1.19000	1.20000
2	1.23210	1.25440	1.27690	1.29960	1.32250	1.34560	1.36890	1.39240	1.41610	1.44000
3	1.36763	1.40493	1.44289	1.48154	1.52087	1.56089	1.60161	1.64303	1.68516	1.72800
4	1.51807	1.57352	1.63047	1.68895	1.74900	1.81064	1.87388	1.93877	2.00533	2.07360
5	1.68505	1.76234	1.84243	1.92541	2.01135	2.10034	2.19244	2.28775	2.38635	2.48831
6	1.87041	1.97382	2.08194	2.19496	2.31305	2.43635	2.56515	2.69954	2.83975	2.98598
7	2.07615	2.21067	2.35259	2.50225	2.66001	2.82621	3.00122	3.18546	3.37930	3.58317
8	2.30453	2.47596	2.65842	2.85256	3.05901	3.27840	3.51142	3.75883	4.02137	4.29980
9	2.55802	2.77307	3.00401	3.25192	3.51785	3.80295	4.10836	4.43542	4.78542	5.15976
10	2.83940	3.10584	3.39453	3.70718	4.04553	4.41142	4.80678	5.23379	5.69463	6.19171
11	3.15173	3.47853	3.83381	4.22618	4.65236	5.11724	5.62393	6.17587	6.77663	7.43001
12	3.49842	3.89596	4.33447	4.81785	5.35021	5.93600	6.57998	7.28752	8.06419	8.91605
13	3.88325	4.36347	4.89794	5.49234	6.15273	6.88576	7.69858	8.59927	9.59638	10.69925
14	4.31040	4.88708	5.53467	6.26126	7.07564	7.98747	9.00732	10.14712	11.41968	12.83910
15	4.78454	5.47353	6.25416	7.13783	8.13698	9.26546	10.53856	11.97360	13.58941	15.40691
16	5.31084	6.13035	7.06720	8.13711	9.35752	10.74793	12.33010	14.12883	16.17139	18.48827
17	5.89503	6.86599	7.98593	9.27631	10.76114	12.46760	14.42620	16.67201	19.24394	22.18591
18	6.54347	7.68991	9.02409	10.57498	12.37530	14.46241	16.87863	19.67294	22.90027	26.62308
19	7.26325	8.61269	10.19721	12.05546	14.23158	16.77638	19.74799	23.21407	27.25130	31.94768
20	8.06220	9.64621	11.52283	13.74321	16.36630	19.46059	23.10510	27.39236	32.42903	38.33719
21	8.94901	10.80376	13.02079	15.66724	18.82124	22.57428	27.03296	32.32320	38.59053	46.00461
22	9.93343	12.10020	14.71347	17.86063	21.64441	26.18616	31.62852	38.14134	45.92271	55.20549
23	11.02609	13.55221	16.62619	20.36110	24.89105	30.37592	37.00534	45.00676	54.64798	66.24637
24	12.23896	15.17848	18.78758	23.21162	28.62468	35.23607	43.29719	53.10793	65.03107	79.49683
25	13.58523	16.99988	21.23095	26.46124	32.91837	40.87383	50.65649	62.66731	77.38693	95.39497
26	15.07960	19.03986	23.98982	30.16577	37.85609	47.41362	59.26805	73.94736	92.09041	114.47389
27	16.73833	21.32463	27.10846	34.38895	43.53448	54.99976	69.34354	87.25783	109.58749	137.36862
28	18.57954	23.88358	30.63252	39.20335	50.06462	63.79970	81.13185	102.96411	130.40907	164.84224
29	20.62328	26.74960	34.61472	44.69179	57.57428	74.00764	94.92419	121.49756	155.18671	197.81067
30	22.89183	29.95955	39.11458	50.94858	66.21037	85.84883	111.06117	143.36697	184.67207	237.37262

TABLE B-1

Compound Sum of $1 for N Years

Interest Rates

N	0.21	0.22	0.23	0.24	0.25	0.26	0.27	0.28	0.29	0.30
1	1.21000	1.22000	1.23000	1.24000	1.25000	1.26000	1.27000	1.28000	1.29000	1.30000
2	1.46410	1.48840	1.51290	1.53760	1.56250	1.58760	1.61290	1.63840	1.66410	1.69000
3	1.77156	1.81584	1.86086	1.90662	1.95313	2.00037	2.04838	2.09715	2.14669	2.19699
4	2.14358	2.21533	2.28886	2.36421	2.44141	2.52047	2.60144	2.68435	2.76923	2.85609
5	2.59373	2.70270	2.81530	2.93162	3.05176	3.17579	3.30383	3.43597	3.57230	3.71292
6	3.13841	3.29729	3.46281	3.63520	3.81470	4.00149	4.19586	4.39804	4.60827	4.82679
7	3.79747	4.02269	4.25926	4.50765	4.76837	5.04187	5.32873	5.62949	5.94467	6.27482
8	4.59493	4.90767	5.23889	5.58948	5.96046	6.35275	6.76749	7.20574	7.66862	8.15726
9	5.55986	5.98736	6.44383	6.93096	7.45058	8.00446	8.59470	9.22334	9.89252	10.60443
10	6.72743	7.30457	7.92590	8.59438	9.31323	10.08562	10.91526	11.80588	12.76134	13.78575
11	8.14018	8.91157	9.74885	10.65703	11.64153	12.70787	13.86238	15.11152	16.46213	17.92145
12	9.84960	10.87211	11.99108	13.21471	14.55192	16.01190	17.60519	19.34273	21.23813	23.29787
13	11.91801	13.26396	14.74903	16.38623	18.18988	20.17497	22.35860	24.75868	27.39461	30.28722
14	14.42077	16.18201	18.14128	20.31891	22.73737	25.42044	28.39539	31.69112	35.33905	39.37335
15	17.44911	19.74203	22.31377	25.19543	28.42171	32.02974	36.06212	40.56461	45.58737	51.18530
16	21.11340	24.08527	27.44592	31.24232	35.52713	40.35745	45.79887	51.92268	58.80769	66.54085
17	25.54720	29.38400	33.75847	38.74046	44.40891	50.85036	58.16454	66.46101	75.86191	86.50304
18	30.91206	35.84845	41.52289	48.03815	55.51114	64.07140	73.86890	85.07007	97.86186	112.45387
19	37.40356	43.73506	51.07312	59.56726	69.38892	80.72990	93.81345	108.88963	126.24179	146.18988
20	45.25826	53.35674	62.81990	73.86339	86.73615	101.71960	119.14299	139.37869	162.85185	190.04674
21	54.76244	65.09517	77.26845	91.59058	108.42020	128.16663	151.31152	178.40469	210.07883	247.06059
22	66.26247	79.41603	95.04013	113.57222	135.52524	161.48981	192.16548	228.35793	271.00171	321.17847
23	80.17751	96.88748	116.89926	140.82947	169.40656	203.47702	244.04999	292.29785	349.59204	417.53149
24	97.01466	118.20265	143.78606	174.62848	211.75819	256.38086	309.94312	374.14136	450.97363	542.79077
25	117.38765	144.20712	176.85677	216.53926	264.69751	323.03955	393.62769	478.90063	581.75610	705.62744
26	142.03886	175.93253	217.53368	268.50830	330.87207	407.02954	499.90674	612.99268	750.46509	917.31519
27	171.86688	214.63751	267.56616	332.95020	413.59009	512.85693	634.88110	784.63037	968.09961	1192.50830
28	207.95863	261.85742	329.10620	412.85815	516.98755	646.19946	806.29785	1004.32617	1248.84766	1550.25977
29	251.62975	319.46582	404.80054	511.94385	646.23413	814.21045	1023.99854	1285.53711	1611.01367	2015.33691
30	304.47144	389.74780	497.90405	634.80981	807.79321	1025.90405	1300.47656	1645.48779	2078.20801	2619.93604

TABLE B-2

Compound Amount of an *N* Year Annuity

Interest Rates

N	0.01	0.02	0.03	0.04	0.05	0.06	0.07	0.08	0.09	0.10
1	1.00000	1.00000	1.00000	1.00000	1.00000	1.00000	1.00000	1.00000	1.00000	1.00000
2	2.01000	2.02000	2.03000	2.04000	2.05000	2.06000	2.07000	2.08000	2.09000	2.10000
3	3.03010	3.06040	3.09090	3.12160	3.15250	3.18360	3.21490	3.24640	3.27810	3.31000
4	4.06039	4.12160	4.18362	4.24646	4.31012	4.37461	4.43994	4.50611	4.57312	4.64099
5	5.10099	5.20403	5.30913	5.41632	5.52562	5.63708	5.75073	5.86660	5.98470	6.10509
6	6.15200	6.30811	6.46840	6.63297	6.80190	6.97530	7.15328	7.33592	7.52331	7.71559
7	7.21351	7.43427	7.66245	7.89828	8.14198	8.39381	8.65400	8.92279	9.20041	9.48714
8	8.28563	8.58295	8.89231	9.21421	9.54907	9.89743	10.25977	10.63661	11.02843	11.43585
9	9.36848	9.75460	10.15907	10.58277	11.02652	11.49127	11.97795	12.48753	13.02098	13.57942
10	10.46215	10.94968	11.46384	12.00608	12.57783	13.18073	13.81639	14.48652	15.19285	15.93735
11	11.56676	12.16867	12.80774	13.48631	14.20671	14.97157	15.78353	16.64543	17.56018	18.53107
12	12.68241	13.41203	14.19197	15.02576	15.91703	16.86984	17.88835	18.97705	20.14056	21.38416
13	13.80922	14.68026	15.61771	16.62677	17.71286	18.88200	20.14052	21.49519	22.95319	24.52254
14	14.94729	15.97385	17.08623	18.29184	19.59848	21.01489	22.55034	24.21478	26.01894	27.97476
15	16.09674	17.29330	18.59879	20.02350	21.57838	23.27576	25.12883	27.15195	29.36061	31.77220
16	17.25769	18.63914	20.15672	21.82442	23.65727	25.67227	27.88782	30.32408	33.00304	35.94939
17	18.43024	20.01190	21.76140	23.69737	25.84010	28.21257	30.83994	33.74998	36.97327	40.54428
18	19.61450	21.41211	23.41422	25.64525	28.13208	30.90529	33.99870	37.44997	41.30083	45.59866
19	20.81061	22.84033	25.11662	27.67104	30.53865	33.75957	37.37857	41.44594	46.01785	51.15849
20	22.01868	24.29712	26.87009	29.77785	33.06555	36.78511	40.99504	45.76158	51.15941	57.27429
21	23.23883	25.78304	28.67616	31.96893	35.71880	39.99217	44.86465	50.42247	56.76370	64.00166
22	24.47118	27.29866	30.53642	34.24767	38.50470	43.39166	49.00514	55.45624	62.87238	71.40176
23	25.71585	28.84460	32.45248	36.61754	41.42989	46.99512	53.43546	60.89270	69.53082	79.54187
24	26.97296	30.42146	34.42603	39.08221	44.50133	50.81477	58.17589	66.76408	76.78853	88.49599
25	28.24265	32.02986	36.45877	41.64548	47.72635	54.86360	63.24815	73.10516	84.69942	98.34550
26	29.52502	33.67043	38.55249	44.31126	51.11261	59.15536	68.67648	79.95354	93.32228	109.17996
27	30.82024	35.34380	40.70903	47.08368	54.66818	63.70462	74.48270	87.34978	102.72119	121.09785
28	32.12839	37.05064	42.93027	49.96700	58.40154	68.52684	80.69643	95.33771	112.96599	134.20752
29	33.44962	38.79163	45.21814	52.96564	62.32155	73.63838	87.34511	103.96466	124.13281	148.62814
30	34.78406	40.56741	47.57465	56.08423	66.43756	79.05661	94.45920	113.28177	136.30464	164.49083

TABLE B-2

Compound Amount of an N Year Annuity

Interest Rates

N	0.11	0.12	0.13	0.14	0.15	0.16	0.17	0.18	0.19	0.20
1	1.00000	1.00000	1.00000	1.00000	1.00000	1.00000	1.00000	1.00000	1.00000	1.00000
2	2.11000	2.12000	2.13000	2.14000	2.15000	2.16000	2.17000	2.18000	2.19000	2.20000
3	3.34210	3.37440	3.40690	3.43960	3.47250	3.50560	3.53890	3.57240	3.60610	3.64000
4	4.70973	4.77933	4.84979	4.92114	4.99337	5.06649	5.14050	5.21543	5.29125	5.36800
5	6.22779	6.35284	6.48026	6.61009	6.74237	6.87713	7.01438	7.15420	7.29659	7.44159
6	7.91285	8.11518	8.32268	8.53550	8.75372	8.97747	9.20682	9.44195	9.68291	9.92991
7	9.78325	10.08900	10.40462	10.73046	11.06677	11.41386	11.77197	12.14149	12.52269	12.91588
8	11.85940	12.29967	12.75721	13.23271	13.72678	14.24007	14.77319	15.32694	15.90199	16.49904
9	14.16393	14.77563	15.41563	16.08527	16.78578	17.51846	18.28461	19.08577	19.92336	20.79881
10	16.72194	17.54869	18.41963	19.33719	20.30363	21.32141	22.39296	23.52118	24.70877	25.95839
11	19.56134	20.65453	21.81415	23.04437	24.34915	25.73282	27.19974	28.75496	30.40341	32.15028
12	22.71307	24.13306	25.64995	27.27055	29.00150	30.85005	32.82363	34.93082	37.18004	39.58032
13	26.21149	28.02901	29.98441	32.08839	34.35170	36.78604	39.40363	42.21832	45.24422	48.49637
14	30.09473	32.39247	34.88234	37.58073	40.50443	43.67178	47.10219	50.81758	54.84059	59.19562
15	34.40512	37.27954	40.41699	43.84198	47.58005	51.65926	56.10950	60.96469	66.26027	72.03471
16	39.18965	42.75307	46.67114	50.97980	55.71701	60.92471	66.64804	72.93828	79.84967	87.11162
17	44.50049	48.88341	53.73834	59.11690	65.07452	71.67264	78.97813	87.06711	96.02106	105.92989
18	50.39551	55.74939	61.72426	68.39319	75.83566	84.14023	93.40433	103.73912	115.26500	128.11580
19	56.93898	63.43929	70.74834	78.96815	88.21095	98.60263	110.28296	123.41206	138.16527	154.73888
20	64.20222	72.05197	80.94554	91.02361	102.44254	115.37901	130.03094	146.62613	165.41636	186.68653
21	72.26442	81.69818	92.46837	104.76680	118.80884	134.83960	153.13605	174.01869	197.84760	225.02371
22	81.21346	92.50194	105.48915	120.43404	137.63008	157.41388	180.16901	206.34189	236.43613	271.02832
23	91.14688	104.60213	120.20261	138.29466	159.27449	183.60004	211.79753	244.48323	282.35864	326.23364
24	102.17297	118.15433	136.82880	158.65576	184.16554	213.97595	248.80287	289.48999	337.00659	392.17998
25	114.41193	133.33279	155.61638	181.86739	212.79022	249.21202	292.09888	342.59790	402.03760	471.97359
26	127.99715	150.33267	176.84633	208.32863	245.70859	290.08569	342.75537	405.26514	479.42432	567.37036
27	143.07674	169.37253	200.83615	238.49440	283.56445	337.49927	402.02319	479.21240	571.51465	681.84421
28	159.81506	190.69716	227.94461	272.88330	327.09888	392.49902	471.36670	566.47021	681.10205	819.21265
29	178.39461	214.58073	258.57690	312.08643	377.16333	456.29858	552.49854	669.43433	811.51099	981.05039
30	199.01788	241.33034	293.19141	356.77808	434.73755	530.30615	647.42261	790.93188	966.69751	1181.86323

TABLE B-2

Compound Amount of an N Year Annuity
Interest Rates

N	0.21	0.22	0.23	0.24	0.25	0.26	0.27	0.28	0.29	0.30
1	1.00000	1.00000	1.00000	1.00000	1.00000	1.00000	1.00000	1.00000	1.00000	1.00000
2	2.21000	2.22000	2.23000	2.24000	2.25000	2.26000	2.27000	2.28000	2.29000	2.30000
3	3.67410	3.70840	3.74290	3.77760	3.81250	3.84760	3.88290	3.91840	3.95410	3.99000
4	5.44565	5.52424	5.60376	5.68422	5.76563	5.84797	5.93128	6.01555	6.10079	6.18699
5	7.58923	7.73957	7.89262	8.04843	8.20703	8.36844	8.53272	8.69990	8.87002	9.04308
6	10.18296	10.44226	10.70792	10.98005	11.25879	11.54422	11.83654	12.13587	12.44232	12.75600
7	13.32137	13.73955	14.17074	14.61525	15.07349	15.54571	16.03239	16.53391	17.05058	17.58278
8	17.11881	17.76224	18.42999	19.12289	19.84186	20.58757	21.36113	22.16339	22.99524	23.85759
9	21.71376	22.66991	23.66887	24.71237	25.80232	26.94032	28.12862	29.36913	30.66385	32.01485
10	27.27362	28.65726	30.11269	31.64334	33.25290	34.94478	36.72331	38.59247	40.55637	42.61926
11	34.00104	35.96182	38.03857	40.23770	42.56612	45.03038	47.63857	50.39835	53.31770	56.40500
12	42.14120	44.87338	47.78741	50.89471	54.20764	57.73824	61.50093	65.50986	69.77983	74.32645
13	51.99080	55.74548	59.77849	64.10942	68.75955	73.75011	79.10612	84.85258	91.01596	97.62431
14	63.90880	69.00943	74.52751	80.49565	86.94943	93.92511	101.46472	109.61127	118.41057	127.91153
15	78.32956	85.19114	92.66879	100.81456	109.68680	119.34555	129.86011	141.30238	153.74962	167.28488
16	95.77867	104.93347	114.98256	126.00999	138.10851	151.37529	165.92223	181.86699	199.33699	218.47018
17	116.89207	129.01874	142.42848	157.25232	173.63564	191.73274	211.72110	233.78967	258.14453	285.01099
18	142.43927	158.40274	176.18695	195.99278	218.04454	242.58310	269.88550	300.25049	334.00635	371.51392
19	173.35133	194.25119	217.70984	244.03093	273.55566	306.65430	343.75439	385.32056	431.86816	483.96777
20	210.75490	237.98625	268.78296	303.59814	342.94458	387.38403	437.56763	494.20996	558.10986	630.15747
21	256.01294	291.34277	331.60278	377.46143	429.68066	489.13352	556.71045	633.58862	720.96167	820.20410
22	310.77539	356.43774	408.87109	469.05200	538.10083	617.27002	708.02197	811.99316	931.04028	1067.26465
23	377.03781	435.85376	503.91113	582.62402	673.62598	778.73977	900.18726	1040.35107	1202.04199	1388.41312
24	457.21533	532.74121	620.81030	723.45337	843.03247	982.23657	1144.23706	1332.64893	1551.63403	1805.97461
25	554.22998	650.94385	764.59619	898.08179	1054.79053	1238.61743	1454.18018	1706.79028	2002.60767	2348.76538
26	671.61743	795.15088	941.45288	1114.62085	1319.48804	1561.65698	1847.80786	2185.69092	2584.36377	3054.39282
27	813.65625	971.08325	1158.98633	1383.12915	1650.86011	1968.68652	2347.71460	2798.68359	3334.82886	3971.70801
28	985.52295	1185.72070	1426.55249	1716.07935	2063.95020	2481.54346	2982.59570	3583.31396	4302.92578	5164.21484
29	1193.48145	1447.57813	1755.65869	2128.93750	2580.93774	3127.74292	3788.89355	4587.63672	5551.17344	6714.47266
30	1445.11108	1767.04395	2160.45923	2640.88135	3227.17188	3941.95337	4812.89063	5873.17188	7162.78516	8729.80859

TABLE B-3

Present Value of $1 Due at the End of N Years
Interest Rates

N	0.01	0.02	0.03	0.04	0.05	0.06	0.07	0.08	0.09	0.10
1	0.99010	0.98039	0.97087	0.96154	0.95238	0.94340	0.93458	0.92593	0.91743	0.90909
2	0.98030	0.96117	0.94260	0.92456	0.90703	0.89000	0.87344	0.85734	0.84168	0.82645
3	0.97059	0.94232	0.91514	0.88900	0.86384	0.83962	0.81630	0.79383	0.77219	0.75132
4	0.96099	0.92385	0.88849	0.85481	0.82271	0.79210	0.76290	0.73503	0.70843	0.68302
5	0.95147	0.90573	0.86261	0.82193	0.78353	0.74726	0.71299	0.68059	0.64993	0.62092
6	0.94205	0.88798	0.83749	0.79032	0.74622	0.70496	0.66635	0.63017	0.59627	0.56448
7	0.93273	0.87056	0.81310	0.75992	0.71069	0.66506	0.62275	0.58349	0.54704	0.51316
8	0.92349	0.85350	0.78941	0.73069	0.67684	0.62742	0.58201	0.54027	0.50187	0.46651
9	0.91435	0.83676	0.76642	0.70259	0.64461	0.59190	0.54394	0.50025	0.46043	0.42410
10	0.90530	0.82035	0.74410	0.67557	0.61392	0.55840	0.50835	0.46320	0.42241	0.38555
11	0.89634	0.80427	0.72243	0.64958	0.58469	0.52679	0.47510	0.42889	0.38754	0.35050
12	0.88746	0.78850	0.70139	0.62460	0.55684	0.49698	0.44402	0.39712	0.35554	0.31863
13	0.87868	0.77304	0.68096	0.60058	0.53033	0.46884	0.41497	0.36770	0.32618	0.28967
14	0.86998	0.75788	0.66113	0.57748	0.50507	0.44231	0.38782	0.34046	0.29925	0.26333
15	0.86137	0.74302	0.64187	0.55527	0.48102	0.41727	0.36245	0.31524	0.27454	0.23940
16	0.85284	0.72846	0.62318	0.53391	0.45812	0.39365	0.33874	0.29189	0.25187	0.21763
17	0.84440	0.71417	0.60502	0.51338	0.43630	0.37137	0.31658	0.27027	0.23108	0.19785
18	0.83604	0.70017	0.58740	0.49363	0.41553	0.35035	0.29587	0.25025	0.21200	0.17986
19	0.82776	0.68644	0.57030	0.47465	0.39574	0.33052	0.27651	0.23171	0.19449	0.16351
20	0.81957	0.67298	0.55369	0.45639	0.37690	0.31181	0.25842	0.21455	0.17843	0.14865
21	0.81145	0.65979	0.53756	0.43884	0.35895	0.29416	0.24152	0.19866	0.16370	0.13513
22	0.80342	0.64685	0.52190	0.42196	0.34186	0.27751	0.22572	0.18394	0.15018	0.12285
23	0.79547	0.63417	0.50670	0.40573	0.32558	0.26180	0.21095	0.17032	0.13778	0.11168
24	0.78759	0.62173	0.49194	0.39013	0.31008	0.24698	0.19715	0.15770	0.12641	0.10153
25	0.77979	0.60954	0.47762	0.37512	0.29531	0.23300	0.18425	0.14602	0.11597	0.09230
26	0.77207	0.59759	0.46370	0.36069	0.28125	0.21982	0.17220	0.13520	0.10640	0.08391
27	0.76443	0.58588	0.45020	0.34682	0.26786	0.20737	0.16093	0.12519	0.09761	0.07628
28	0.75686	0.57439	0.43709	0.33348	0.25510	0.19564	0.15041	0.11592	0.08955	0.06935
29	0.74937	0.56313	0.42436	0.32066	0.24295	0.18456	0.14057	0.10733	0.08216	0.06304
30	0.74195	0.55208	0.41200	0.30832	0.23138	0.17412	0.13137	0.09938	0.07537	0.05731

TABLE B-3

Present Value of $1 Due at the End of N Years

Interest Rates

N	0.11	0.12	0.13	0.14	0.15	0.16	0.17	0.18	0.19	0.20
1	0.90090	0.89286	0.88496	0.87719	0.86957	0.86207	0.85470	0.84746	0.84034	0.83333
2	0.81162	0.79719	0.78315	0.76947	0.75614	0.74316	0.73051	0.71819	0.70617	0.69445
3	0.73119	0.71178	0.69305	0.67497	0.65752	0.64066	0.62437	0.60863	0.59342	0.57870
4	0.65873	0.63552	0.61332	0.59208	0.57175	0.55229	0.53365	0.51579	0.49867	0.48225
5	0.59345	0.56743	0.54276	0.51937	0.49718	0.47611	0.45611	0.43711	0.41905	0.40188
6	0.53464	0.50663	0.48032	0.45559	0.43233	0.41044	0.38984	0.37043	0.35214	0.33490
7	0.48166	0.45235	0.42506	0.39964	0.37594	0.35383	0.33320	0.31393	0.29592	0.27908
8	0.43393	0.40388	0.37616	0.35056	0.32690	0.30503	0.28478	0.26604	0.24867	0.23257
9	0.39093	0.36061	0.33289	0.30751	0.28426	0.26295	0.24341	0.22546	0.20897	0.19381
10	0.35219	0.32197	0.29459	0.26975	0.24719	0.22668	0.20804	0.19107	0.17560	0.16151
11	0.31729	0.28748	0.26070	0.23662	0.21494	0.19542	0.17781	0.16192	0.14757	0.13459
12	0.28584	0.25668	0.23071	0.20756	0.18691	0.16846	0.15198	0.13722	0.12401	0.11216
13	0.25752	0.22918	0.20417	0.18207	0.16253	0.14523	0.12989	0.11629	0.10421	0.09346
14	0.23200	0.20462	0.18068	0.15971	0.14133	0.12520	0.11102	0.09855	0.08757	0.07789
15	0.20901	0.18270	0.15989	0.14010	0.12290	0.10793	0.09489	0.08352	0.07359	0.06491
16	0.18829	0.16312	0.14150	0.12289	0.10687	0.09304	0.08110	0.07078	0.06184	0.05409
17	0.16963	0.14565	0.12522	0.10780	0.09293	0.08021	0.06932	0.05998	0.05196	0.04507
18	0.15282	0.13004	0.11081	0.09456	0.08081	0.06914	0.05925	0.05083	0.04367	0.03756
19	0.13768	0.11611	0.09807	0.08295	0.07027	0.05961	0.05064	0.04308	0.03670	0.03130
20	0.12404	0.10367	0.08678	0.07276	0.06110	0.05139	0.04328	0.03651	0.03084	0.02608
21	0.11174	0.09256	0.07680	0.06383	0.05313	0.04430	0.03699	0.03094	0.02591	0.02174
22	0.10067	0.08264	0.06796	0.05599	0.04620	0.03819	0.03162	0.02622	0.02178	0.01811
23	0.09069	0.07379	0.06015	0.04911	0.04018	0.03292	0.02702	0.02222	0.01830	0.01510
24	0.08171	0.06588	0.05323	0.04308	0.03493	0.02838	0.02310	0.01883	0.01538	0.01258
25	0.07361	0.05882	0.04710	0.03779	0.03038	0.02447	0.01974	0.01596	0.01292	0.01048
26	0.06631	0.05252	0.04168	0.03315	0.02642	0.02109	0.01687	0.01352	0.01086	0.00874
27	0.05974	0.04689	0.03689	0.02908	0.02297	0.01818	0.01442	0.01146	0.00913	0.00728
28	0.05382	0.04187	0.03265	0.02551	0.01997	0.01567	0.01233	0.00971	0.00767	0.00607
29	0.04849	0.03738	0.02889	0.02238	0.01737	0.01351	0.01053	0.00823	0.00644	0.00506
30	0.04368	0.03338	0.02557	0.01963	0.01510	0.01165	0.00900	0.00698	0.00542	0.00421

TABLE B-3

Present Value of $1 Due at the End of N Years

Interest Rates

N	0.21	0.22	0.23	0.24	0.25	0.26	0.27	0.28	0.29	0.30
1	0.82645	0.81967	0.81301	0.80645	0.80000	0.79365	0.78740	0.78125	0.77519	0.76923
2	0.68301	0.67186	0.66098	0.65036	0.64000	0.62988	0.62000	0.61035	0.60093	0.59172
3	0.56448	0.55071	0.53738	0.52449	0.51200	0.49991	0.48819	0.47684	0.46583	0.45517
4	0.46651	0.45140	0.43690	0.42297	0.40960	0.39675	0.38440	0.37253	0.36111	0.35013
5	0.38555	0.37000	0.35520	0.34111	0.32768	0.31488	0.30268	0.29104	0.27993	0.26933
6	0.31863	0.30328	0.28878	0.27509	0.26214	0.24991	0.23833	0.22737	0.21700	0.20718
7	0.26333	0.24859	0.23478	0.22185	0.20972	0.19834	0.18766	0.17764	0.16822	0.15937
8	0.21763	0.20376	0.19088	0.17891	0.16777	0.15741	0.14777	0.13878	0.13040	0.12259
9	0.17986	0.16702	0.15519	0.14428	0.13422	0.12493	0.11635	0.10842	0.10109	0.09430
10	0.14865	0.13690	0.12617	0.11636	0.10737	0.09915	0.09161	0.08470	0.07836	0.07254
11	0.12285	0.11221	0.10258	0.09383	0.08590	0.07869	0.07214	0.06617	0.06075	0.05580
12	0.10153	0.09198	0.08340	0.07567	0.06872	0.06245	0.05680	0.05170	0.04709	0.04292
13	0.08391	0.07539	0.06780	0.06103	0.05498	0.04957	0.04473	0.04039	0.03650	0.03302
14	0.06934	0.06180	0.05512	0.04922	0.04398	0.03934	0.03522	0.03155	0.02830	0.02540
15	0.05731	0.05065	0.04481	0.03969	0.03518	0.03122	0.02773	0.02465	0.02194	0.01954
16	0.04736	0.04152	0.03644	0.03201	0.02815	0.02478	0.02183	0.01926	0.01700	0.01503
17	0.03914	0.03403	0.02962	0.02581	0.02252	0.01967	0.01719	0.01505	0.01318	0.01136
18	0.03235	0.02790	0.02408	0.02082	0.01801	0.01561	0.01354	0.01176	0.01022	0.00889
19	0.02674	0.02286	0.01958	0.01679	0.01441	0.01239	0.01066	0.00918	0.00792	0.00681
20	0.02210	0.01874	0.01592	0.01354	0.01153	0.00983	0.00839	0.00717	0.00614	0.00526
21	0.01826	0.01536	0.01294	0.01092	0.00922	0.00780	0.00661	0.00561	0.00476	0.00405
22	0.01509	0.01259	0.01052	0.00880	0.00738	0.00619	0.00520	0.00438	0.00369	0.00311
23	0.01247	0.01032	0.00855	0.00710	0.00590	0.00491	0.00410	0.00342	0.00286	0.00240
24	0.01031	0.00846	0.00695	0.00573	0.00472	0.00390	0.00323	0.00267	0.00222	0.00184
25	0.00852	0.00693	0.00565	0.00462	0.00378	0.00310	0.00254	0.00209	0.00172	0.00142
26	0.00704	0.00568	0.00460	0.00372	0.00302	0.00246	0.00200	0.00163	0.00133	0.00109
27	0.00582	0.00466	0.00374	0.00300	0.00242	0.00195	0.00158	0.00127	0.00103	0.00084
28	0.00481	0.00382	0.00304	0.00242	0.00193	0.00155	0.00124	0.00100	0.00080	0.00065
29	0.00397	0.00313	0.00247	0.00195	0.00155	0.00123	0.00098	0.00078	0.00062	0.00050
30	0.00328	0.00257	0.00201	0.00158	0.00124	0.00097	0.00077	0.00061	0.00048	0.00038

TABLE B-3

Present Value of $1 Due at the End of N Years

Interest Rates

N	0.31	0.32	0.33	0.34	0.35	0.36	0.37	0.38	0.39	0.40
1	0.76336	0.75758	0.75188	0.74627	0.74074	0.73529	0.72993	0.72464	0.71942	0.71429
2	0.58272	0.57392	0.56532	0.55692	0.54870	0.54066	0.53279	0.52510	0.51757	0.51020
3	0.44482	0.43479	0.42506	0.41561	0.40644	0.39754	0.38890	0.38051	0.37235	0.36443
4	0.33956	0.32939	0.31959	0.31016	0.30107	0.29231	0.28387	0.27573	0.26788	0.26031
5	0.25921	0.24953	0.24029	0.23146	0.22301	0.21493	0.20720	0.19980	0.19272	0.18593
6	0.19787	0.18904	0.18067	0.17273	0.16520	0.15804	0.15124	0.14479	0.13865	0.13281
7	0.15104	0.14321	0.13584	0.12890	0.12237	0.11621	0.11040	0.10492	0.09975	0.09486
8	0.11530	0.10850	0.10214	0.09620	0.09064	0.08545	0.08058	0.07603	0.07176	0.06776
9	0.08802	0.08219	0.07680	0.07179	0.06714	0.06283	0.05882	0.05509	0.05163	0.04840
10	0.06719	0.06227	0.05774	0.05357	0.04974	0.04620	0.04293	0.03992	0.03714	0.03457
11	0.05129	0.04717	0.04341	0.03998	0.03684	0.03397	0.03134	0.02893	0.02672	0.02469
12	0.03915	0.03574	0.03264	0.02984	0.02729	0.02498	0.02287	0.02096	0.01922	0.01764
13	0.02989	0.02707	0.02454	0.02227	0.02021	0.01837	0.01670	0.01519	0.01383	0.01260
14	0.02281	0.02051	0.01845	0.01662	0.01497	0.01350	0.01219	0.01101	0.00995	0.00900
15	0.01742	0.01554	0.01387	0.01240	0.01109	0.00993	0.00890	0.00798	0.00716	0.00643
16	0.01329	0.01177	0.01043	0.00925	0.00822	0.00730	0.00649	0.00578	0.00515	0.00459
17	0.01015	0.00892	0.00784	0.00691	0.00609	0.00537	0.00474	0.00419	0.00370	0.00328
18	0.00775	0.00676	0.00590	0.00515	0.00451	0.00395	0.00346	0.00304	0.00267	0.00234
19	0.00591	0.00512	0.00443	0.00385	0.00334	0.00290	0.00253	0.00220	0.00192	0.00167
20	0.00451	0.00388	0.00333	0.00287	0.00247	0.00213	0.00184	0.00159	0.00138	0.00120
21	0.00345	0.00294	0.00251	0.00214	0.00183	0.00157	0.00135	0.00115	0.00099	0.00085
22	0.00263	0.00223	0.00188	0.00160	0.00136	0.00115	0.00098	0.00084	0.00071	0.00061
23	0.00201	0.00169	0.00142	0.00119	0.00101	0.00085	0.00072	0.00061	0.00051	0.00044
24	0.00153	0.00128	0.00107	0.00089	0.00074	0.00062	0.00052	0.00044	0.00037	0.00031
25	0.00117	0.00097	0.00080	0.00066	0.00055	0.00046	0.00038	0.00032	0.00027	0.00022
26	0.00089	0.00073	0.00060	0.00050	0.00041	0.00034	0.00028	0.00023	0.00019	0.00016
27	0.00068	0.00056	0.00045	0.00037	0.00030	0.00025	0.00020	0.00017	0.00014	0.00011
28	0.00052	0.00042	0.00034	0.00028	0.00022	0.00018	0.00015	0.00012	0.00010	0.00008
29	0.00040	0.00032	0.00026	0.00021	0.00017	0.00013	0.00011	0.00009	0.00007	0.00006
30	0.00030	0.00024	0.00019	0.00015	0.00012	0.00010	0.00008	0.00006	0.00005	0.00004

TABLE B-4

Present Value of $1 Per Year For N Years

Interest Rates

N	0.01	0.02	0.03	0.04	0.05	0.06	0.07	0.08	0.09	0.10
1	0.99010	0.98039	0.97087	0.96154	0.95238	0.94340	0.93458	0.92593	0.91743	0.90909
2	1.97040	1.94156	1.91347	1.88610	1.85941	1.83339	1.80802	1.78327	1.75911	1.73554
3	2.94099	2.88389	2.82861	2.77509	2.72325	2.67301	2.62432	2.57710	2.53130	2.48685
4	3.90197	3.80773	3.71710	3.62990	3.54596	3.46511	3.38722	3.31213	3.23973	3.16987
5	4.85345	4.71347	4.57971	4.45183	4.32949	4.21237	4.10020	3.99271	3.88966	3.79079
6	5.79550	5.60144	5.41720	5.24214	5.07571	4.91734	4.76655	4.62288	4.48593	4.35527
7	6.72822	6.47201	6.23030	6.00206	5.78639	5.58240	5.38930	5.20638	5.03297	4.86843
8	7.65172	7.32550	7.01971	6.73276	6.46324	6.20981	5.97131	5.74665	5.53484	5.33494
9	8.56607	8.16226	7.78613	7.43535	7.10785	6.80172	6.51525	6.24690	5.99527	5.75904
10	9.47136	8.98262	8.53023	8.11091	7.72177	7.36012	7.02360	6.71009	6.41768	6.14459
11	10.36770	9.78689	9.25266	8.76050	8.30646	7.88691	7.49870	7.13898	6.80522	6.49508
12	11.25516	10.57539	9.95405	9.38510	8.86330	8.38388	7.94271	7.53609	7.16076	6.81372
13	12.13384	11.34843	10.63500	9.98568	9.39363	8.85273	8.35768	7.90380	7.48694	7.10338
14	13.00382	12.10631	11.29613	10.56316	9.89870	9.29503	8.74550	8.24426	7.78619	7.36672
15	13.86518	12.84934	11.93800	11.11843	10.37973	9.71231	9.10795	8.55950	8.06073	7.60611
16	14.71802	13.57779	12.56117	11.65234	10.83784	10.10596	9.44669	8.85140	8.31261	7.82375
17	15.56242	14.29196	13.16620	12.16572	11.27415	10.47733	9.76327	9.12167	8.54368	8.02159
18	16.39845	14.99213	13.75360	12.65935	11.68968	10.82768	10.05914	9.37192	8.75568	8.20145
19	17.22621	15.67858	14.32389	13.13400	12.08542	11.15820	10.33565	9.60363	8.95017	8.36496
20	18.04578	16.35155	14.87758	13.59039	12.46231	11.47001	10.59407	9.81818	9.12861	8.51361
21	18.85722	17.01132	15.41514	14.02923	12.82126	11.76417	10.83559	10.01684	9.29231	8.64874
22	19.66063	17.65817	15.93704	14.45119	13.16312	12.04168	11.06131	10.20078	9.44249	8.77159
23	20.45609	18.29233	16.44373	14.85692	13.48870	12.30348	11.27226	10.37110	9.58028	8.88327
24	21.24367	18.91405	16.93567	15.24705	13.79877	12.55046	11.46941	10.52880	9.70668	8.98480
25	22.02345	19.52359	17.41328	15.62217	14.09408	12.78347	11.65366	10.67482	9.82265	9.07710
26	22.79552	20.12117	17.87698	15.98286	14.37533	13.00328	11.82586	10.81002	9.92905	9.16100
27	23.55994	20.70703	18.32718	16.32968	14.64319	13.21066	11.98679	10.93521	10.02666	9.23728
28	24.31679	21.28142	18.76425	16.66316	14.89829	13.40629	12.13720	11.05113	10.11621	9.30663
29	25.06615	21.84454	19.18860	16.98381	15.14124	13.59085	12.27776	11.15846	10.19837	9.36967
30	25.80809	22.39662	19.60059	17.29213	15.37262	13.76497	12.40913	11.25783	10.27374	9.42698

TABLE B-4

Present Value of $1 Per Year For N Years
Interest Rates

N	0.11	0.12	0.13	0.14	0.15	C.16	0.17	0.18	0.19	0.20
1	0.90090	0.89286	0.88496	0.87719	0.86957	0.86207	0.85470	0.84746	0.84034	0.83333
2	1.71252	1.69005	1.66810	1.64666	1.62571	1.60523	1.58522	1.56564	1.54650	1.52778
3	2.44372	2.40183	2.36116	2.32163	2.28323	2.24589	2.20959	2.17428	2.13992	2.10648
4	3.10245	3.03735	2.97448	2.91372	2.85498	2.79818	2.74324	2.69007	2.63859	2.58873
5	3.69590	3.60478	3.51724	3.43309	3.35216	3.27430	3.19935	3.12718	3.05764	2.99061
6	4.23054	4.11141	3.99756	3.88868	3.78449	3.68474	3.58919	3.49761	3.40978	3.32551
7	4.71220	4.56376	4.42262	4.28832	4.16043	4.03857	3.92239	3.81154	3.70570	3.60459
8	5.14613	4.96764	4.79879	4.63888	4.48733	4.34359	4.20717	4.07758	3.95437	3.83716
9	5.53706	5.32826	5.13167	4.94639	4.77159	4.60655	4.45058	4.30303	4.16334	4.03097
10	5.88925	5.65023	5.42627	5.21613	5.01878	4.83323	4.65862	4.49410	4.33894	4.19248
11	6.20653	5.93771	5.68697	5.45275	5.23372	5.02865	4.83643	4.65602	4.48651	4.32706
12	6.49237	6.19438	5.91767	5.66031	5.42063	5.19711	4.98841	4.79324	4.61051	4.43922
13	6.74989	6.42356	6.12184	5.84239	5.58316	5.34234	5.11830	4.90953	4.71472	4.53268
14	6.98189	6.62818	6.30252	6.00210	5.72449	5.46753	5.22932	5.00808	4.80228	4.61057
15	7.19089	6.81087	6.46241	6.14220	5.84739	5.57546	5.32421	5.09159	4.87587	4.67548
16	7.37919	6.97400	6.60391	6.26509	5.95425	5.66850	5.40531	5.16237	4.93771	4.72956
17	7.54882	7.11964	6.72913	6.37289	6.04718	5.74871	5.47463	5.22235	4.98967	4.77464
18	7.70164	7.24968	6.83995	6.46745	6.12798	5.81785	5.53387	5.27318	5.03334	4.81220
19	7.83932	7.36579	6.93801	6.55040	6.19825	5.87746	5.58451	5.31626	5.07003	4.84350
20	7.96336	7.46946	7.02479	6.62317	6.25935	5.92885	5.62779	5.35276	5.10087	4.86958
21	8.07510	7.56202	7.10159	6.68699	6.31248	5.97315	5.66478	5.38370	5.12678	4.89132
22	8.17577	7.64466	7.16956	6.74298	6.35868	6.01133	5.69640	5.40992	5.14856	4.90943
23	8.26646	7.71845	7.22970	6.79209	6.39886	6.04425	5.72342	5.43214	5.16685	4.92453
24	8.34817	7.78433	7.28293	6.83517	6.43379	6.07263	5.74652	5.45097	5.18223	4.93711
25	8.42178	7.84315	7.33003	6.87296	6.46417	6.09710	5.76626	5.46692	5.19515	4.94759
26	8.48809	7.89567	7.37172	6.90611	6.49058	6.11819	5.78313	5.48045	5.20601	4.95632
27	8.54784	7.94257	7.40861	6.93519	6.51355	6.13637	5.79755	5.49191	5.21514	4.96360
28	8.60166	7.98444	7.44125	6.96070	6.53353	6.15204	5.80987	5.50162	5.22280	4.96967
29	8.65015	8.02182	7.47014	6.98308	6.55090	6.16556	5.82041	5.50985	5.22925	4.97472
30	8.69383	8.05520	7.49570	7.00270	6.56600	6.17720	5.82941	5.51682	5.23466	4.97894

TABLE B-4

Present Value of $1 Per Year For N Years
Interest Rates

N	0.21	0.22	0.23	0.24	0.25	0.26	0.27	0.28	0.29	0.30
1	0.82645	0.81967	0.81301	0.80645	0.80000	0.79365	0.78740	0.78125	0.77519	0.76923
2	1.50946	1.49154	1.47399	1.45682	1.44000	1.42353	1.40740	1.39160	1.37612	1.36095
3	2.07394	2.04224	2.01137	1.98130	1.95200	1.92344	1.89559	1.86844	1.84195	1.81611
4	2.54045	2.49364	2.44827	2.40428	2.36160	2.32019	2.28000	2.24097	2.20306	2.16624
5	2.92599	2.86364	2.80347	2.74539	2.68928	2.63507	2.58267	2.53201	2.48299	2.43557
6	3.24462	3.16692	3.09226	3.02047	2.95142	2.88498	2.82100	2.75938	2.70000	2.64275
7	3.50795	3.41551	3.32704	3.24232	3.16114	3.08332	3.00867	2.93702	2.86821	2.80212
8	3.72538	3.61927	3.51792	3.42122	3.32891	3.24073	3.15643	3.07579	2.99861	2.92471
9	3.90545	3.78629	3.67311	3.56550	3.46312	3.36566	3.27278	3.18421	3.09970	3.01900
10	4.05409	3.92319	3.79927	3.68186	3.57050	3.46481	3.36440	3.26892	3.17806	3.09154
11	4.17694	4.03540	3.90185	3.77569	3.65640	3.54350	3.43653	3.33509	3.23881	3.14734
12	4.27846	4.12738	3.98524	3.85137	3.72511	3.60595	3.49333	3.38679	3.28589	3.19026
13	4.36237	4.20277	4.05304	3.91239	3.78009	3.65552	3.53806	3.42718	3.32240	3.22328
14	4.43171	4.26457	4.10817	3.96161	3.82407	3.69486	3.57328	3.45873	3.35069	3.24868
15	4.48902	4.31522	4.15298	4.00130	3.85925	3.72608	3.60100	3.48339	3.37263	3.26821
16	4.53638	4.35674	4.18942	4.03330	3.88740	3.75086	3.62284	3.50264	3.38963	3.28324
17	4.57553	4.39077	4.21904	4.05911	3.90992	3.77052	3.64003	3.51769	3.40281	3.29480
18	4.60788	4.41867	4.24312	4.07993	3.92793	3.78613	3.65357	3.52944	3.41303	3.30369
19	4.63461	4.44153	4.26270	4.09672	3.94234	3.79852	3.66423	3.53863	3.42095	3.31053
20	4.65671	4.46027	4.27862	4.11026	3.95387	3.80835	3.67262	3.54580	3.42709	3.31579
21	4.67497	4.47564	4.29156	4.12117	3.96309	3.81615	3.67923	3.55141	3.43185	3.31984
22	4.69006	4.48823	4.30208	4.12998	3.97047	3.82234	3.68443	3.55579	3.43554	3.32296
23	4.70253	4.49855	4.31063	4.13708	3.97638	3.82725	3.68853	3.55921	3.43840	3.32535
24	4.71284	4.50701	4.31759	4.14280	3.98110	3.83115	3.69175	3.56188	3.44062	3.32719
25	4.72135	4.51394	4.32324	4.14742	3.98487	3.83425	3.69429	3.56397	3.44234	3.32861
26	4.72839	4.51963	4.32784	4.15115	3.98790	3.83671	3.69629	3.56560	3.44367	3.32970
27	4.73421	4.52428	4.33157	4.15415	3.99031	3.83865	3.69787	3.56687	3.44470	3.33051
28	4.73902	4.52810	4.33461	4.15657	3.99225	3.84020	3.69911	3.56787	3.44550	3.33118
29	4.74300	4.53123	4.33708	4.15852	3.99380	3.84143	3.70008	3.56864	3.44612	3.33168
30	4.74628	4.53380	4.33909	4.16010	3.99503	3.84240	3.70085	3.56925	3.44660	3.33206

TABLE B-4

Present Value of $1 Per Year For N Years

Interest Rates

N	0.31	0.32	0.33	0.34	0.35	0.36	0.37	0.38	0.39	0.40
1	0.76336	0.75758	0.75188	0.74627	0.74074	0.73529	0.72993	0.72464	0.71942	0.71429
2	1.34608	1.33150	1.31720	1.30319	1.28944	1.27595	1.26272	1.24974	1.23700	1.22449
3	1.79090	1.76629	1.74226	1.71880	1.69588	1.67349	1.65162	1.63025	1.60935	1.58892
4	2.13046	2.09567	2.06185	2.02805	1.99695	1.96580	1.93549	1.90598	1.87723	1.84923
5	2.38966	2.34521	2.30214	2.26041	2.21996	2.18074	2.14269	2.10578	2.06995	2.03516
6	2.58753	2.53425	2.48281	2.43315	2.38516	2.33878	2.29393	2.25057	2.20860	2.16797
7	2.73857	2.67746	2.61866	2.56205	2.50753	2.45498	2.40433	2.35548	2.30834	2.26284
8	2.85387	2.78596	2.72079	2.65825	2.59817	2.54043	2.48491	2.43151	2.38010	2.33060
9	2.94189	2.86815	2.79759	2.73004	2.66531	2.60326	2.54373	2.48660	2.43173	2.37900
10	3.00908	2.93042	2.85533	2.78361	2.71504	2.64945	2.58666	2.52652	2.46887	2.41357
11	3.06036	2.97759	2.89874	2.82359	2.75189	2.68342	2.61800	2.55545	2.49559	2.43826
12	3.09951	3.01332	2.93139	2.85343	2.77917	2.70840	2.64088	2.57642	2.51481	2.45590
13	3.12940	3.04040	2.95593	2.87569	2.79939	2.72676	2.65757	2.59161	2.52864	2.46850
14	3.15222	3.06091	2.97438	2.89231	2.81436	2.74026	2.66976	2.60261	2.53859	2.47750
15	3.16963	3.07644	2.98825	2.90471	2.82545	2.75019	2.67865	2.61059	2.54575	2.48393
16	3.18292	3.08821	2.99869	2.91396	2.83367	2.75749	2.68515	2.61637	2.55090	2.48852
17	3.19307	3.09713	3.00653	2.92087	2.83976	2.76286	2.68989	2.62056	2.55460	2.49180
18	3.20082	3.10388	3.01243	2.92602	2.84426	2.76681	2.69335	2.62359	2.55727	2.49414
19	3.20673	3.10900	3.01686	2.92986	2.84760	2.76971	2.69587	2.62579	2.55918	2.49581
20	3.21125	3.11288	3.02019	2.93273	2.85007	2.77184	2.69771	2.62738	2.56056	2.49701
21	3.21469	3.11582	3.02270	2.93487	2.85191	2.77341	2.69906	2.62854	2.56155	2.49786
22	3.21732	3.11804	3.02458	2.93647	2.85326	2.77457	2.70004	2.62938	2.56227	2.49847
23	3.21933	3.11973	3.02600	2.93766	2.85427	2.77541	2.70075	2.62998	2.56278	2.49891
24	3.22086	3.12100	3.02707	2.93855	2.85501	2.77604	2.70128	2.63042	2.56315	2.49922
25	3.22203	3.12197	3.02787	2.93922	2.85556	2.77649	2.70166	2.63074	2.56341	2.49944
26	3.22292	3.12270	3.02847	2.93971	2.85597	2.77683	2.70194	2.63097	2.56360	2.49960
27	3.22360	3.12326	3.02892	2.94008	2.85627	2.77708	2.70214	2.63113	2.56374	2.49971
28	3.22412	3.12368	3.02926	2.94036	2.85650	2.77726	2.70229	2.63126	2.56384	2.49979
29	3.22452	3.12400	3.02952	2.94056	2.85666	2.77740	2.70240	2.63134	2.56391	2.49985
30	3.22482	3.12424	3.02971	2.94072	2.85679	2.77749	2.70247	2.63141	2.56396	2.49989